# ERROR PATTERNS IN COMPUTATION

## Using Error Patterns to Help Each Student Learn

### TENTH EDITION

### Robert B. Ashlock
Professor Emeritus
Covenant College

**Allyn & Bacon**

Boston   New York   San Francisco
Mexico City   Montreal   Toronto   London   Madrid   Munich   Paris
Hong Kong   Singapore   Tokyo   Cape Town   Sydney

Series Editor: Kelly Villella Canton
Series Editorial Assistant: Annalea Manalili
Marketing Manager: Darcy Betts Prybella
Editorial Production Service: Connie Strassburg, GGS
Manufacturing Buyer: Megan Cochran
Electronic Composition: GGS
Cover Administrator: Linda Knowles

---

Library of Congress Cataloging-in-Publication Data

Ashlock, Robert B.
    Error patterns in computation : using error patterns to help each student
learn / Robert B. Ashlock.–10th ed.
        p. cm.
    Includes bibliographical references.
    ISBN-13: 978-0-13-500910-9
    ISBN-10: 0-13-500910-3
    1. Arithmetic—Study and teaching (Elementary)    I. Title.
    QA135.5.A782 2010
    372.7'2044—dc22

                                                          2008045371

10 9 8 7 6          RRD-VA 12 11

**Allyn & Bacon**
**is an imprint of**

ISBN-10: 0-13-500910-3
ISBN-13: 978-0-13-500910-9

# About the Author

**Robert B. Ashlock** began his career in the public schools of Indiana, teaching in the elementary grades and serving as an administrator. He completed his doctorate at Indiana University, where he majored in elementary education with a focus on mathematics education.

For 15 years, while at the College Park campus of the University of Maryland, he taught courses about teaching mathematics to children. He developed a graduate program for teachers with students experiencing difficulty learning mathematics, and a clinic program for children and youth who needed help learning mathematics.

Throughout his career he served as a consultant and spoke at regional and national meetings of mathematics educators. As he moved into retirement years, he continued to work with preservice and in-service teachers as they studied how to help children learn mathematics. He now spends less time with professional activities and more time with his family.

# Contents

# Preface

We want to help our students learn to think mathematically. Mere skill in computing is not our primary concern.

Even so, computation in its many forms—estimation, mental computation, the use of calculators, and paper-and-pencil procedures—continues to have a significant role in both the learning of mathematics and in solving problems in the world around us.

We hope all of our students will understand what they study; we want them to succeed in mathematics and to enjoy solving problems—but sometimes they learn erroneous concepts and procedures. It is very important that we be alert to the erroneous learnings of our students.

This book was written for those who are willing to listen carefully to what each student says and to make thoughtful analyses of each student's work—teachers who want to discover misconceptions and erroneous procedures learned. Thereby, they can focus instruction more effectively. This book was written to help teachers, whatever the level, to look at *all* student work diagnostically.

Most of Part One focuses on detecting the misconceptions and systematic errors many students make, especially when computing with paper and pencil. Readers observe that students actually do learn misconceptions and error patterns. They consider reasons students may have learned specific erroneous procedures, and they learn strategies for helping those students. Many of the instructional strategies described are useful when teaching *any* student—whether that student has experienced difficulty under previous instruction or not. In Part Two, help is provided for assessment and for instruction that is focused on the needs of each student. Diagnostic teaching is the goal.

The erroneous patterns of students are not due to carelessness alone nor are they due to insufficient practice. Students make connections, observe patterns, and make inferences during instruction. In the case of an error pattern, that which has been learned does not always produce correct answers. Some incorrect procedures produce correct answers part of the time; when this happens students are reinforced in their belief that they have learned the desired concepts and skills.

You will find looking for misconceptions and error patterns to be a very worthwhile assessment activity because you will gain specific knowledge about each student's strengths, and you will be able to base future instruction on what students actually know and can do.

## NEW TO THIS EDITION

The tenth edition has been updated throughout. Emphases on the *Principles and Standards for School Mathematics*, by the National Council of Teachers of Mathematics (NCTM), are highlighted even more than in the previous edition. Early in the text readers experience the reality of student misconceptions and error patterns, then they focus extensively on assessment and instruction in order to learn how they can teach more diagnostically. In this edition, there is *greater emphasis* on:

- Formative assessment and diagnosis
- Understanding operations
- Making connections
- Big ideas that need to be emphasized repeatedly; for example, *there* are *many names for a number.*
- Using representations
- Teaching so that students can *use* what they learn
- Open-ended assessment
- Using classroom discourse
- Assessing dispositions
- Using problem writing for diagnosis

Chapter length is more uniform throughout the book than in previous editions, and each chapter closes with a list of thoughts and questions for further reflection. New appendixes focus on meanings of operations and thematic units. Also, a greater number of ideas and resources are highlighted with sidebars.

## ORGANIZATION OF THE TEXT

This book is organized into two parts and concludes with additional resources. In Part One, the reader considers the place of computation within our age of calculators, and the misconceptions and error patterns that students learn in spite of our good intentions. Then the reader gains direct experience with many of the misconceptions and error patterns that real students have learned in various areas of mathematics. Readers identify patterns within the written work of students and consider instruction to help particular students, comparing their ideas with those of the author. Additional practice identifying error patterns is provided in five chapters. Experience has shown that direct involvement through simulation, as provided in this text, helps both preservice and in-service teachers become more proficient at diagnosing and correcting computational procedures. They gain skill by actually looking for patterns, making decisions, and planning instruction.

In Part Two, readers consider what they can do to diagnose misconceptions and error patterns in computation and in other mathematical topics, and how to teach diagnostically, providing data-driven instruction. Additional resources include a glossary and an extensive annotated bibliography for assessment and for instruction.

Questions for further reflection are provided at the end of each chapter. Activities and assignments are included in appendixes; examples include game-like activities, a diagnostic interview, and a sample thematic unit.

## ACKNOWLEDGMENTS

I wish to express appreciation for the encouragement of many classroom teachers who have shown great interest in this book over the years, and to acknowledge the help of teachers, former students, and their students. These colleagues have identified many of the error patterns presented.

I also wish to thank my colleagues who served as text reviewers: Elaine Beck, Louisiana State University at Alexandria; Yolanda De La Cruz, Arizona State University; Juli K. Dixon, University of Central Florida; Neal Grandgenett, University of Nebraska at Omaha; and John Piel, University of North Carolina Charlotte.

*—Robert B. Ashlock*
*December, 2008*

# Misconceptions and Error Patterns

This book is designed to help us improve mathematics instruction in our classrooms by becoming more diagnostically oriented. Diagnosis should be continuous throughout instruction.

Why do our students sometimes learn misconceptions and erroneous procedures when learning to compute? How important is it to teach paper-and-pencil computation procedures in our age of calculators and computers? Part One addresses these questions, and the need for conceptually oriented instruction.

As we teach our students, we need to be alert to misconceptions and error patterns they may learn. Part One provides many opportunities to identify misconceptions and error patterns in student papers and to think about why these students may have used the procedures they did. You learn what might be done to help students who are experiencing such difficulties.

In Chapters 2 through 8, student papers are presented so you can study them and infer what the student was actually thinking and doing when completing the paper. Then you turn to a page where the difficulty is discussed, and you have an opportunity to think about instructional activities that may help the student. Suggested activities are described and you can compare your ideas with those of the author.

Some papers include a few correct answers even though the student's thinking will not always lead to a correct result. When this happens, students are encouraged to believe that their thinking is correct and their procedure is satisfactory.

# CHAPTER 1

# Computation, Misconceptions, and Error Patterns

> **Number and Operations Standard**
>
> Instructional programs from prekindergarten through grade 12 should enable all students to—
>
> - *understand numbers, ways of representing numbers, relationships among numbers, and number systems;*
> - *understand meanings of operations and how they relate to one another;*
> - *compute fluently and make reasonable estimates.*[1]

In this age of calculators and computers, do our students actually need to learn paper-and-pencil procedures? We want our students to understand mathematical concepts and to compute fluently, but how does this relate to students learning to do paper-and-pencil procedures when calculators are so readily available?

As we examine these and other questions in this chapter, we will find that even in our technological age, paper-and-pencil computation is often needed. True, paper-and-pencil procedures constitute only one alternative for computing— though it often makes sense to use such procedures. It is also true that while our students are learning to compute with paper and pencil, their knowledge of basic facts, numeration concepts, and various principles can be further developed— knowledge needed for doing other forms of computation.

## ■ Instruction in Mathematics

Our society is drenched with data. We have long recognized that verbal literacy is essential to our well-being as a society; now we recognize that quantitative literacy or *numeracy* is also essential.

Accordingly, our goals are changing. We want to see instructional programs enable students to understand and use mathematics in a technological world.

We are not interested in students just doing arithmetic in classrooms; we want to see the operations of arithmetic applied in real-world contexts where students observe and organize data. We no longer assume that students must be skillful with computation before they can actually begin investigating interesting topics in mathematics.

Instruction in mathematics is moving toward covering fewer topics but in greater depth and toward making connections between mathematical ideas. Increasingly, mathematics is being perceived as a science of patterns rather than a collection of rules. In truth, there are those who characterize algebra as *generalized* arithmetic, and there are those who even propose that ". . . the teaching and learning of arithmetic be conceived as the foundation for algebra."[2]

Number and Operations is only one of the five content standards for grades pre-K through 12 in *Principles and Standards for School Mathematics,* published in 2000 by the National Council of Teachers of Mathematics (NCTM). But computation, including the basic facts of arithmetic, is often involved when the other four content standards are learned and applied: Algebra, Geometry, Measurement, and Data Analysis and Probability. Moreover, application in every grade of the five process standards frequently entails the basic facts of arithmetic and computation: Problem Solving, Reasoning and Proof, Communication, Connections, and Representation. The basic facts and different methods of computation are very much a part of standards-based instruction in mathematics today.

The computations of arithmetic are not being ignored. The importance of computation is made clear in *Principles and Standards for School Mathematics*.

> **Knowing basic number combinations—the single-digit addition and multiplication pairs and their counterparts for subtraction and division—is essential. Equally essential is computational fluency—having and using efficient and accurate methods for computing.**[3]

Number and Operations were later highlighted for grades pre-K through 8 by NCTM in their *Curriculum Focal Points*.

# ■ Computational Fluency

If our students are to have computational fluency, if they are to have and use efficient and accurate methods for computing, they need conceptual understanding—"comprehension of mathematical concepts, operations, and relations" and procedural fluency—"skill in carrying out procedures flexibly, accurately, efficiently, and appropriately." Both are aspects of mathematical proficiency as defined by the Mathematics Learning Study Committee of the National Research Council.[4]

Increasingly we need to integrate arithmetic and all of the mathematics we teach with the world of our students, including their experiences with other subject areas. In order to solve problems encountered in the world around them, our students need to know not only how to compute a needed number, but also *when* to compute. In order for them to know when to use specific operations, we need to emphasize the meanings of operations during instruction.

Furthermore, in order for our students to gain computational fluency, they need to be able to use different methods of computation in varied problem-solving situations.

> Part of being able to compute fluently means making smart choices about which tools to use and when. Students should have experiences that help them learn to choose among mental computation, paper-and-pencil strategies, estimation, and calculator use. The particular context, the question, and the numbers involved all play roles in those choices.[5]

If we focus on paper-and-pencil procedures but do not introduce other methods of computing, our students are apt to believe that the process of computing is limited to paper-and-pencil procedures.

When students have a problem to solve, there are decisions to be made before any required computation begins. Consider this part of a conversation overheard in a student math group led by Chi. Calculators were available and students were free to use one if they needed it, but the teacher also encouraged other methods of exact computation: mental computation and paper-and-pencil procedures.

| CHI: | We have three word problems to solve. Here's Problem A. *You are to help the class get ready for art class. There are 45 pounds of clay for 20 people. How many pounds do you give each person?* |
|---|---|
| RAUL: | We need an exact answer. Each person should get the same amount. |
| TERRY: | I don't think we need to use the calculator. Each person gets a little more than two pounds . . . but how much more? |
| SONJA: | That's easy, just divide 45 by 20. The students proceed to divide 45 by 20 with paper and pencil. |
| CHI: | Here's Problem B. *Wanda's scores for three games of darts are 18, 27, and 39. What is her average score?* |
| RAUL: | Another exact answer. |
| CHI: | Shall we get the calculator? |
| SONJA: | I can do it in my head. |
| TERRY: | I don't see how. I'm going to use paper; it's easy. |
| SONJA: | Round each number up . . . 20 + 30 + 40 is 90 . . . divided by 3 is 30. But we need to subtract: 2 and 3 (that's 5) and one more . . . 6 divided by 3 is 2. Two from 30 is 28. Her average score is 28. |
| TERRY: | That's what I got, too. |

Different methods of computation are listed in Figure 1.1. Because an approximation is often sufficient, the first decision a student must make is whether an exact number is needed. In regard to exact computation, paper-and-pencil procedures constitute only one of the methods of computation available.

**FIGURE 1.1**   Methods of computation.

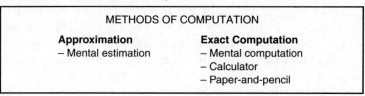

METHODS OF COMPUTATION

**Approximation**                    **Exact Computation**
– Mental estimation                  – Mental computation
                                     – Calculator
                                     – Paper-and-pencil

**FIGURE 1.2**   Decisions about calculation in problem situations requiring computation.

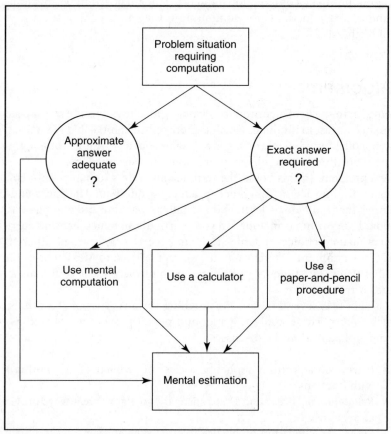

*Source:* Based on a chart in *Curriculum and Evaluation Standards for School Mathematics* (Reston, VA: National Council of Teachers of Mathematics, 1989), p. 9.

The diagram in Figure 1.2 focuses on decisions about the method of computation to be used for solving a particular problem. The actual teaching of different methods of computation is addressed in Chapter 10.

When a solution to $300 - 25 = \square$ is needed by a fourth grader, mental computation is likely the most appropriate method to use. But there are times when a paper and pencil strategy is the most efficient procedure for an individual. When a calculator is not immediately available and an exact answer is needed for the sum of two or three multi-digit numbers, it often makes sense to use a paper-and-pencil procedure.

Because computational procedures are tools for helping us solve problems, whenever possible the *context* for teaching different methods of computation should be a problem-solving situation; we need to keep focused on problem solving as we teach computation procedures. The *goal* of instruction in computation today continues to be computational fluency. Students need to be able to use efficient and accurate methods for computing if they are to enjoy success in most areas of mathematics.

## ■ Algorithms

It is common to speak of algorithmic *thinking,* which uses specific step-by-step procedures, in contrast to thinking, which is more self-referential and recursive. Polya's four-step model for problem solving is an example of algorithmic thinking.[6]

An algorithm is a step-by-step procedure for accomplishing a task, such as solving a problem. In this book, the term usually refers to paper-and-pencil procedures for finding a sum, difference, product, or quotient. The paper-and-pencil procedures that individuals learn and use differ over time and among cultures. If a "standard" algorithm is included in your curriculum, remember that curriculum designers made a choice. If some students have already learned different algorithms (for example, a different way to subtract learned in Mexico or in Europe), remember that these students' procedures are quite acceptable if they always provide the correct number.

Usiskin lists several reasons for teaching various types of algorithms, a few of which follow. These apply to paper-and-pencil procedures as well as to the other types of algorithms he discusses.[7]

- *Power.* An algorithm applies to a class of problems (e.g., multiplication with fractions).
- *Reliability and accuracy.* Done correctly, an algorithm always provides the correct answer.
- *Speed.* An algorithm proceeds directly to the answer.
- *A record.* A paper-and-pencil algorithm provides a record of how the answer was determined.
- *Instruction.* Numeration concepts and properties of operations are applied.

As we teach paper-and-pencil procedures, we need to remember that our students are learning and applying concepts as they are learning procedures.

# ■ Conceptual Learning and Procedural Learning

The importance of conceptual learning is stressed by NCTM in *Principles and Standards for School Mathematics*. Conceptual learning in mathematics always focuses on ideas and on generalizations that make connections among ideas. In contrast, procedural learning focuses on skills and step-by-step procedures.[8]

Sadly, procedures are sometimes taught without adequately connecting the steps to mathematical ideas. Both conceptual learning and procedural learning are necessary, but procedural learning needs to be tied to conceptual learning and to real-life applications. Procedural learning *must* be based on concepts already learned. There is evidence that learning rote procedures before learning concepts and how they are applied in those procedures actually interferes with later meaningful learning.[9]

In order for concepts to build on one another, ideas need to be understood and woven together. As a part of their increasing number sense, our younger students need to understand principles and concepts associated with whole numbers and numerals for whole numbers. Then, students begin to make reasonable estimates and accurate mental computations.

Students need to understand the meaning of each operation (and not just do the computations), so they can decide which operation is needed in particular situations. Otherwise, they do not know which button to push on a calculator or which paper-and-pencil procedure to use.

Conceptual understanding is *so* important that some mathematics educators stress the invention of algorithms by young students; they fear that early introduction of standard algorithms may be detrimental and not lead to understanding important concepts.[10] Understanding the concepts and reasoning involved in an algorithm does lead to a more secure mastery of that procedure. It is also true that standard algorithms *can* be taught so that students understand the concepts and reasoning associated with specific procedures.

Paper-and-pencil procedures that we teach actually involve more than procedural knowledge; they entail conceptual knowledge as well. Many of the instructional activities described in this book are included because students need to understand specific concepts. Our students are not merely mechanical processors; they are involved conceptually as they learn—even when we teach procedures.

> [I]nstruction can emphasize conceptual understanding without sacrificing skill proficiency . . . understanding does not detract from skill proficiency and may even enhance it.[11]

It has long been recognized that instruction should balance conceptual understanding and skill proficiency. One of the classic publications of mathematics education is William Brownell's "Meaning and Skill—Maintaining the Balance," published originally in 1956 but reprinted twice by the National Council of Teachers of Mathematics, once as recently as 2003.[12]

It must be recognized that as a student uses a specific paper-and-pencil procedure over time, it becomes more automatic. The student employs increasingly less conceptual knowledge and more procedural knowledge, a process researchers sometimes call "proceduralization."

## ■ Paper-and-Pencil Procedures Today

Even with calculators and computers available, our students need to acquire skill with paper-and-pencil procedures. Writing in *Educational Leadership,* Loveless and Coughlan conclude:

> We would simply like all students to learn how to add, subtract, multiply, and divide using whole numbers, fractions, and decimals—and accurately compute percentages—by the end of 8th grade. Only by mastering these skills will students have the opportunity to learn higher-level mathematics.[13]

NCTM's *Principles and Standards for School Mathematics* clearly supports teaching computation skills:

> [S]tudents must become fluent in arithmetic computation—they must have efficient and accurate methods that are supported by an understanding of numbers and operations. "Standard" algorithms for arithmetic computation are one means of achieving this fluency.[14]

Although needed arithmetic computation skills include estimation, mental computation, and using calculators, it is noteworthy that our students also need to be able to use appropriate paper-and-pencil algorithms when it makes sense to do so.

Students sometimes learn error patterns as we teach these procedures. We can teach diagnostically and carefully observe what our students do, looking for misconceptions and error patterns in their written work.

## ■ Learning Misconceptions and Error Patterns

All of us, including our students, make mistakes from time to time. Some individuals suggest that if you don't make mistakes, you are probably not working on hard enough problems—and *that's* a big mistake.

However, there is a difference between the careless mistakes we all make, and *misconceptions* about mathematical ideas and procedures. Students learn concepts, and sometimes they also learn misconceptions—in spite of whatever we try to teach them. Error patterns in computation often reveal misconceptions our students have learned.

The mathematical ideas and procedures (or rules) a student learns may be correct or they may be full of misconceptions, but the *process* of learning those ideas and procedures is basically the same. During experiences with a concept or a process (or a procedure), a student focuses on whatever the experiences appear to have in common and connects that information to information already known.

Consider the student whose only school experiences with the number idea we call *five* involve manila cards with black dots in the familiar domino pattern (Figure 1.3a). That student may draw from those experiences a notion of five that includes many or all of the characteristics his experiences had in common: possibly black on manila paper, round dots, or a specific configuration. One of the author's own students, when presenting to her students the configuration associated with Stern pattern boards (Figure 1.3b) was told, "That's not five. Five doesn't look like that."

More young students will name as a triangle the shape in Figure 1.3c than the shape in Figure 1.3d; yet both are triangles. Again, configuration (or even the orientation of the figure) may be a common characteristic of a child's limited range of experiences with triangles.

Dr. Geoffrey Matthews, who organized the Nuffield Mathematics Teaching Project in England, told about a child who computed correctly one year but missed half of the problems the next year. As the child learned to compute, he adopted the rule, "Begin on the side by the piano." The next school year the child was in a room with the piano on the other side, and he was understandably confused about where to start computing.

Concept cards, which are often used in learning centers, also illustrate concept formation (Figure 1.4). As a student examines a concept card, he sees a name

**FIGURE 1.3**  Patterns for five and triangles.

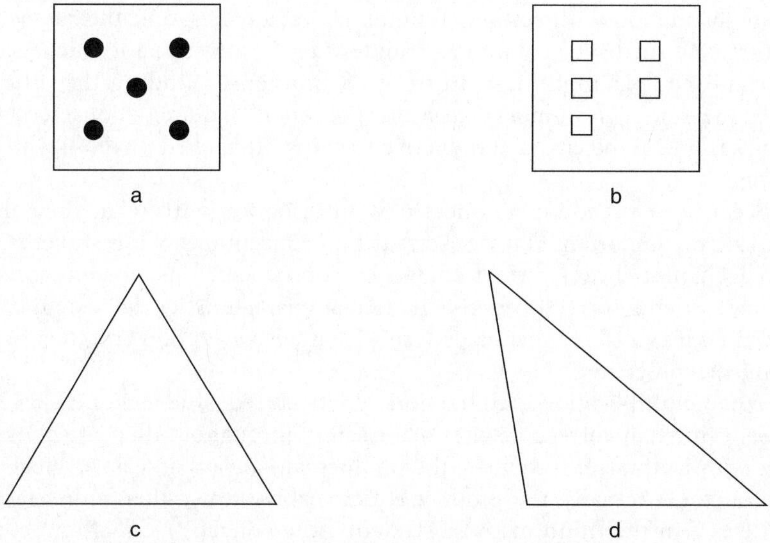

**FIGURE 1.4**   Concept card for rhombus.

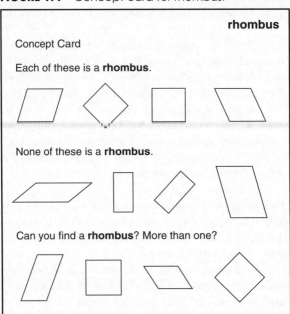

or label, such as *rhombus*. Examples of a rhombus and non-examples of a rhombus are both shown on the card, and the student must decide what a rhombus is. Finally, the card provides an opportunity to test out his newly derived definition.

Students often learn erroneous concepts and processes similarly. They look for commonalities among their initial contacts with an idea or procedure. They form an abstraction with certain common characteristics, and their concept or algorithm is formed. The common attributes may be very specific, such as crossing out a digit, placing a digit in front of another, or finding the difference between two one-digit numbers (regardless of order). Failure to consider enough examples is one of the errors of inductive learning often cited by those who study thinking.

Because our students connect new information with what they already know, it is very important that we assess the preconceptions of our students. Prior knowledge is not always correct knowledge; misconceptions are common. Even when our students correctly observe particular characteristics that examples have in common, they may connect a pattern with a misconception and thereby learn an erroneous procedure.

When multiplication with fractions is introduced, students often have difficulty believing that correct answers make sense; throughout their previous experiences with factors and products, the product was always at least as great as the smaller factor. (Actually, the product is noticeably greater than either factor in most cases.) In the mind of these students, the concept *product* had come to include the idea of a greater number because this was common throughout most of their experiences with products.

From time to time, an erroneous procedure produces a correct answer. When it does, use of the error pattern is reinforced. For example, a student may decide that "rounding whole numbers to the nearest ten" means erasing the units digit and writing a zero. The student is correct about half of the time!

There are many reasons why students tend to learn patterns of error. It most certainly is not the intentional result of our instruction. Yet all too often, individual students do not have all the prerequisite understandings and skills they need when introduced to new ideas and procedures. When this happens, they may "grab at straws." A teacher who introduces paper-and-pencil procedures while a particular student still needs to work out problems with concrete aids encourages that student to try to memorize a complex sequence of mechanical acts, thereby prompting the student to adopt simplistic procedures that can be remembered. Because incorrect algorithms do not usually result in correct answers, it would appear that a student receives limited positive reinforcement for continued use of erroneous procedures. But students sometimes hold tenaciously to incorrect procedures, even during instruction that confronts their beliefs directly.

Students often invent similar rules when introduced to the sign for equals. For example, they may decide "The equals sign means 'the answer turns out to be.'"

Students who learn erroneous patterns *are* capable of learning. Typically, these students have what we might call a learn*ed* disability, not a learn*ing* disability. The rules that children construct are derived from their search for meaning; a sensible learning process is involved. This is true even for the erroneous rules they invent, though such rules may involve a distortion or a poor application. Sometimes students overgeneralize or overspecialize while learning.[15]

## Overgeneralizing

Most of us are prone to overgeneralize on occasion; we "jump to a conclusion" before we have adequate data at hand. Examples of overgeneralizing abound in many areas of mathematics learning. Several interesting examples were observed by project staff at the University of Maryland during their study of misconceptions among secondary school students.[16] At the University of Pittsburgh, Mack studied the development of students' understanding of fractions during instruction, and she also observed students overgeneralizing.[17]

Consider the following examples of overgeneralizing.

- What is a sum? Sometimes students decide that a sum is the number written on the right side of an equals sign.

$$4 + 2 = 6$$
$$6 - 2 = 4$$

Both are considered sums.

- Consider students who believe that all three of these figures are triangles.

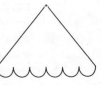

Graeber reports an interesting speculation on this situation.

> **These students may be reasoning from a definition of triangle position. Extension of this definition to simple closed curves that are not polygons may lead to this error of including such shapes in the set of triangles.**[18]

- Sometimes students are exposed to right triangles like these:

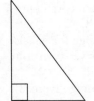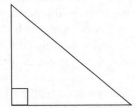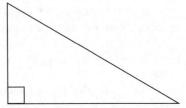

And they conclude that a right angle is oriented to the right as well as measuring 90 degrees.

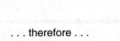

a right angle            . . . therefore . . .            a left angle

- The student who believes that 2y means 20 + y may be overgeneralizing from expressions like 23 = 20 + 3.
- Other students always use 10 for regrouping, even when computing with measurements.

$$\begin{array}{r} 3 \text{ gal. } 2 \text{ qt.} \\ - 1 \text{ gal. } 3 \text{ qt.} \\ \hline \end{array} \longrightarrow \begin{array}{r} \overset{2}{3} \text{ gal. } \overset{1}{2} \text{ qt.} \\ - 1 \text{ gal. } 3 \text{ qt.} \\ \hline \end{array}$$

- Students sometimes think of the longest side of a triangle as a hypotenuse. They assume the Pythagorean Theorem applies even when the triangle is not a right triangle.[19]

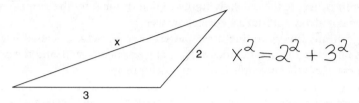

## Overspecializing

Other misconceptions and erroneous procedures are generated when a student overspecializes during the learning process. The resulting procedures are restricted inappropriately. For example, students know that in order to add or subtract fractions, the fractions must have like denominators. Sometimes students believe that multiplication and division of fractions require like denominators.

It is quite common for students to restrict their concept of altitude of a triangle to only that which can be contained within the triangle.

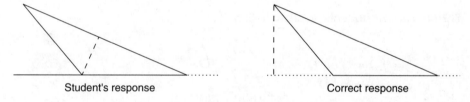

Student's response                                    Correct response

As we diagnose students who are experiencing difficulty, we need to be alert for both overgeneralization and overspecialization. We need to probe deeply as we examine written work—looking for misconceptions and erroneous procedures that form patterns across examples—and try to find out why specific procedures were learned.

## ■ Error Patterns in Computation

As our students learn concepts and computation procedures, many students—even students who invent their own algorithms—learn error *patterns*. Sometimes the words a teacher says are used (inappropriately) by a student when forming an error pattern. Chapters 2 through 8 include specific examples of error patterns—systematic procedures and applications of concepts students learn that often do not provide the correct answer.

Errors *can* be a positive thing. In many cultures, errors are regarded as an opportunity to reflect and learn. Furthermore, errors are often viewed as part of the "messiness" of doing mathematics.

Rather than warning our students about errors to avoid, we can use errors as catalysts for learning by approaching errors as problem-solving situations. For example, a group of students can examine an erroneous procedure and use reasoning with concepts they already know to determine why the strategy that was used does not always produce a correct answer.[20]

Algorithms incorporating error patterns are sometimes called *buggy algorithms*. A buggy algorithm includes at least one erroneous step, and the procedure does not consistently accomplish the intended purpose.

As we teach computation procedures, we need to remember that our students are not necessarily learning what we think we are teaching; we need to keep our eyes and ears open to find out what our students are *actually* learning. We need to be alert for error patterns!

We can look for patterns as we examine student work, and note the different strategies for computing that our students develop. Of course, we observe that results are correct or incorrect; but we also need to look for evidence that indicates *how each student is thinking*. One way of getting at that thinking is to encourage students to show or describe how they obtained their answers, as can be seen for six students' solutions to 25 + 37 in Figure 1.5.

**FIGURE 1.5**   Six students' solutions to 25 + 37.

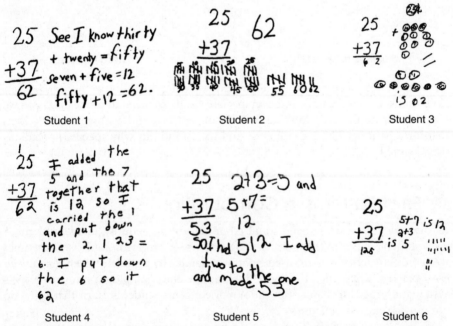

*Source:* Reproduced from Principles and Standards for School Mathematics (Reston, VA: National Council of Teachers of Mathematics, 2000) p. 85, by permission of National Council of Teachers of Mathematics.

**FIGURE 1.6**   Sample student paper.

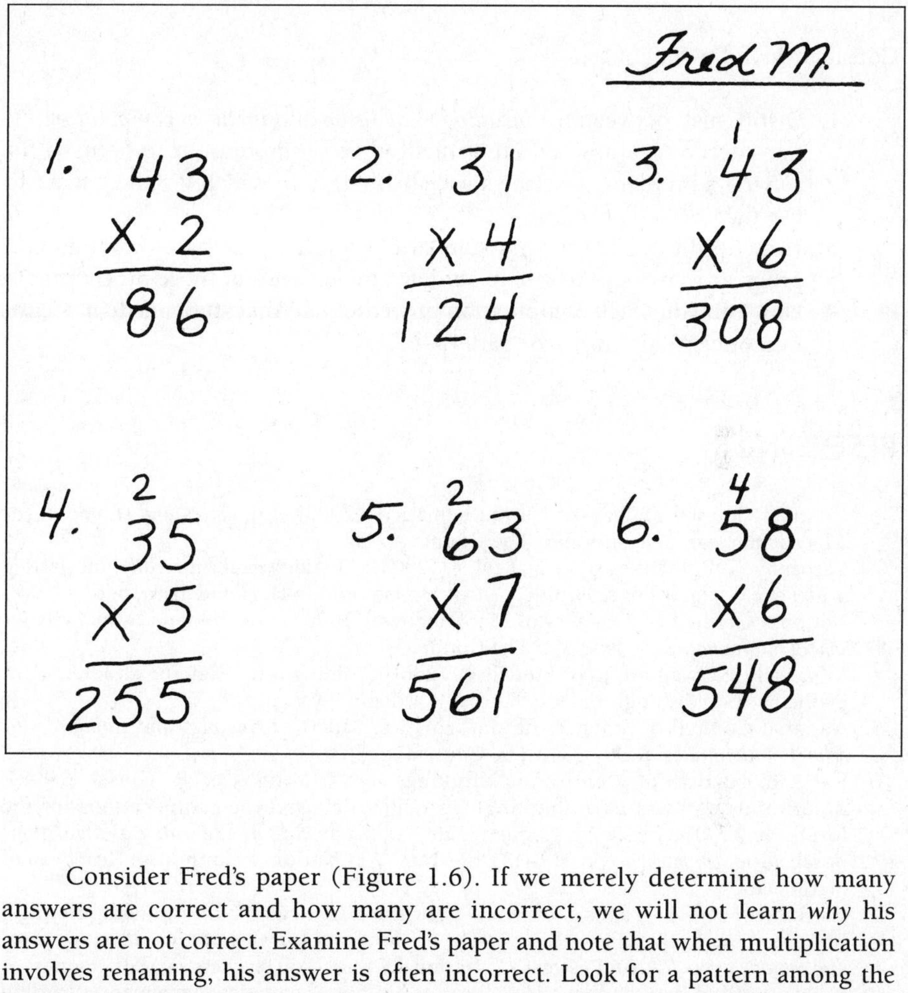

Fred M.

1.   43
    × 2
    ----
     86

2.   31
    × 4
    ----
    124

3.   ⁴3
    × 6
    ----
    308

4.   ²
     35
    × 5
    ----
    255

5.   ²
     63
    × 7
    ----
    561

6.   ⁴
     58
    × 6
    ----
    548

Consider Fred's paper (Figure 1.6). If we merely determine how many answers are correct and how many are incorrect, we will not learn *why* his answers are not correct. Examine Fred's paper and note that when multiplication involves renaming, his answer is often incorrect. Look for a pattern among the incorrect responses; observe that he seems to be adding his "crutch" and then multiplying. This can be verified by studying other examples and briefly interviewing Fred.

Because we observed Fred's error pattern, instruction can be modified as needed. The algorithm may be reviewed as a written record of multiplying "one part at a time" (an application of distributing multiplication over addition), or a modification of the algorithm itself may be suggested so that the "crutch" is recorded with a small half-space digit written below the line. (See Error Pattern M-W-2 in Chapter 3.)

Rather than just scoring papers, we need to examine each student's paper diagnostically—looking for patterns, hypothesizing possible causes, and verifying our ideas. As we learn about each student, we will find that a student's paper is sometimes a problem or puzzle to be solved.

## FURTHER REFLECTION

Consider the following questions:

1. Distinguish between *the meaning of addition* and *addition computation.*
2. For each of the four different methods of computation to be used for solving a problem, describe a social situation in which it makes sense to use that particular method.
3. How do the NCTM *process* standards support teaching of computation procedures in ways that help students make sense of those procedures?
4. How can you teach computation procedures so that students do *not* learn misconceptions and error patterns?

## REFERENCES

1. National Council of Teachers of Mathematics. (2000). *Principles and standards for school mathematics.* Reston, VA: The Council, p. 32.
2. Carpenter, T. P., Franke, M. L., & Levi, L. (2003). *Thinking mathematically: Integrating arithmetic & algebra in elementary school.* Portsmouth, NH: Heinemann, p. 6.
3. National Council of Teachers of Mathematics. (2000). *Principles and standards for school mathematics.* Reston, VA: The Council, p. 32.
4. Kilpatrick, J., Swafford, J., & Findell, B. (2001). Adding it up: Helping children learn mathematics. Washington, DC: National Academy Press, p. 116.
5. National Council of Teachers of Mathematics. (2000). *Principles and standards for school mathematics.* Reston, VA: The Council, p. 36.
6. For a discussion of algorithmic thinking, see T. Mingus & R. Grassl (1998). Algorithmic and recursive thinking: Current beliefs and their implications for the future. In L. Morrow & M. Kenney (Eds.), *The teaching and learning of algorithms in school mathematics* (pp. 32–43). Reston, VA: National Council of Teachers of Mathematics.
7. Usiskin, Z. (1998). Paper-and-pencil algorithms in a calculator-and-computer age. In L. Morrow & M. Kenney (Eds.), *The teaching and learning of algorithms in school mathematics* (pp. 7–20). Reston, VA: National Council of Teachers of Mathematics.
8. It is recognized that mathematics educators are not in complete agreement regarding definitions of procedural and conceptual knowledge. Readers may want to study the debate in the following research commentaries:
   - Star, J. R. (2005). Reconceptualizing procedural knowledge. *Journal for Research in Mathematics Education 36*(5), 404–411.
   - Baroody, A. J., Feil, Y., & Johnson, A. R. (2007). An alternative reconceptualization of procedural and conceptual knowledge. *Journal for Research in Mathematics Education 38*(2), 115–131. A rejoinder by Star follows.
9. For example, see D. D. Pesek & D. Kirshner (2000). Interference of instrumental instruction in subsequent relational learning. *Journal for Research in Mathematics Education 31*(5), 524–540.
10. For example, see C. Kamii & A. Dominick (1998). The harmful effects of algorithms in grades 1–4. In L. Morrow & M. Kenney (Eds.), *The teaching and learning of algorithms in school mathematics* (pp. 130–140). Reston, VA: National Council of Teachers of Mathematics.

11. Hiebert, J. (2000). What can we expect from research? *Mathematics Teaching in the Middle School* 5(7), 415.
12. Brownell, W. A. (1956). Meaning and skill—Maintaining the balance. *The Arithmetic Teacher* 3(4), 129–136. Reprinted (February 2003). *Teaching Children Mathematics* 9(6), 311–316.
13. Loveless, T., & Coughlan, J. (2004). The arithmetic gap. *Educational Leadership* 61(5), 58.
14. National Council of Teachers of Mathematics. (2000). *Principles and standards for school mathematics.* Reston, VA: The Council, p. 35.
15. For a discussion of intuitive rules students seem to follow as they develop particular misconceptions, see R. Stavy & D. Tirosh (2000). *How students (mis-)understand science and mathematics: Intuitive rules.* New York: Teachers College Press.
16. See A. O. Graeber (1992). *Methods and materials for preservice teacher education in diagnostic and prescriptive teaching of secondary mathematics: Project final report.* (NSF funded grant). College Park, MD: University of Maryland, pp. 4–4 through 4–7.
17. Mack, N. K. (1995). Confounding whole-number and fraction concepts when building on informal knowledge. *Journal for Research in Mathematics Education* 26(5), 422–441.
18. A. O. Graeber, op. cit., p. 4–5.
19. Ibid., pp. 4–12.
20. Eggleton, P. J., & Moldavan, C. C. (2001). The value of mistakes. *Mathematics Teaching in the Middle School* 7(1).

# CHAPTER 2

# Error Patterns:
# Addition and Subtraction
## with Whole Numbers

When planning instruction, we need to consider sufficient student data to divulge any *patterns* of incorrect and immature computations.

On the following pages, you will find examples of papers on which students practiced adding and subtracting whole numbers. With these simulated student papers, you have the opportunity to develop your own skill in identifying error patterns. These papers contain the error patterns of real students observed by teachers in ordinary school settings; they are like students in our own classrooms.

Look for a pattern of errors, then check your findings by using the error pattern yourself with the examples provided. Be careful not to decide on the error pattern too quickly. (Students often make hasty decisions and, as a result, adopt the kind of erroneous procedures presented in this book.) When you think you see a pattern, verify your hypothesis by looking at the other examples on the student's paper.

As you read about each student's procedure, think about needed instruction. It is always important for a teacher to have in mind more than one instructional strategy, so try to think of at least two different activities to help the student. Compare your ideas with the author's suggestions.

Each error pattern has been labeled to facilitate discussion: A-W for addition of whole numbers and S-W for subtraction of whole numbers.

## ■ Identifying Patterns

### Error Pattern A-W-1

*There were 7 cookies on the plate, but Mother put 8 more cookies on the plate. How many cookies are on the plate now?*

Gary said that there are 14 cookies on the plate now. Look at his written work carefully. Can you find the error pattern he has followed?

Name _Gary_

A. 7 + 8 = *14*

B. 8 + 6 = *13*

C. 7 + 6 = *12*

D. 8 + 5 = *12*

Did you find Gary's error pattern? Check yourself by using his error pattern to determine these sums.

E. 7 + 7 = —— F. 6 + 8 = ——

Next, turn to Error Pattern A-W-1 on page 25 to see if you were able to identify the error pattern. *Why* might Gary use such a procedure?

## Error Pattern A-W-2

*Collins has 74 nickels in his nickel jar, and 56 dimes in his dime jar. How many coins does Collins have in his two coin jars?*

Mike came up with an answer that is over a thousand. Obviously, he is not estimating yet. Can you find the error pattern he followed?

Name *Mike*

A.
$$\begin{array}{r} 74 \\ +56 \\ \hline 1210 \end{array}$$

B.
$$\begin{array}{r} 35 \\ +92 \\ \hline 127 \end{array}$$

C.
$$\begin{array}{r} 67 \\ +18 \\ \hline 715 \end{array}$$

D.
$$\begin{array}{r} 56 \\ +97 \\ \hline 1413 \end{array}$$

Did you find his error pattern? Check yourself by using his error pattern to determine these sums.

E.
$$\begin{array}{r} 43 \\ +65 \\ \hline \end{array}$$

F.
$$\begin{array}{r} 88 \\ +39 \\ \hline \end{array}$$

Next, turn to Error Pattern A-W-2 on page 25 to see if you were able to identify the error pattern. How is Mike finding his answers? Why might he use such a procedure?

## Error Pattern A-W-3

Mary gets some correct sums, but many of her answers are not even reasonable. What error pattern is Mary following in her written work?

Name _Mary_

A.
$$\begin{array}{r} 432 \\ +265 \\ \hline 697 \end{array}$$

B.
$$\begin{array}{r} 74 \\ +43 \\ \hline 18 \end{array}$$

C.
$$\begin{array}{r} 38\overset{4}{5} \\ +667 \\ \hline 9\ 1\ 16 \end{array}$$

D.
$$\begin{array}{r} 5\overset{..}{6}\overset{..}{3} \\ +545 \\ \hline 1\ 1\ 8 \end{array}$$

Check to see if you found Mary's pattern by using her erroneous procedure to compute these examples.

E.
$$\begin{array}{r} 254 \\ +535 \\ \hline \end{array}$$

F.
$$\begin{array}{r} 618 \\ +782 \\ \hline \end{array}$$

Why might Mary or any student use such a procedure? Is she estimating? What can you say about her number sense? Next, turn to page 27 to see if you were able to identify her error pattern.

## Error Pattern A-W-4

*There were 56 students in Ms. Jones's gym class. Six more students were placed in the class. How many students are in the class now?*

When Carol adds, she gets many of her answers correct, but she came up with 17 students for this problem. That is not even close. What is wrong? Can you find the error pattern she followed?

Name _Carol_

A.
$$\begin{array}{r} 56 \\ +\ 6 \\ \hline 17 \end{array}$$

B.
$$\begin{array}{r} 18 \\ +30 \\ \hline 48 \end{array}$$

C.
$$\begin{array}{r} 8 \\ +16 \\ \hline 15 \end{array}$$

D.
$$\begin{array}{r} 42 \\ +56 \\ \hline 98 \end{array}$$

E.
$$\begin{array}{r} 85 \\ +\ 6 \\ \hline 19 \end{array}$$

Did you find her error pattern? Check yourself by using her procedure to determine these sums.

F.  26        G.  60        H.  74
+   3        + 24        +  5

What does Carol understand about numerals and estimating? What can you say about her number sense? Why might she be using such a procedure? To make sure you have identified her procedure, turn to page 27.

## Error Pattern A-W-5

Dorothy does not seem to be thinking about what she is doing as she practices addition with paper and pencil. Her answers are quite unreasonable. Can you find her pattern of errors?

Name *Dorothy*

A.
'75
+   8
—————
1 6 3

B.
'67
+   4
—————
1 1 1

C.
'84
+   9
—————
1 8 3

D.
'59
    6
—————
1 2 5

Did you find Dorothy's procedure? What does Dorothy really understand about numerals and place value? What does she not yet understand? Will giving her more examples like this help her? Make sure you found her procedure by using her error pattern to compute these examples.

E.  46        F.  98
+   8         +  3

When you have completed Examples E and F, turn to page 28 and see if you identified the pattern. Why might Dorothy be using such a procedure?

## Error Pattern S-W-1

Cheryl was very successful with paper-and-pencil subtraction until recently. Has she become careless, or is there another reason for her present difficulty? Look carefully at Cheryl's written work. What error pattern did she follow?

Note: Cheryl used a different procedure for one of the examples.

Name *Cheryl*

| A. | B. | C. | D. |
|---|---|---|---|
| $\begin{array}{r}3\,2 \\ -\,1\,6 \\ \hline 1\,6\end{array}$ | $\begin{array}{r}2\,4\,5 \\ -\,1\,3\,7 \\ \hline 1\,1\,2\end{array}$ | $\begin{array}{r}5\,2\,4 \\ -\,2\,9\,8 \\ \hline 3\,7\,4\end{array}$ | $\begin{array}{r}1\,3\,5 \\ -\,6\,7 \\ \hline 1\,3\,2\end{array}$ |

Did you find her error pattern? Check yourself by using her procedure for these examples.

E.
$$\begin{array}{r}4\,5\,8 \\ -\,3\,7\,2 \\ \hline\end{array}$$

F.
$$\begin{array}{r}2\,4\,1 \\ -\,9\,6 \\ \hline\end{array}$$

What does Cheryl understand about subtraction? What does she understand about numerals and place value? What does she not understand? Why might a student use such a procedure? We call the answer to a subtraction example a "difference." Would that have anything to do with her use of this procedure? Now turn to Error Pattern S-W-1 on page 30 to see if you were able to identify the error pattern.

## Error Pattern S-W-2

George recently learned to regroup (or "rename"), and at first he got correct answers. But soon there were difficulties when he met simple problems like the following:

*Pat had 197 pieces in his set of plastic building materials. But he traded 43 of them for some baseball cards. How many pieces are in his set of building materials now?*

Look carefully at George's written work. Is he using estimation? What does he understand about numeration and subtraction? What does he *not* understand? What error pattern did he follow?

Name _George_

A.
$$\begin{array}{r} 1\,\overset{8}{\cancel{9}}\,7 \\ -\quad 4\,3 \\ \hline 1\,4\,1\,4 \end{array}$$

B.
$$\begin{array}{r} 1\,\overset{6}{\cancel{8}}\,6 \\ -\quad 2\,3 \\ \hline 1\,4\,1\,3 \end{array}$$

C.
$$\begin{array}{r} 3\,\overset{7}{\cancel{8}}\,4 \\ -\quad 5\,9 \\ \hline 3\,2\,5 \end{array}$$

Did you find his error pattern? Check yourself by using his procedure for these examples.

D.
$$\begin{array}{r} 2\,7\,3 \\ -\quad 3\,8 \\ \hline \end{array}$$

E.
$$\begin{array}{r} 2\,8\,5 \\ -\quad 6\,3 \\ \hline \end{array}$$

Why might a student use such a procedure? Now turn to Error Pattern S-W-2 on page 32 to see if you identified the error pattern.

## Error Pattern S-W-3

Donna's answers seem reasonable to her, and most of them are correct. But she keeps getting incorrect answers when she subtracts. Look carefully at her written work. Do you find an error pattern?

Name _Donna_

A.
$$\begin{array}{r} 1\,4\,7 \\ -\quad 2\,0 \\ \hline 1\,2\,0 \end{array}$$

B.
$$\begin{array}{r} 6\,2\,4 \\ -\,3\,2\,3 \\ \hline 3\,0\,1 \end{array}$$

C.
$$\begin{array}{r} 5\,2\,7 \\ -\,3\,0\,4 \\ \hline 2\,0\,3 \end{array}$$

D.
$$\begin{array}{r} 8\,0\,5 \\ -\,2\,0\,1 \\ \hline 6\,0\,4 \end{array}$$

Did you find her pattern? Check yourself by using her procedure for these examples.

E.  446
  − 302

F.  760
  − 230

Why might a student use such a procedure? Has Donna learned something that she is using inappropriately? Now turn to Error Pattern S-W-3 on page 33 to see if you actually found Donna's pattern of errors.

## Error Pattern S-W-4

Barbara seemed to be doing well with subtraction until recently. Look carefully at her written work. Can you find a pattern of errors?

Name **Barbara**

A.
  6 7 8
− 2 4 8
  4 4 5

B.
  3 2 5
− 1 5 1
  1 7 4

C.
  7 2 6
− 3 4 9
  2 8 7

D.
  4 3 4
− 2 7 6
    6 8

What does she know how to do? What does she *not* understand? Do you think she is using estimation? Make sure you found the pattern by using her procedure for these examples.

E.  436
  − 172

F.  625
  − 348

What might have caused Barbara to begin using such a procedure? Turn to Error Pattern S-W-4 on page 35 to see if you actually found Barbara's pattern of errors.

# ■ Planning Instruction

## Error Pattern A-W-1
*(from Gary's paper on page 19)*

If you discovered Gary's procedure, you completed Examples E and F as shown.

E. 7 + 7 = _____ *13*            F. 6 + 8 = _____ *13*

     During an interview with his teacher, Gary admitted he uses his fingers to count addition sums. So his teacher gave him an addition example and said, "Lots of boys and girls use their fingers. Show me how you use *your* fingers." Gary counted out the first addend, then used the last finger already used as the first finger for counting out the second addend.

     How would you help Gary find simple sums as needed? Are your suggestions among the following?

1. *Make sets of marks.* Let the child make a set of marks for the first addend, then a set for the second addend. Ask, "Are there 10?" Let the child circle 10 marks, and count on to find the total number.
2. *Use an all-new set.* Explain that the finger that was counted twice cannot be a part of both sets. For the second number, an *all-new* set is needed.
3. *Count sets of objects and fingers.* Put a row of objects on the table and let the child count off a set for the first addend, then a set for the second addend. (Note when the first set is complete and the fact that the next object is part of a new set.) The total amount in both sets can then be counted. Repeat the same activity, but let the child use his fingers to make sets.

## Error Pattern A-W-2
*(used by Mike on page 19)*

Using the error pattern, Examples E and F would be completed as shown.

E.  4 3
   + 6 5
   1 0 8

F.  8 8
   + 3 9
   1 1 1 7

     The ones were added and recorded, then the tens were added and recorded (or vice versa). The sum of the ones and the sum of the tens were each recorded without regard to place value in the sum. Note that Mike may have applied some knowledge of place value in his work with the two addends; i.e., he may have treated the 88 in Example F as 8 tens and 8 ones, and his answer as 11 tens and

17 ones. It is also probable that Mike may have merely thought, "8 plus 9 equals 17, and 8 plus 3 equals 11." I have found many students who think through such a problem in this way; some of these students also emphasize that you add 8 and 9 first because "you add the ones first."

Mike has the idea of adding ones with ones—possibly from work with bundles of sticks and single sticks. He apparently knows he should consider all of the single sticks together. He *may* know a rule for exchanging or regrouping 10 single sticks for one bundle of 10, but if he does, he has not applied the rule to these examples. Previous instruction may not have given adequate emphasis to the mechanics of recording sums.

If you were Mike's teacher, how would you help him? Are your suggestions among the following?

**Note:** Be sure to extend your diagnosis. Let Mike "think out loud" for you. Unless you do this, you will not even know whether he is adding the ones or the tens first.

1. *Use bundles of 10 and single sticks.* Show both addends, then "make a 10" as may have been done in past instruction. Emphasize that we always need to start with the single sticks. Apply a rule for exchanging or regrouping if it is possible. Then make 10 bundles of 10, if possible. With paper and pencil, record what is done *step by step*.

2. *Provide the student with a set of numerals (0 through 9) and a frame for the answer.* Each box of the frame should be of a size that will enclose only one digit. Let the student use the cardboard or plastic numerals to record sums for problems. This activity should help the student remember to apply the rule for exchanging.

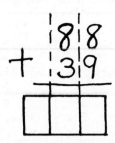

3. *Play chip-trading games.* To develop the idea for exchanging many for one, play games in which the values of chips are defined in terms of our numeration place-value pattern. However, it is easier to begin with bases less than 10. A child rolls a die and receives as many units as indicated on the die. He then exchanges for higher-valued chips according to the rule of the game (five for one if base five, 10 for one if base ten). Play proceeds similarly. The first child to get a specific chip of a high value wins. Such games are described in *Chip Trading Activities, Book I*.[1]

## Error Pattern A-W-3
*(from Mary's paper on page 20)*

If you used Mary's error pattern, you completed Examples E and F as they are shown.

E.
$$
\begin{array}{r}
2\ 5\ 4 \\
+5\ 3\ 5 \\
\hline
7\ 8\ 9
\end{array}
$$

F.
$$
\begin{array}{r}
{}^{3\ 2} \\
6\ 1\ 8 \\
+7\ 8\ 2 \\
\hline
1\ 1\ 1\ 2
\end{array}
$$

This pattern is a reversal of the procedure used in the usual algorithm—without regard for place value. Addition is performed from left to right, and, when the sum of a column is 10 or greater, the left figure is recorded and the right figure is placed above the next column to the right.

If you were Mary's teacher, what corrective procedures might you follow? Are your suggestions among the following?

1. *Estimate sums.* Even *before* computing, the sum can be estimated. For instance, in Example F, it can be determined in advance that the sum is more than 1,300.
2. *Use base ten blocks and show the sum.* Have her use base-ten blocks to show both addends, and challenge her to show the total amount with as few pieces of wood as possible, (Ten of one size can always be traded for the next larger size.) Then have her examine her written work again. Can she make up a rule to help her remember to make 10 if she can? Activities such as this can also be done with Montessori Golden Beads, or with single sticks and bundles of ten (and bundles of one hundred as needed).
3. *Use a game-like activity with a pattern board, base blocks, and a bank.* Help students understand place values and begin computation with units by making the algorithm a written record of moves in a game-like activity. A pattern board serves as an organizing center. Appendix D describes such activities and includes an illustration for addition with whole numbers.

## Error Pattern A-W-4
*(from Carol's paper on page 20)*

If you found Carol's error pattern, your results are the same as the erroneous computation shown.

F.
$$
\begin{array}{r}
2\ 6 \\
+\ \ 3 \\
\hline
1\ 1
\end{array}
$$

G.
$$
\begin{array}{r}
6\ 0 \\
+2\ 4 \\
\hline
8\ 4
\end{array}
$$

H.
$$
\begin{array}{r}
7\ 4 \\
+\ \ 5 \\
\hline
1\ 6
\end{array}
$$

Carol misses examples in which one of the addends is written as a single digit. When working such examples, she adds the three digits as if they were all units. When both addends are two-digit numbers, she appears to add correctly. However, it is quite probable that Carol is not applying any knowledge of place value with either type of example. She may be merely adding units in every case. (When both addends are two-digit numbers, she adds units in straight columns. When one addend is a one-digit number, she adds the three digits along a curve.) If this is the way Carol is thinking, she will probably experience even more failure and frustration when she begins to add and subtract examples that require renaming.

An interview with Carol may provide very helpful information. Is she able to explain the examples that were worked correctly? Does she identify tens and units? Does she reason that units must be added to units, and tens must be added to tens?

How would you help Carol? Are your ideas among the following possibilities?

1. *Play Pick-a-Number.* This game stresses the different values a digit may signify in various positions. Use cards with 0 through 9. Each player draws a form like this:

   One player picks a card and reads the number, and each player writes that number in one of the spaces. Repeat until all blanks are full. The player showing the greatest number wins.

2. *Show each addend.* After the student shows both addends with base-ten blocks or with bundles of 10 and single sticks, have her collect the units and record the total number of units. She may then collect the tens and record the total number of tens.

3. *Draw a line to separate tens and units.* This procedure may help with the mechanics of notation if the student understands the need to add units to units and tens to tens.

$$
\begin{array}{c|c}
T & U \\ \hline
 & 3 \\
+\,2 & 6 \\ \hline
2 & 9
\end{array}
\qquad
\begin{array}{c|c}
T & U \\ \hline
6 & 0 \\
+\,2 & 4 \\ \hline
8 & 4
\end{array}
\qquad
\begin{array}{c|c}
T & U \\ \hline
7 & 4 \\
+ & 5 \\ \hline
7 & 9
\end{array}
$$

## Error Pattern A-W-5

*(from Dorothy's paper on page 21)*

Using Dorothy's error pattern, Examples E and F would be computed as shown.

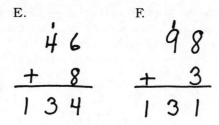

E.
```
  . 
  4 6
+   8
-----
1 3 4
```

F.
```
  .
  9 8
+   3
-----
1 3 1
```

Dorothy is not having difficulty with basic number facts, but higher decade addition situations are confusing her. She tries to use the regular addition algorithm; however, when she adds the tens column, she adds in the one-digit number again.

If Dorothy has been introduced to the multiplication algorithm, she may persist in seeing similar patterns for computation whenever numerals are arranged as she has seen them in multiplication examples. Changing operations when the arrangement of digits is similar is difficult for some children. An interview with Dorothy may help you determine if she really knows how to add problems like these. When working with a child who tends to carry over one situation into her perception of another, avoid extensive practice on any single procedure at a given time.

How would you help Dorothy replace her erroneous pattern with a correct procedure? Are your suggestions among the ideas that follow?

**Note:** The following suggestions assume the student is *not* confusing these higher decade situations with multiplication.

1. *Explain using units and tens.* Let the student explain the addition to you in terms of units (or ones) and tens. If her understanding of place value is adequate, this procedure may be sufficient to clear up the difficulty. It may be necessary to have her use base-ten blocks or a place-value chart.
2. *Label units and tens.* Have the student label each column. The use of squared paper may also help if only one digit is written in each square.

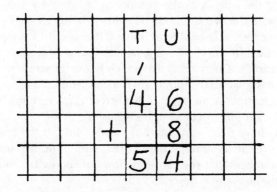

3. *Make higher decade sequences.* Help the student discover the pattern illustrated, then have her complete similar sequences. She may want to make up a few patterns all on her own.

$$6 \quad\quad 16 \quad\quad 26 \quad\quad 36$$
$$+8 \quad\quad +8 \quad\quad +8 \quad\quad +8$$
$$\overline{14} \quad\quad \overline{24} \quad\quad \overline{34} \quad\quad \overline{44} \quad \cdots \bullet$$

## Error Pattern S-W-1
*(from Cheryl's paper on page 22)*

Using the error pattern, Examples E and F would be computed as shown.

$$
\text{E.} \quad
\begin{array}{r}
458 \\
-372 \\
\hline
126
\end{array}
\qquad\qquad
\text{F.} \quad
\begin{array}{r}
241 \\
-96 \\
\hline
255
\end{array}
$$

Did you identify the error pattern? As a general rule, the ones are subtracted and recorded, then the tens are subtracted and recorded, and so on. Apparently Cheryl is considering each position (ones, tens, and so on) as a separate subtraction problem. In Example E, she probably would not think of the numbers 458 and 372, but only of 8 and 2, 5 and 7, and 4 and 3, Further, in subtracting single-digit numbers, she does not conceive of the upper figure (minuend) as the number in a set and the lower figure (subtrahend) as the number in a subset. When subtracting ones, Cheryl may think of the larger of the two numbers as the number of the set, and the smaller as the number to be removed from the set. Or she may merely compare the two single-digit numbers much as she would match sets one to one or place rods side by side to find a difference. In Example F, she would think, "1 and 6, the difference is 5." She uses the same procedure when subtracting tens and hundreds. Cheryl may have merely overgeneralized commutativity for addition and assumed that subtraction is also commutative.

Note that Example A on page 22 is correct. This example includes much smaller numbers than the other examples. It may be that Cheryl counted from 16 to 32, or she may have used some kind of number line. If she did think of 32 as "20 plus 12" in order to subtract, it may be that she applies renaming procedures only to smaller numbers that she can somehow conceptualize, but she breaks up larger numbers in the manner described above.

Has Cheryl heard rules in the classroom or at home that she is applying in her own way? Perhaps she has heard, "Always subtract the little number from the big one" and "Stay in the column when you subtract."

If you were Cheryl's teacher, what would you do? You need to extend your diagnosis by interviewing her and letting her think out loud as she works similar examples. Does she use the erroneous procedures only with greater numbers? Does she, on her own initiative, question the reasonableness of her answers? (In Example F, the result is greater than the minuend!)

How might you help Cheryl correct the error pattern? Are your ideas among those that follow?

1. *Use bundles of 100, bundles of 10, and single sticks.* Let the student show the "number altogether," that is, the minuend or sum shown by the upper numeral. Pose the problem of removing the number of sticks shown by the lower numeral. Any verbal problems presented in this context should describe take-away rather than comparison situations. Trading or exchanging may be needed. Eventually, guidance should be provided to help the student remove units first, then tens, and so on.

2. *Use a learning center for renaming.* For Cheryl and others with similar difficulties, a simple learning center could be set up to help them rename a minuend and select the most useful name for that number in a specific subtraction problem. One possibility is to have a sorting task in which the child decides which cards show another name for a given number and which show an entirely different number. A second task would be to consider all the different names for the given number and decide which of the names would be most useful for computing subtraction examples that have the given number as the minuend. Ask, "Which name will let us use the subtraction facts we know?"

3. *Use base-ten blocks.* Proceed as in Activity 1.
4. *Use a place-value chart.* Proceed similarly.

**So that students**
     **do *not* overgeneralize strategies,**

- intermix addition and subtraction problems early, and
- intermix two-digit and three-digit problems early.

## Error Pattern S-W-2

*(from George's paper on page 23)*

Did you identify the error pattern George used?

D.
$$\begin{array}{r} 2\ \overset{6}{\cancel{7}}\ ^{1}3 \\ -\ \ \ 3\ 8 \\ \hline 2\ 3\ 5 \end{array}$$

E.
$$\begin{array}{r} 2\ \overset{7}{\cancel{8}}\ ^{1}5 \\ -\ \ \ 6\ 3 \\ \hline 2\ /1/2 \end{array}$$

George has learned to "borrow," or rename, in subtraction. In fact, he renames whether he needs to or not. It is possible that George would be able to rename one ten as 10 ones, and it is also possible that he could interpret the answer (in Example E) as 2 hundreds, 1 ten, and 12 ones. But his final answer does not account for conventional place-value notation.

You have observed that the answer to Example D is correct. George's procedure is correct for a subtraction example that requires renaming tens as ones. However, George has overgeneralized. He does not distinguish between examples that require renaming and examples that do not require renaming. The fact that some of his answers are correct may reinforce his perception that the procedure he is using is appropriate for all subtraction examples.

How would you help George replace his error pattern with a correct computational procedure? Are your suggestions among those that follow?

**Note:** Helpful instruction will emphasize (1) the ability to distinguish between subtraction problems requiring regrouping in order to use basic subtraction facts and subtraction problems not requiring regrouping, and, (2) mechanics of notation.

1. *Use a physical representation for the minuend (sum).* If the minuend of Example E is represented physically (with base blocks for example), questions can be posed, such as, "Can I take away 3 units *without* trading?" or "When do I need to trade, and when is it not necessary for me to trade?"

2. *Replace computation with yes or no.* Focus on the critical skill of distinguishing by presenting a row of subtraction problems for which the differences are *not* to be computed. Have the child simply write yes or no for each example to indicate the decision whether regrouping is or is not needed. If this is difficult, physical materials should be available for the child to use. (See Activity 1.)

3. *Use a number line and estimate.* Let the student use a number line to help with the estimate. A number line showing at least hundreds and tens may be helpful for this purpose. Ask, "Will the answer be more than a hundred? Less than a hundred?"

## Error Pattern S-W-3

*(from Donna's paper on page 23)*

Did you find Donna's error pattern?

E.
$$446$$
$$-302$$
$$\overline{\phantom{00}104}$$

F.
$$760$$
$$-230$$
$$\overline{530}$$

Although Donna subtracts $0 - 0 = 0$ correctly, she consistently writes "0" for the missing addend (difference) whenever the known addend (subtrahend) is zero. She may be confusing this situation with multiplication fact in which zero is a factor. At any rate, she writes nine of the subtraction facts incorrectly because of this one difficulty.

We ought to be able to help Donna with a problem of this sort. How would you help her? Are your ideas among those that follow?

1. *Use base blocks or bundled sticks to picture the computation.* Show the sum (the minuend) of a given subtraction problem.

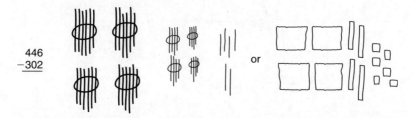

446
−302

Sit beside the student and arrange the materials so that units are to the right and hundreds to the left as in the algorithm. For Example E, let the student remove the number (of sticks or blocks) shown by the given addend, beginning with the units. After the student removes a subset of 2 units, *you* record the fact that 4 units remain. After the student removes an empty set of tens, you record the fact that 4 tens remain, and so on. For another example, you remove the subset while the *student* records the number remaining each time.

2. *Try a sorting game.* If the student has been introduced to the multiplication facts for zero, there may be confusion between the zero property for multiplication and the zero properties for other operations. For the zero facts of arithmetic, prepare cards similar to the ones shown.

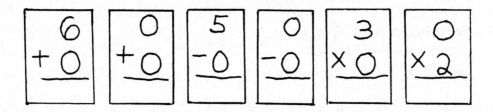

(Vertical notation is suggested in this case because it appears in the algorithm. It may be appropriate to include division number sentences as well, e.g., $0 \div 3 =$ .) To create an individual activity or a game for two, the cards can be sorted into two sets—those with zero for the answer and those that do not have zero for an answer.

3. *Use a calculator.* Have the student try several examples of adding a zero, subtracting a zero, and multiplying by zero. Then ask her to state a generalization or rule for each operation. Have her compare the rules to see how they are alike or different.

## Error Pattern S-W-4

*(from Barbara's paper on page 24)*

Did you find Barbara's error pattern?

E.
$$\begin{array}{r} \overset{3}{\cancel{4}}\overset{1}{3}6 \\ -172 \\ \hline 264 \end{array}$$

F.
$$\begin{array}{r} \overset{4}{\cancel{6}}\overset{1}{2}5 \\ -348 \\ \hline 187 \end{array}$$

Barbara appeared to be doing well with subtraction until recently, when renaming more than once was introduced. She apparently had been thinking something like, "Take 1 from 4 and put the 1 in front of the 3" (Example E). Now she has extended this procedure so that, in Example F, she thinks, "In order to subtract (i.e., in order to use a simple subtraction combination), I need a 1 in front of the 5 and a 1 in front of the 2. Take *two* 1s from the 6. . . ." Note that if Barbara had not been showing her work with crutches of some sort, it would have been much more difficult to find the pattern.

Help is needed—promptly—before she reinforces her error pattern with further practice. How would you help her? Are your suggestions among those that follow?

1. *Teach both situations, one column at a time.* Present problem situations involving subtraction with two two-digit numbers—situations that involve regrouping a ten as ones, and situations that do not. Make sure students can distinguish between these situations and do the computation required before introducing two three-digit numbers. Again, teach both situations together and focus on distinguishing between situations that require regrouping a hundred as tens from those that do not.

Note: Asking a student to check his computation may accomplish little in this situation. "Adding up" may only confirm that individual subtraction facts have been correctly recalled. The following activities are suggested to help a student keep in mind the *total quantity* from which a lesser number is being subtracted.

2. *Use base-ten blocks to show the sum (minuend).* Pointing to the known addend (subtrahend), ask, "Do we need to trade so we can remove this many? What trading must we do?" As appropriate, trade a ten for ones and *immediately* record the action; as appropriate, trade a hundred for tens and record that action. Stress the need to proceed step by step. Let the student trade and remove blocks while you record the action, then reverse the process. While you trade and remove blocks (thinking aloud as you do), let the student make the record.

3. *Use a game-like activity with a pattern board, base blocks, and a bank.* Help students understand place values and the algorithm itself by making it a written record of moves in a game-like activity. A pattern board serves as an organizing center. Appendix D describes such activities and includes an illustration for subtraction with whole numbers.

> When students learn one algorithm without adequate conceptual grounding and are then taught another algorithm, they sometimes confuse the two procedures. Carlos learned the equal-additions algorithm (also called the European-Latino algorithm), but was later taught the procedure commonly taught in the United States. What he is doing now makes no sense mathematically because he is combining the algorithms in a mechanical way.[2] Can you figure out what he is doing?
>
> $$\begin{array}{r} \overset{\overset{1}{3}\ \ \overset{}{15}}{\cancel{45}} \\ -\ 29 \\ \hline 66 \end{array} \qquad \begin{array}{r} \overset{\overset{1}{4}\ \ \overset{}{12}}{\cancel{52}} \\ -34 \\ \hline 88 \end{array} \qquad \begin{array}{r} \overset{\overset{1}{5}\ \ \overset{}{12}}{\cancel{62}} \\ -\ 17 \\ \hline 75 \end{array}$$

## CONCLUSION

Help students learn to choose when an estimate is needed and when an exact answer is needed; help them learn to choose the most appropriate way to get that exact answer when they are to add or subtract. Many times the most appropriate procedure is a paper-and-pencil procedure.

As you help students learn addition and subtraction procedures, focus on concepts and number sense. Prompt them to make a habit of asking, "Is it reasonable?" Continuously emphasize estimation. And help students monitor their own learning, possibly by keeping a journal.

During instruction, make sure each student is aware of his or her strengths. Help individuals take note of progress as it is made. Proceed in very small steps, if necessary, to ensure successful experiences.

Diagnosis is a continuous process. It continues even during instructional activity as you observe a student at work. Keep looking for patterns.

## FURTHER REFLECTION

Consider the following questions:

1. *Before* a student learns algorithms for adding and subtracting whole numbers, should that student understand place values and the *pattern* of place values within multi-digit numerals? Why?
2. How would you determine if a particular student understands multi-digit numerals for whole numbers?
3. Show an error pattern in adding or subtracting whole numbers that was likely caused by misunderstanding a particular mathematical concept or principle. Also, show an error pattern in adding or subtracting whole numbers caused primarily by misunderstanding the mechanics of notation.
4. Think of what teachers sometimes say to students that might prompt students to adopt one of the error patterns illustrated in this chapter.

## ADDITIONAL PRACTICE

Can you describe the error pattern in each of the following papers? A key is provided on page 233.

PAPER 1

A.
$$35$$
$$+28$$
$$\overline{\phantom{0}18}$$

B.
$$24$$
$$+17$$
$$\overline{\phantom{0}14}$$

C.
$$43$$
$$+26$$
$$\overline{\phantom{0}15}$$

PAPER 2

A.
$$47$$
$$-\phantom{0}3$$
$$\overline{14}$$

B.
$$65$$
$$-\phantom{0}2$$
$$\overline{43}$$

C.
$$78$$
$$-\phantom{0}4$$
$$\overline{34}$$

PAPER 3
The store had a sale of red and blue shirts. There were 46 red shirts left after the sale, and 28 blue shirts were left. How many shirts were left after the sale?

$$\underline{\phantom{00}18\phantom{00}}$$

# REFERENCES

1. Chip Trading Activities, originally published by Scott Resources, Inc., are available from suppliers of materials for elementary school mathematics. They include a sequence of games and other activities that involve trading colored chips. Activities emphasize the pattern of grouping in our numeration system.
2. See P. Ron (1998). My family taught me this way. In L. J. Morrow and M. J. Kenney (Eds.). *The teaching and learning of algorithms in school mathematics* (pp. 115–119). Reston, VA: National Council of Teachers of Mathematics.

# CHAPTER 3

# Error Patterns:
# Multiplication and Division
## with Whole Numbers

In this chapter you will find examples of papers in which students practiced multiplying and dividing whole numbers. These papers may be like some you will encounter in your own classroom.

Look for a pattern, then check your findings by using the procedure with the examples provided for that purpose. When you think you see the pattern, make sure by looking at the other examples on the paper.

As you read about each student's procedure, think about needed instruction. Can you think of at least two different activities to help the student? Compare your ideas with the author's suggestions.

Each error pattern has been labeled to facilitate discussion: M-W for multiplication with whole numbers, and D-W for division with whole numbers.

## ▨ Identifying Patterns

### Error Pattern M-W-1

*The new park is in the shape of a parallelogram measuring 46 meters along the base and having a height of 26 meters. What is the area of the new park?*

Bob is proud that he really knows his multiplication facts. When his math group multiplies by one-digit numbers, he gets the correct answer, but now he often gets an incorrect product.

Look carefully at Bob's written work for these problems. His place-value columns are aligned carefully, but he is having difficulty. What error pattern is he following?

Name _Bob_

A.
$$\overset{2}{4}6$$
$$\times \ 24$$
$$184$$
$$102$$
$$1204$$

B.
$$'76$$
$$\times \ 32$$
$$152$$
$$228$$
$$2432$$

C.
$$\overset{5}{4}8$$
$$\times \ 57$$
$$336$$
$$250$$
$$2836$$

Did you find his error pattern? Check yourself by using his procedure for Examples D and E.

D.
$$98$$
$$\times 56$$

E.
$$86$$
$$\times 45$$

Do you think Bob is using estimation, or can you tell? What does he *not* yet understand? Turn to Error pattern M-W-1 on page 45 to see if you identified the error pattern.

## Error Pattern M-W-2

Previously, Joe experienced some success multiplying by a one-digit factor; however, this practice paper suggests a difficulty. The products are not correct, and it is important that Joe receive help before he does more practice exercises. It is a common error pattern. Can you find it?

Name _Joe_

A.
$$\overset{2}{2}7$$
$$\times 4$$
$$168$$

B.
$$\overset{2}{3}4$$
$$\times 6$$
$$304$$

C.
$$\overset{3}{4}5$$
$$\times 7$$
$$495$$

Did you find his error pattern? What does Joe understand correctly? What does Joe need to understand and apply in this situation? Check yourself by using his procedure for Examples D and E.

D.
$$68 \\ \times\ 5$$

E.
$$29 \\ \times\ 3$$

After you finish Examples D and E, turn to page 47 to see if you were able to identify the error pattern. What could possibly have caused Joe to learn such a procedure?

## Error Pattern M-W-3

Doug seems to multiply correctly by a one-digit multiplier, but now he is having trouble with two- and three-digit multipliers. Can you find his error pattern?

Name __Doug__

A.
$$3\overset{1}{1}3 \\ \times\ 4 \\ \overline{1\ 2\ 5\ 2}$$

B.
$$210 \\ \times 15 \\ \overline{210}$$

C.
$$5\overset{1}{2}4 \\ \times 34 \\ \overline{1\ 5\ 7\ 6}$$

D.
$$4\overset{1}{3}3 \\ \times 226 \\ \overline{8\ 7\ 8}$$

Did you find his pattern? What does Doug do correctly? He seems to be confused by two- and three-digit multipliers. What is he confusing with the multiplication algorithm?

Check yourself by using Doug's error pattern for Examples E and F.

E.  6 2 1
    x   2 3

F.  5 1 7
    x 4 6 3

After Examples E and F are completed, turn to page 48 to learn if you have correctly identified Doug's procedure. What instruction might you initiate with Doug or any student using such a procedure?

## Error Pattern D-W-1

*At the factory, there are 176 sponges to be placed 2 in a bag. How many bags will be needed?*

Jim's quotient for this problem is not even reasonable. Obviously, he is not using estimation. What he is actually doing may surprise you. Can you find his error pattern?

Name *Jim*

A.
233
2⟌176

B.
221
4⟌824

C.
231
3⟌713

Did you find the procedure? Check yourself by using Jim's procedure for Examples D and E.

D.
3⟌639

E.
4⟌518

Why might Jim be using this procedure? Do you suppose the teacher could have said anything that he is applying inappropriately?

After completing Examples D and E, turn to Error Pattern D-W-1 on page 50 and learn if you correctly identified Jim's error pattern. What instructional procedures might you use to help Jim or any other student using this procedure?

## Error Pattern D-W-2

Clearly, Gail does not understand division as a relationship between two factors and a reasonable product. Her division computation is neat, with columns aligned, but the quotients she computes are usually incorrect. Look carefully at her written work. Can you find the error pattern she has followed?

Name *Gail*

A.
```
    4 4
  2)8 8
    8
    ‾‾
    8
    8
    ‾
```

B.
```
      1 4
  4)1 6 4
    1 6
    ‾‾
      4
      4
      ‾
```

C.
```
      6 7
  3)2 2 8
    2 1
    ‾‾
      1 8
      1 8
      ‾‾
```

D.
```
      3 9
  5)4 6 5
    4 5
    ‾‾
      1 5
      1 5
      ‾‾
```

Did you find the procedure? Check yourself by using the error pattern to compute these examples.

E.
```
  3)7 5
```

F.
```
  6)5 1 6
```

Why might Gail be using this procedure? Turn to Error Pattern D-W-2 on page 51 and see if you identified her error pattern. Can you think of a way to help Gail?

## Error Pattern D-W-3

John has been doing well with much of his work in division, but recently he began having difficulty. Can you find his error pattern?

Name *John*

A.
$$
\begin{array}{r}
6\,5\,\text{R}\,1 \\
7\,\overline{)4\,5\,6} \\
4\,2 \\
\hline
3\,6 \\
3\,5 \\
\hline
1
\end{array}
$$

B.
$$
\begin{array}{r}
9\,4\,\text{R}\,2 \\
6\,\overline{)5\,4\,2\,6} \\
5\,4 \\
\hline
2\,6 \\
2\,4 \\
\hline
2
\end{array}
$$

C.
$$
\begin{array}{r}
6\,7\,\text{R}\,4 \\
8\,\overline{)4\,8\,6\,0} \\
4\,8 \\
\hline
6\,0 \\
5\,6 \\
\hline
4
\end{array}
$$

D.
$$
\begin{array}{r}
5\,4\,\text{R}\,3 \\
8\,\overline{)4\,0\,3\,5} \\
4\,0 \\
\hline
3\,5 \\
3\,2 \\
\hline
3
\end{array}
$$

Do you think John is using estimation? Try his procedure with these examples.

E.
$$9\,\overline{)2\,7\,2\,1}$$

F.
$$6\,\overline{)4\,2\,5\,0}$$

After you complete Examples E and F, turn to page 53 to see if you correctly identified John's error pattern. Why might John be using such a procedure? What instructional procedures might you use to help him?

## ■ Planning Instruction

### Error Pattern M-W-1
*(used by Bob on page 40)*

Did you find the error pattern Bob used?

Consider Example E. When multiplying 5 ones times 6 ones, Bob recorded the 3 tens as a reminder above the 8 tens so he would add 3 tens to the product of 5 and 8 tens. However, the reminder recorded when multiplying by ones was *also* used when multiplying by tens.

D.

$$
\begin{array}{r}
\overset{4}{9}\,8 \\
\times\ 5\,6 \\
\hline
5\,8\,8 \\
4\,9\,0 \\
\hline
5\,4\,8\,8
\end{array}
$$

E.

$$
\begin{array}{r}
\overset{3}{8}\,6 \\
\times\ 4\,5 \\
\hline
4\,3\,0 \\
3\,5\,4 \\
\hline
3\,9\,7\,0
\end{array}
$$

Note that the answers to Example B on page 40 and Example D above are correct. Bob's error pattern may have gone undetected because he gets enough correct answers—enough positive reinforcement—to convince him that he is using a correct procedure. There may have been enough correct answers to cause Bob's busy teacher to conclude that Bob was merely careless. But Bob is *consistently* applying an erroneous procedure.

How would you help Bob with this all-too-common problem? Are your suggestions among the following?

**Note:** The following activities emphasize place value, the distributive property, and proper mechanics of notation.

1. *Use more partial products and no reminder.* The algorithm that follows can be related to an array partitioned twice. When the student is able to use this algorithm with ease, let him try to combine the first two partial products (and also the last two) by *remembering* the number of tens (and the number of hundreds). In this situation, do not encourage use of a written reminder.

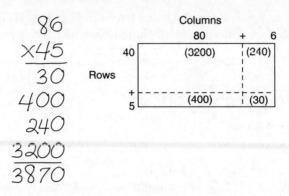

2.  *Make two problems.* Have the student multiply by ones and then by tens
    in two separate problems. As he computes the product in this way,
    encourage him to try remembering his reminder number (rather than
    writing it) "because they are sometimes confusing in multiplication and
    division." When he can compute each easily without recording a
    reminder, you may want to suggest that he convert to a more standard
    algorithm.

3.  *Record tens within partial products.* Instead of writing a "reminding
    number" above the example, use lightly written, half-sized numerals
    within each of the partial products to record the number of tens to be
    remembered.

Caution: There is a very real danger in proceeding to a standard algorithm too quickly. Often, a new, more efficient procedure is best introduced as a shortcut for an already understood algorithm. Whenever zeros help a student think in terms of place value, do not insist that the units zero in the second partial product be dropped.

---

## Use Reminders?

Written reminder numbers are to be encouraged if they are useful and help the student understand what he is doing. But they can be confusing when multiplying by a two-digit multiplier. Also, questions such as $5 \times 86 = \boxed{\phantom{x}}$ occur within division computation, where use of a written reminder is impractical. For these reasons, students should be encouraged to remember numbers in multiplication rather than writing a reminder.

---

## Error Pattern M-W-2
*(from Joe's paper on page 40)*

Did you find the error pattern Joe uses?

D.
$$
\begin{array}{r}
\overset{4}{6}\,8 \\
\times\ \ \ 5 \\
\hline
5\,0\,0
\end{array}
$$

E.
$$
\begin{array}{r}
\overset{2}{2}\,9 \\
\times\ \ \ 3 \\
\hline
1\,2\,7
\end{array}
$$

Joe is using an erroneous procedure that is all too frequently adopted by students. He adds the reminding number *before* multiplying the tens figure, whereas the algorithm requires that the tens figure be multiplied first. In Example D, he thought, "6 plus 4 equals 10 and 5 times 10 equals 50" instead of "5 times 6 equals 30 and 30 plus 4 equals 34." It may be that when Joe learned the addition algorithm involving regrouping, his teacher reminded him repeatedly, "The first thing you do is to add the number you carry." Some teachers drill children on such a rule, and it is little wonder that children sometimes apply the rule in inappropriate contexts.

How would you help Joe? Are your suggestions among the following?

1. *Use partial products.* Such an algorithm is easily developed as a step-by-step record of what is done when an array is partitioned. Help the student determine the order in which the multiplication and addition occur, lead him to generalize, and state the sequence.

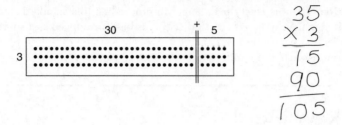

2. *Write the reminder below the bar.* Instead of the student writing a reminder in the conventional way, have him make a small numeral below the bar to remind him to add *just before* recording a product.

$$\begin{array}{r} 2\,9 \\ \times\ \ \ 3 \\ \hline {}_2\ \ 7 \end{array} \qquad\qquad \begin{array}{r} 2\,9 \\ \times\ \ \ 3 \\ \hline {}_8^2\ 7 \end{array}$$

## Error Pattern M-W-3
*(from Doug's paper on page 41)*

Did you find Doug's error pattern? If so, you completed Examples E and F as they are shown.

E.
$$\begin{array}{r} 6\,2\,1 \\ \times\ \ \ 2\,3 \\ \hline 1\,2\,4\,3 \end{array}$$

F.
$$\begin{array}{r} 5\,\overset{2}{1}\,7 \\ \times\ 4\,6\,3 \\ \hline 2\,0\,8\,1 \end{array}$$

The procedure used by Doug is a blend of the algorithm for multiplying by a one-digit multiplier and the conventional addition algorithm. Each column is approached as a separate multiplication. When the multiplicand has more digits than the multiplier, the left-most digit of the multiplier continues to be used.

You may meet Doug in your own classroom. How would you help him? Are your ideas among the following?

1. *Use the distributive property.* Have the student rewrite the problem as two problems. Later, the two products can be related to partial products in the conventional algorithm.

$$621 \quad \rightarrow \quad 621 \qquad 621$$
$$\times \quad 23 \qquad \times \quad 20 \qquad \times \quad 3$$
$$\qquad\qquad\qquad \underline{\phantom{xxx}} \qquad \underline{\phantom{xxx}}$$
$$\qquad\qquad\qquad ? \qquad\qquad ?$$

If the student does not understand why the sum of the two products is the same number as the product in the original problem, partition an array and label the parts. If the student does not understand the concept of an array, begin with small numbers.

$$2 \times 3$$

Then use rectangles to represent arrays with greater numbers.

23 × 621

621

| 20 + 3 | (20 × 621) |
|---|---|
| | (3 × 621) |

2. *Use a paper mask.* To help the student focus on multiplying the entire upper figure (multiplicand) by one place value at a time, cover the multiplier so only one digit at a time will show. After multiplication by the units digit is completed, the mask can be moved to the left so that only the tens digit is visible. Later, the hundreds digit can be highlighted. With each digit, emphasize the need to do a complete multiplication problem. Also stress proper placement of each partial product.

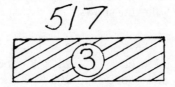

3. *Use a calculator.* Use a calculator to compute each partial product. Make sure the correct values are multiplied; for 23 × 621, multiply 3 × 621 then 20 × 621.

## Error Pattern D-W-1

*(used by Jim on page 42)*

Did you find the erroneous procedure Jim used?

D.
$$3\overline{)639} = 213$$

E.
$$4\overline{)518} = 142$$

Example D is correct and it does not give many clues to Jim's thinking. Example E illustrates Jim's thinking more completely. Apparently Jim ignores place value in the dividend and quotient, and he thinks of each digit as "ones." Furthermore, he considers one digit of the dividend and the one-digit divisor as two numbers "to be divided." The greater of the two (whether the divisor or a digit within the dividend) is divided by the lesser and the result is recorded. Jim has probably learned something like, "a smaller number goes into a larger number." The remainder is ignored.

**Note:** To help the student who has adopted such an error pattern, select activities that emphasize place values in the dividend and stress the total quantity of the dividend. Procedures that can be understood in relation to concrete referents are needed instead of an assortment of rules to be applied in a mechanical way. In essence, a division algorithm needs to be reintroduced.

1. *Use manipulatives to redevelop the algorithm.* Teach the algorithm as a step-by-step record of activities with manipulatives. For the problem 54 ÷ 3 = ? the dividend can be shown as 5 tens and 4 units using base-ten blocks, Cuisenaire rods, single sticks and bundles, or Montessori Golden Beads. See the game-like activity for division described in Appendix D.

2. *Focus on skill in multiplying multiples of powers of 10 by a single digit.* This skill, used in the above activities, may need to be developed independently of a division algorithm. Patterns can be observed from such data, as the following shows.

$$2 \times 3 = 6 \qquad\qquad 2 \times 3 = 6$$
$$2 \times 30 = 60 \qquad\qquad 20 \times 3 = 60$$
$$2 \times 300 = 600 \qquad\qquad 200 \times 3 = 600$$

Have the student describe the pattern orally. Consider this conversation.

STUDENT: You find the numbers (digits) for the multiplication fact, then you count the zeros and write the same number of zeros. Then you are done.

TEACHER: That's a great rule, but does it always work? Try your rule with these examples, then use your calculator to see if the rule always works.

3. *Estimate quotient figures.* Use open number sentences such as $3 \times ? \leq 54$ with the rule that the number to be found is the largest multiple of a power of 10 that will make the number sentence true.

## Error Pattern D-W-2
*(from Gail's paper on page 43)*

Using Gail's incorrect procedure. Examples E and F would be computed as shown.

E.
$$
\begin{array}{r}
5\,2 \\
3\overline{\smash{\big)}\,7\,5} \\
6\,0 \\
\hline
1\,5 \\
1\,5 \\
\hline
\end{array}
$$

F.
$$
\begin{array}{r}
6\,8 \\
6\overline{\smash{\big)}\,5\,1\,6} \\
4\,8\,0 \\
\hline
3\,6 \\
3\,6 \\
\hline
\end{array}
$$

Did you find the error pattern? In the ones column Gail records the first quotient figure she determines, and in the tens column she records the second digit she determines. In other words, the answer is recorded right to left. In the usual algorithms for addition, subtraction, and multiplication of whole numbers, the answer is recorded right to left. Perhaps Gail assumes it is appropriate to do the same with the division algorithm.

It is quite probable that, for Example E, Gail thinks "7 divided by 3" (or perhaps "3 times what number is 7") rather than, "75 divided by 3." The quotient for a shortcut expression such as "7 divided by 3" would indeed be 2 units. Shortcuts in thinking and the standard algorithm for division may have been introduced too soon.

What would you do if you were Gail's teacher? What corrective steps might you take? Are your suggestions among those that follow?

1. *Estimate the quotient before computing.* Frequently, quotients resulting from the erroneous algorithm are quite unreasonable. If intelligent estimating is followed by computing, and the estimate and the quotient are then compared, the student may rethink her computational procedure.

2. *Redevelop an algorithm.* Give the student base blocks and a problem such as 75 divided by 3. Then have the student work out the answer using the blocks, possibly with the game-like activity for division in Appendix D. Make sure the quotient is recorded step by step, using appropriate place values. After the written record is completed, have the student reflect on the written procedure and how it differs from what she has been doing.

3. *Develop skill in multiplying numbers by powers of 10.* This skill is necessary for meaningful use of any of the division algorithms. A series of equations can be written to facilitate observation of patterns.

$$6 \times 4 = 24$$
$$6 \times 40 = 240$$
$$6 \times 400 = 2400$$

4. *Use a different algorithm.* At least temporarily, choose an algorithm that shows the value of each partial quotient. In each of the algorithms in Example F, the 8 in the quotient is first shown as 80, thereby emphasizing proper placement of quotient figures. After the student is able to use such an algorithm, a transition to the standard algorithm can be made, if desired, by recording quotients differently. In Example F-3, the first quotient figure would be recorded as 8 in the tens place instead of 80.

F-1

$$
\begin{array}{r}
6\overline{)516} \\
480 = 80 \times 6 \\
\hline
36 \\
36 = \phantom{00}6 \times 6 \\
\hline
86 \times 6
\end{array}
$$

F-2

$$
\begin{array}{r|l}
6\overline{)516} & \\
480 & 80 \\
\hline
36 & \\
36 & 6 \\
\hline
& 86
\end{array}
$$

F-3

$$
\begin{array}{r}
86 \\
6 \\
80 \\
6\overline{)516} \\
480 \\
\hline
36 \\
36 \\
\hline
\end{array}
$$

5. *Emphasize place value in estimating quotient figures.* Let the student use open number sentences such as $3 \times ? \leq 70$ and $3 \times ? \leq 15$ while thinking through Example E. Number sentences should be completed remembering the following: When dividing 7 tens, the missing number is the largest multiple of 10 that will make the number sentence true. For $3 \times ? \leq 70, ? = 20$. Similarly, when dividing 15 ones, the missing number is the largest multiple of one that will make the number sentence true.

## Error Pattern D-W-3
*(from John's paper on page 44)*

If you found John's error pattern, you completed Examples E and F as they are shown.

E.

$$9\overline{)2721} \quad 3\,2\,r3$$
$$\underline{27}$$
$$21$$
$$\underline{18}$$
$$3$$

F.

$$6\overline{)4250} \quad 7\,8\,r2$$
$$\underline{42}$$
$$50$$
$$\underline{48}$$
$$2$$

John has difficulty with examples that include a zero in the tens place of the quotient. Whenever he cannot divide in the tens place, he proceeds to the ones place, but without recording a zero to show that there are no tens. He may believe that "zero is nothing." Also, careless placement of figures in the quotient may contribute to John's problem.

How would you help John? Are your ideas among the following?

1. *Estimate the quotient before beginning computation.* Have the student determine how many digits are in the quotient, then record an estimated quotient. This may be sufficient to overcome the problem, especially if careless writing of quotient figures is a major cause of the difficulty.
2. *Use lined paper turned 90°.* It may be that letting the student use vertically lined paper (or cross-sectioned paper) will clear up the problem. When such forms are used for practice, the omission of one digit becomes very obvious.

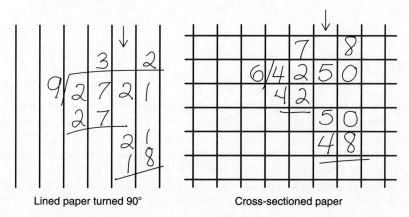

Lined paper turned 90°                    Cross-sectioned paper

3. *Use the pyramid algorithm.* At least temporarily, use an algorithm that emphasizes place value. If the pyramid algorithm has been learned by the student earlier in the instructional program, ask him to solve some of the troublesome examples using it to see if he can figure out why he is having difficulty now. If the pyramid algorithm is new to the student, he may enjoy trying a new procedure that is a bit easier to understand.

$$
\begin{array}{r}
6\ 0\ 7\ r\ 4 \\
7 \\
6\ 0\ 0 \\
8\,\overline{)4\ 8\ 6\ 0} \\
4\ 8\ 0\ 0 \\
\hline
6\ 0 \\
5\ 6 \\
\hline
4
\end{array}
$$

4. *Use base-ten blocks and a game-like activity.* Teach the algorithm as a step-by-step record of activities with base-ten blocks, using the game-like activity for division described in Appendix D. For Example E ($2721 \div 9 = ?$) the two 10-blocks cannot be distributed among nine sets; it is therefore necessary to exchange the two 10-blocks for an equal number—an equal amount of wood—for 20 unit-blocks. But before exchanging, *make sure the student records in the algorithm with a zero that no 10-blocks are being distributed* among the nine sets.

## CONCLUSION

Keep looking for patterns while teaching multiplication and division procedures. Continuously emphasize the need for reasonable answers. Build on students' strengths.

During diagnosis and instruction, notice how your students use language—the specific meanings they associate with words and phrases.

When students use manipulative, be sure they connect what they observe with the written procedure you are teaching.

## FURTHER REFLECTION

Consider the following questions:

1. In Error Pattern M-W-2 Joe added the reminding number before multiplying the tens number, whereas the algorithm requires that the tens number be multiplied first. Why is it necessary to multiply the tens number before adding the reminding number?
2. In Error Pattern D-W-3 John apparently thought that zero is nothing, and therefore it can be ignored. Is zero nothing? Is zero a number? Is zero a numeral? Is zero a place holder? What is zero? Can you think of other computations where zero is often a problem?
3. When a missing number is needed, how important is it for students to estimate? Should they estimate before or after they compute the needed number?
4. Students learning to multiply and divide with whole numbers are a bit older than students learning to add and subtract. As we teach students to multiply and divide with whole numbers, do we really need to use two- and three-dimensional representations? Why?

## ADDITIONAL PRACTICE

Can you describe the error pattern in the following paper? A key is provided on page 233.

PAPER 4

A.

$$
\begin{array}{r}
3\ 6 \\
\times\ 2\ 5 \\
\hline
1\ 8\ 0 \\
1\ 0\ 2 \\
\hline
1\ 2\ 0\ 0
\end{array}
$$

B.

$$
\begin{array}{r}
7\ 8 \\
\times\ 4\ 3 \\
\hline
2\ 3\ 4 \\
3\ 3\ 2 \\
\hline
3\ 5\ 5\ 4
\end{array}
$$

C.

$$
\begin{array}{r}
6\ 5 \\
\times\ 3\ 7 \\
\hline
4\ 5\ 5 \\
2\ 2\ 5 \\
\hline
2\ 7\ 0\ 5
\end{array}
$$

CHAPTER 4

# Misconceptions and Error Patterns:
# Concepts and Equivalence
## with Fractions and Decimals

Papers in this chapter involve fraction concepts, equivalent fractions, and decimals. The procedures students used resulted in many incorrect answers.

Can you find the patterns that characterize each student's responses? Check your findings by using the error pattern with the examples provided for that purpose. Verify your hypothesis by looking at the other examples on the student's paper.

As you read about a student's procedure, think about what you need to do to help the student. It is always wise to have in mind more than one strategy, so try to conceive of at least two different activities. Then compare your suggestions with those recorded in this text. To facilitate discussion of the error patterns, each pattern is labeled to indicate fraction concepts (F-C), decimal equivalents (D-E), or fraction equivalents (F-E).

## ◼ Identifying Patterns

### Error Pattern F-C-1

Gretchen completed her worksheet with ease, but only one example is correct. What does she understand? What does she *not* yet understand? At times she uses an erroneous procedure. Can you find her error pattern?

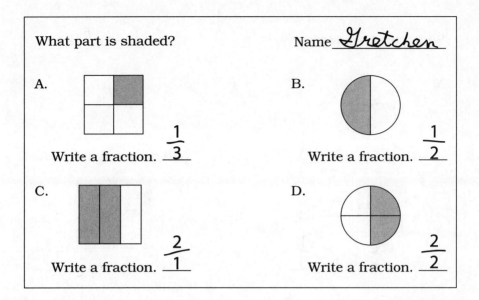

Why do you think Gretchen responded correctly to Example B? Make sure you found her error pattern by using her procedure for these.

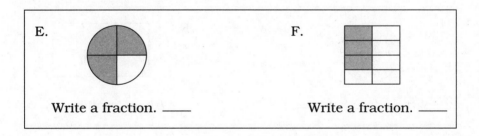

Now, turn to Error Pattern F-C-1 on page 61 and see if you identified her procedure. How will you help Gretchen so that she will have correct associations for fraction symbols?

## Error Pattern F-C-2

Carlos was asked to complete a worksheet to show that he understands certain fraction concepts. What does he understand? What does he *not* yet understand? Find his error pattern.

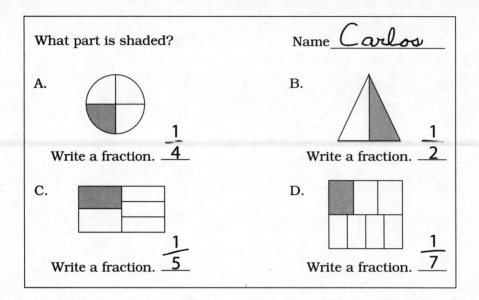

What part is shaded?          Name _Carlos_

A.          Write a fraction. $\frac{1}{4}$

B.          Write a fraction. $\frac{1}{2}$

C.          Write a fraction. $\frac{1}{5}$

D.          Write a fraction. $\frac{1}{7}$

Make sure you know what Carlos is doing by using his procedure for these examples.

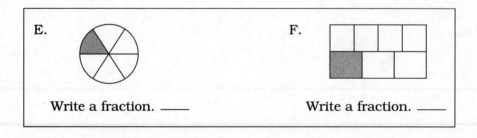

E.          Write a fraction. ____

F.          Write a fraction. ____

Now, turn to Error Pattern F-C-2 on page 62 and see if you identified his procedure. Why might he be responding in this way?

## Error Pattern D-E-1

Even though Tonya *can* name place values within decimals, she is struggling with very basic decimal concepts as she compares decimals. At some point during instruction she made an incorrect inference. What is her error pattern?

Name __Tonya__

Write <, >, or =.

A.  0.3 ___<___ 0.4          B.  0.2 ___<___ 0.02

C.  0.03 ___>___ 0.3          D.  0.1 ___=___ 0.1

E.  0.2 ___<___ 0.03          F.  0.001 ___>___ 0.02

Find out if you correctly identified Tonya's error pattern by using her procedure to complete Examples G and H.

G. 0.04 _____ 0.5          H. 0.9 _____ 0.01

Now turn to page 63, where Tonya's pattern is described. How could you help her and any others using this pattern?

## Error Pattern F-E-1

Jill needs to determine the simplest terms for each fraction. Some are already in simplest terms, but some fractions need to be changed to simpler terms.

What procedure is she using? This error pattern is difficult to find. You may have to interview Jill and listen to her explanation of how she changed each fraction.

Name __Jill__

A. $\dfrac{4}{9} = \dfrac{2}{3}$          B. $\dfrac{3}{9} = \dfrac{1}{3}$

C. $\dfrac{3}{8} = \dfrac{1}{4}$          D. $\dfrac{4}{8} = \dfrac{3}{4}$

Even though she was using an error pattern, Jill actually did change some fractions to simplest terms. Find out if you correctly identified Jill's procedure by using her error pattern to complete Examples E and F.

E.
$$\frac{3}{4} =$$

F.
$$\frac{2}{8} =$$

Next, turn to page 64, where Jill's pattern is described. How might you help Jill or others using such a pattern?

## Error Pattern F-E-2

If Sue understands basic fraction concepts and what *equals* means, she certainly is not applying that knowledge. She appears to be following some rules she constructed somehow, perhaps from phrases she heard in the classroom.

Sue tried to change each fraction to lowest or simplest terms, but her results are quite unreasonable. Can you find her error pattern?

---

Name _Sue_

A. $\dfrac{4}{8} = \dfrac{2}{8}$     B. $\dfrac{6}{8} = \dfrac{1}{8}$     C. $\dfrac{2}{4} = \dfrac{2}{4}$

D. $\dfrac{7}{7} = \dfrac{1}{7}$     E. $\dfrac{4}{6} = \dfrac{1}{6}$     F. $\dfrac{9}{3} = \dfrac{3}{9}$

---

Use Sue's procedure with these fractions to learn if you found her pattern.

G. $\dfrac{3}{6} =$                                H. $\dfrac{6}{4} =$

After Examples G and H are completed, turn to page 67 to see if you found Sue's error pattern. How would you help Sue or any student using such a procedure? Where would you begin?

## ■ Planning Instruction

### Error Pattern F-C-1
*(from Gretchen's paper on page 57)*

If you completed Examples E and F using the procedure Gretchen used, you completed them as follows.

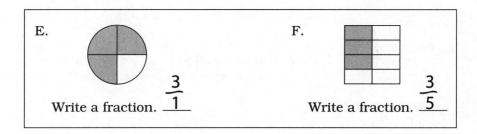

Apparently Gretchen understands that the number of shaded parts is indicated by the numerator. She then counts the number of parts not shaded and records that number (rather than the total number of equivalent parts) as the denominator for her fraction.

Gretchen's response to Example B (on page 57) is not consistent with the procedure she used. She may have memorized a specific connection between a semicircular shape and one half; for her, a semicircular region may be "what one half looks like."

How would you help Gretchen correct her error pattern? Are your suggestions among those that follow?

> Students *must* understand how a fractional part is related to the unit.

1. *Start with the whole.* Have the student "build" the fraction for a given unit region by thinking about the whole unit. "How many equal-sized parts are there *altogether* in the whole square (circle, etc.)? Write that number." Then have the student put a "roof" over that number, and write the number of shaded parts on top. Be sure to have the student read each fraction she makes, and read them top-to-bottom: "one of four parts, that's one fourth; two of three parts, that's two thirds; and so on." A set can be used in place of a unit region—possibly with two colors.

2. *Color parts, then record.* For each of these rectangular strips, have the student record the total number of equal-size parts, then make a line above each numeral (to show that it is the total number of equal-size parts), and then color one or more parts in each strip. Finally, have the student write the number of *colored* parts above the total number of parts. Ask, "How much of each strip is colored?"

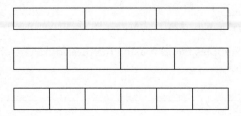

3. *Play an online visual fractions game.* For example, Find Grampy-Strict names fractional parts of a unit along a line, but also requires the concept "lowest terms." See http://www.visualfractions.com/FindGrampstrict.html.

## Error Pattern F-C-2
*(from Carlos's paper on page 58)*

If you completed Examples E and F using the procedure Carlos used, you completed them as follows.

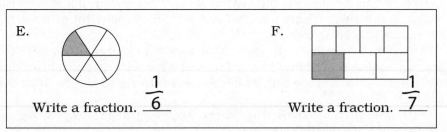

Carlos associates the denominator of the fraction with the total number of parts indicated, and the numerator with the number of shaded parts.

However, he apparently fails to understand that these associations apply *only* when *all* shaded parts are equivalent. Each fractional part needs to be the same part of the whole unit; each needs to cover the same area within the unit region.

Carlos needs to make sure that all parts are equivalent. When they are not equivalent, he needs to determine how much of the unit region each individual shaded part covers, and write a fraction with this in mind.

How would you help Carlos? Are the instructional activities you suggest among those that follow?

1. *Select fourths.* Give the student partially shaded regions similar to these and have the student select all that show one fourth. Have the student

explain (to you or to another student) why each shaded region does or does not show one fourth.

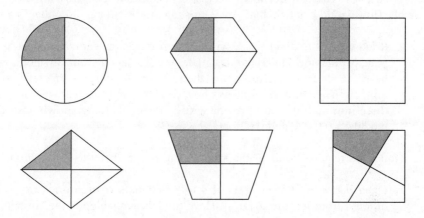

2. *Focus on equal area.* In using fractional parts of a unit region as the model for a fraction, the parts do not have to be the same shape, but they *do* have to be the same size; that is, they must have the same area. They have to cover the same amount of surface. Have the student identify which of the following regions are divided into equal-size parts, and which are not so divided.

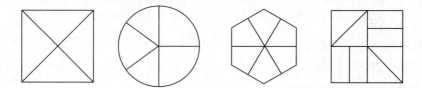

## Error Pattern D-E-1
*(from Tonya's paper on page 59)*

Did you find Tonya's pattern?

G.  0.04 _____>_____ 0.5        H.  0.9 _____<_____ 0.01

When Tonya compares two decimals, she appears to focus primarily on the "size" of the numeral and thinks that a numeral with an additional place is for a greater number because the numeral is longer. She does not compare the total values of the numbers shown.

Tonya may be able to name place values in decimals, but she does not yet understand the total value of a rational number represented with a decimal. She needs to be able to compare decimals successfully before she learns to compute with decimals. How would you help her? Are your suggestions among those that follow?

1. *Relate models to decimals.* Using base-ten blocks or equivalent materials (e.g., Montessori materials) designate one size as one unit (a whole) and have the student determine that the next smallest size is one tenth of a unit, etc. Then have the student show you "one and two tenths," "one and three hundredths," etc. Present written decimals to be shown with the models: 1.03, 0.4, and 0.02.

**Note:** This requires "if-then" thinking: "If this is one, then this is one tenth."

2. *Order decimals.* Present sets of 3 to 5 decimals written on cards to be ordered from least to greatest. Have models available for the student to use if needed when comparing decimals.
3. *Use a zero-to-one number line.* Provide (or have the student make) a number line from zero to one.

Have the student place 0.5 on the number line, then 0.05. Provide guidance as needed. Then on a different zero-to-one number line, have the student place 0.2 followed by 0.05. Discuss patterns observed, and contrast those patterns with the error pattern that was used.

## Error Pattern F-E-1
*(from Jill's paper on page 59)*

Did you find Jill's error pattern?

E.
$$\frac{3}{4} = \frac{1}{2}$$

F.
$$\frac{2}{8} = \frac{1}{4}$$

Jill's computation appears almost random, though several answers are correct. She obviously does not recognize which fractions are already in simplest terms. She explains her procedure as follows:

"4 goes to 2, and 9 goes to 3"
"3 goes to 1, and 9 goes to 3"

For Examples E and F,

"3 goes to 1, and 4 goes to 2"
"2 goes to 1, and 8 goes to 4"

Jill simply associates a specific whole number with each given numerator or denominator. *All* 3s become 1s and *all* 4s become 2s when fractions are to be changed to simplest terms. This procedure is a very mechanical one, requiring no concept of a fraction; however, it does produce correct answers part of the time.

Concepts such as the equivalence of rational numbers develop very *slowly* over time. If students are taught computational procedures before they develop adequate concepts of fractions and equivalent fractions, they are apt to experience difficulty.

Jill has a very real problem. How would you help her replace this erroneous procedure with a correct procedure? Are your suggestions among those that follow?

**Note:** It may be wise to extend the diagnosis to determine if the student is able to interpret a fraction as parts of a region or a set. If the student cannot, instruction should begin with the concept of a fraction. The following activities assume the student has a basic understanding of a fraction even though a mechanical rule for changing a fraction to simplest terms was adopted.

1. *Use fractional parts of regions.* Begin with reference to the unit, then show the given number with fractional parts. Do *not* restrict instruction to pie shapes, but use rectangular shapes as well. Pose the question, "Can we use larger parts to cover exactly what we have?" Record several "experiments" and note the ones that are already in simplest terms. Then look for a mathematical rule for changing, i.e., dividing both numerator and denominator by the same number.

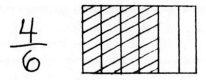

2. *Build an array with fractional parts of a set.* With discs of two colors, make a row for a given fraction.

2 of the 3 discs are white

Then build an array by forming additional rows of discs—rows identical to the first. As each row is formed, count the columns and the discs. Record the equivalent fractions.

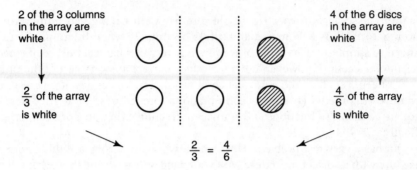

2 of the 3 columns
in the array are
white

$\frac{2}{3}$ of the array
is white

4 of the 6 discs
in the array are
white

$\frac{4}{6}$ of the array
is white

$$\frac{2}{3} = \frac{4}{6}$$

3. *Look for a pattern in a list.* Present a list of *correct* examples similar to the following, and have the student look for a pattern (a mathematical rule) for changing. Test the suggested pattern on other examples. When a correct procedure is found, use it to help determine the fractions that can be changed to simpler terms and those already in simplest terms.

$$\frac{6}{8} = \frac{3}{4}$$

$$\frac{4}{6} = \frac{2}{3}$$

> Two equivalent fractions, decimals, and/or percents can be thought of as two names for the same number.

4. *Make sets of equivalent fractions.* Students can do this by subdividing a region, then continuing to subdivide it again and again. Record the resulting sets of equivalent fractions in order, with the lesser numerator first; then use the sets for finding simplest terms. Look for a relationship between any one fraction and the first fraction in the set.

$$\frac{2}{3} \quad \frac{4}{6} \quad \frac{6}{9} \quad \frac{8}{12} \ldots$$

5. *Play a game.* Play a board game in which players race their pieces forward along a track made up of sections, each of which is partitioned into twelfths. Players roll special dice, draw cards with fraction numerals, or draw unit regions for fractions. Possible fractions include $\frac{1}{2}, \frac{2}{3}, \frac{5}{6}, \frac{3}{4}$, and so forth. Moves forward are for the equivalent number of twelfths. An example of this kind of game can be found in the *Fraction Bars* program.[1]

## Error Pattern F-E-2

*(from Sue's paper on page 60)*

Did you correctly identify Sue's pattern of errors? Many teachers would assume she had responded randomly.

G.
$$\frac{3}{6} = \frac{2}{6}$$

H.
$$\frac{6}{4} = \frac{1}{6}$$

Sue considers the given numerator and denominator as two whole numbers and divides the greater by the lesser to determine the new numerator, ignoring any remainder; then the greater of the two numbers is copied as the new denominator. Perhaps she has observed in the fractions she has seen that the denominator is usually the greater of the two numbers.

There is some evidence that Sue is only manipulating symbols in a mechanistic way and not even interpreting fractions as part of unit regions. For example, her statement that $\frac{3}{6} = \frac{2}{6}$ suggests that an understanding of $\frac{3}{6}$ or $\frac{2}{6}$ as parts of a unit just is not present, or, if it is, it is a behavior associated with something like fraction pies, and it is not applied in other contexts. Also, she probably thinks of *equals* as "results in" instead of "is the same as." Before planning instruction, it may be wise to interview her to determine how she conceptualizes *fractions* and *equals*.

Sue is not unlike many other children who develop mechanistic and unreasonable procedures in arithmetic classes. How would you help her? Are your suggestions among the following?

1. *Match numerals with physical or diagrammatic representations.* To encourage interpretation of a fraction in terms of real-world referents, help the student learn and reinforce these abilities:
   a. Provide a physical representation or a diagram for a fraction, then have the student write the fraction or pick out a numeral card showing "how much." In an activity of this sort, be sure the student understands the given frame of reference, i.e., the unit.
   b. Provide a fraction, and have the student represent the fraction with blocks, parts of a unit region, sets, etc., or draw an appropriate diagram.

2. *Find equivalent numerals on number lines.* Have the student place number lines side by side so that whole numbers match, then look for different fractions that name the same number.

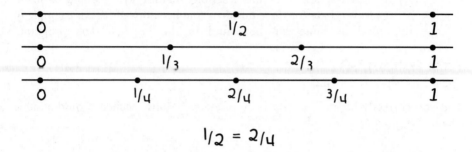

$$1/2 = 2/4$$

3. *Order fraction cards.* Give the student a set of cards, each with a different fraction but with each fraction having the same denominator. Then, let the student sequence the cards, thereby focusing on the fact that $\frac{3}{6} \neq \frac{2}{6}$. (It may be necessary to emphasize that the equality sign means "is the same as.") Encourage the student to refer to physical representations or to diagrams as necessary to verify decisions.

4. *Play "Can you make a whole?"* The student has a need to recognize fractions that can be changed to a mixed number. Give her a set of cards with a fraction on each. Some of the cards should have proper or common fractions; others should have improper fractions. The student can play a game by sorting individual cards into two piles, those which will "make a whole" (those equal to or greater than 1) and those which will "not make a whole." Then after a playing partner or teacher challenges the student by picking two of the sorted cards, the student must use physical representations to prove that the fractions are sorted correctly. If two students are playing, they should take turns sorting and challenging. More specific game rules and scoring procedures (if any) can be agreed upon by the students involved.

## CONCLUSION

Many manipulatives and diagrams are available for modeling quantities expressed as fractions and decimals. Equivalent parts of unit regions, fraction bars, and number lines are examples. Use a variety of models, so that students associate numerals with quantities and not with particular representations.

As you help each student learn procedures for changing a fraction to equivalent fractions or to a decimal, focus on concepts and number sense.

Help students make a habit of asking, "Is it reasonable?" Ask questions like, "Are both numbers more than a half?" "This number is almost one; is this number almost one also?" Continuously emphasize estimation.

Remember that diagnosis continues even during instructional activities as you observe students at work. Keep looking for patterns.

## FURTHER REFLECTION

Consider the following questions:

1. When we introduce fractions to students we use representations, as we should. But some students tend to associate the *shape* of a fractional part (the representation) with a particular fraction—for example, a semicircular region with one half. Why should this association be avoided? How can it be avoided?
2. It is extremely important that our students understand and apply the concept of equivalence; students will avoid many errors if they do. How can we express or talk about equivalence (other than talking about the same number) as we use representations for rational numbers?

## REFERENCE

1. *Fraction Bars,* originally published by Scott Resources, Inc., are available from suppliers of materials for elementary school mathematics. They include many games with fraction bars, cards, spinners, and game mats.

# CHAPTER 5

Error Patterns:
# Addition and Subtraction
## with Fractions and Decimals

Evidences of purely mechanical procedures abound. Such procedures cannot be explained by a student with mathematical principles or physical aids. Students who use mechanical procedures "push symbols around" whenever there are examples to be computed and answers to be determined. Many of the students represented here have been introduced to the standard short-form algorithms too soon. Some students lack very basic understandings of numeration or of the algorithm itself, while others have become careless and confused. Sadly, each student has practiced an erroneous procedure.

Here are examples of papers in which students practiced addition and subtraction with fractions and decimals. Look for a pattern in each paper, then make sure you found the student's procedure by looking at all of the examples on the paper. Check your findings by using the procedure with the examples provided for that purpose.

Accompanying many of the error patterns is a discussion of reasons some students may learn to compute that way. If the procedure produces the correct answer part of the time, the validity of the pattern is confirmed in the student's mind.

As you read about each student's erroneous procedure, think about needed instruction. Compare your ideas with those in this book. Each error pattern has been labeled to facilitate discussion: A-F for addition with fractions, S-F for subtraction with fractions, A-D for addition with decimals, and S-D for subtraction with decimals.

## ■ Identifying Patterns

### Error Pattern A-F-1

*Wes sold bagels from bags of 30 bagels. On Monday, he sold $\frac{4}{5}$ of a bag, then on Tuesday he sold $\frac{2}{3}$ of a different bag. How many full bags of bagels did he sell?*

If Robbie was using estimating skills, he could have thought, "Four fifths is almost one, and two thirds is more than a half. So, the sum is about one and a half." He would have known that six eighths is not a reasonable answer.

Look at Robbie's written work. He is using a common error pattern. Can you find it?

Name __Robbie__

A. $$\frac{4}{5} + \frac{2}{3} = \frac{6}{8}$$

B. $$\frac{1}{4} + \frac{2}{3} = \frac{3}{7}$$

C. $$\frac{7}{8} + \frac{5}{6} = \frac{12}{14}$$

D. $$\frac{3}{7} + \frac{1}{2} = \frac{4}{9}$$

Did you find the pattern? Make sure by using the pattern to compute these examples.

E. $$\frac{3}{4} + \frac{1}{5} =$$

F. $$\frac{2}{3} + \frac{5}{6}$$

What does Robbie understand? What does Robbie *not* yet understand? Can you think of a situation in which Robbie's procedure would actually be correct for the total needed? Think about sports.

Turn to page 78 and see if you identified the pattern. Why might Robbie be using such a procedure?

## Error Pattern A-F-2

Look at Dave's paper. Do you think he is using estimation skills? His error pattern is all too common. Can you find it?

---

Name *Dave*

A.
$$\frac{3}{4} + \frac{2}{3} = \frac{5}{12}$$

B.
$$\frac{6}{8} + \frac{1}{3} = \frac{7}{24}$$

C.
$$\frac{2}{3} + \frac{5}{6} = \frac{7}{18}$$

D.
$$\frac{3}{5} + \frac{2}{3} = \frac{5}{15} = \frac{1}{3}$$

---

Did you find Dave's procedure? Check yourself by using his procedure to compute Examples E and F.

E.
$$\frac{1}{3} + \frac{3}{5} =$$

F.
$$\frac{3}{8} + \frac{4}{5}$$

Dave's difficulty may involve a previous learning that he recalls and applies (inappropriately) when adding examples like these.

Turn to page 80 and see if you identified the procedure.

## Error Pattern A-F-3

Robin knows that before she can add the numbers, she must change unlike fractions so they have a common denominator. She is able to find a common denominator.

Beyond that, her procedure appears to make no sense at all. Even so, she is following a regular error pattern.

Can you find her procedure?

Name Robin

A.
$$\frac{1}{2} = \frac{1}{4}$$
$$+\frac{1}{4} = \frac{1}{4}$$
$$\frac{2}{4}$$

B.
$$\frac{2}{5} = \frac{2}{10}$$
$$+\frac{1}{2} = \frac{1}{10}$$
$$\frac{3}{10}$$

C.
$$\frac{3}{5} = \frac{3}{15}$$
$$+\frac{1}{3} = \frac{1}{15}$$
$$\frac{4}{15}$$

Did you find Robin's procedure? Check yourself by using her procedure to compute Examples D and E.

D.
$$\frac{3}{4}$$
$$+\frac{1}{2}$$

E.
$$\frac{4}{5}$$
$$+\frac{1}{4}$$

What does Robin actually understand? What does Robin *not* yet understand as indicated by her work?

Turn to page 81 and see if you identified the procedure.

## Error Pattern S-F-1

Andrew is able to add with fractions and mixed numbers, but he seems to have difficulty subtracting with mixed numbers.

Clearly, Andrew is *not* using estimating skills. For Example B, he could have thought, "If I subtract two thirds, the results cannot be what I started with." If he pictured a number line in his head for Example C, he would have moved from six to five *and beyond* because "the answer has to be less than five."

Andrew is using an error pattern similar to a common pattern for subtraction of whole numbers. Can you find the error pattern in his work?

---

Name ___Andrew___

A.
$$7\tfrac{1}{2}$$
$$-\ 3$$
$$\overline{4\tfrac{1}{2}}$$

B.
$$8\tfrac{1}{3}$$
$$-\ \tfrac{2}{3}$$
$$\overline{8\tfrac{1}{3}}$$

C.
$$6$$
$$-\ 1\tfrac{1}{4}$$
$$\overline{5\tfrac{1}{4}}$$

D.
$$3\tfrac{1}{4}$$
$$-\ 2\tfrac{3}{4}$$
$$\overline{1\tfrac{3}{4}}$$

---

Did you find the pattern? Make sure by using his procedure to compute these examples.

E.
$$5\tfrac{1}{5}$$
$$-\ 3\tfrac{3}{5}$$

F.
$$3$$
$$-\ 1\tfrac{1}{3}$$

What does Andrew actually understand? What does he *not* yet understand?

Turn to page 82 and see if you identified the procedure correctly. Why might Andrew be using such a procedure?

## Error Pattern S-F-2

*Riva selected a piece of scrap lumber that was $8\tfrac{3}{4}$ feet long. She cut off a board that was $6\tfrac{1}{8}$ feet long. How long was the remaining piece of lumber?*

Chuck chose the correct operation, but followed an error pattern in his computation. Look carefully at his written work and find his procedure.

---

Name  *Chuck*

A.
$$8\tfrac{3}{4} - 6\tfrac{1}{8} = 2\tfrac{2}{4}$$

B.
$$5\tfrac{3}{5} - 2\tfrac{2}{3} = 3\tfrac{1}{5}$$

C.
$$9\tfrac{1}{5} - 1\tfrac{3}{8} = 8\tfrac{2}{3}$$

D.
$$7\tfrac{2}{5} - 4\tfrac{7}{10} = 3\tfrac{5}{5}$$

---

Did you find the procedure? Make sure by using his error pattern to compute these examples.

E.
$$6\tfrac{2}{3} - 3\tfrac{1}{6} =$$

F.
$$4\tfrac{5}{8} - 1\tfrac{3}{4} =$$

What do you think Chuck actually *does* understand about fractions, mixed numbers, and subtraction? What does he *not* yet understand?

Turn to page 83 and see if you identified the procedure.

## Error Pattern S-F-3

If Ann understands what *equals* means, she is not using that knowledge. She appears to have constructed her own procedure using different phrases she heard. Can you determine the faulty procedure she is using?

Name **Ann**

A.

$$2\frac{3}{4} = 2\frac{11}{4}$$
$$-1\frac{1}{2} = 1\frac{3}{4}$$
$$\overline{\qquad\quad 1\frac{8}{4}}$$

B.

$$11\frac{1}{6} = 11\frac{67}{48}$$
$$-3\frac{7}{8} = 3\frac{31}{48}$$
$$\overline{\qquad\quad 8\frac{36}{48}}$$

C.

$$9\frac{1}{3} = 9\frac{28}{3}$$
$$-\quad\frac{2}{3} = \quad\frac{2}{3}$$
$$\overline{\qquad\quad 9\frac{26}{3}}$$

Did you find the error pattern? Make sure by using her procedure to compute these examples.

D.

$$5\;{}^{3}\!/_{8}$$
$$-2\;{}^{1}\!/_{2}$$
$$\overline{\qquad\qquad}$$

E.

$$4\;{}^{1}\!/_{3}$$
$$-1\;{}^{4}\!/_{5}$$
$$\overline{\qquad\qquad}$$

What does Ann understand about fractions and mixed numbers, and about subtraction? What does she *not* yet understand?

Turn to page 84 and see if you identified the procedure correctly. How would you help Ann?

## Error Pattern A-D-1

Harold knows his addition facts. Does he use estimation skills? Examine his work carefully. Can you find the error pattern he is following?

Name __Harold__

A.

$$
\begin{array}{r}
.8 \\
+.4 \\
\hline .12
\end{array}
$$

B.

$$
\begin{array}{r}
.6 \\
+.9 \\
\hline .15
\end{array}
$$

C.

$$
\begin{array}{r}
.4 \\
+.3 \\
\hline .7
\end{array}
$$

D.

$$
\begin{array}{r}
.5 \\
+.8 \\
\hline .13
\end{array}
$$

Did you find the pattern? Make sure by using Harold's procedure to compute these examples.

E.

$$
\begin{array}{r}
.3 \\
+.5 \\
\hline
\end{array}
$$

F.

$$
\begin{array}{r}
.7 \\
+.7 \\
\hline
\end{array}
$$

What does he actually understand about decimals? What does he *not* yet understand?

Turn to page 86 and see if you identified the procedure correctly. Why might Harold be using such a procedure?

## Error Pattern S-D-1

Les has learned to align place-value columns correctly, yet he sometimes has difficulty when subtracting with decimals. Can you determine his procedure?

Name _Les_

A.
$$87 - .31 = ?$$

B.
$$99.4 - 27.86 = ?$$

C.
$$200 - .65 = ?$$

$$
\begin{array}{r}
87 \\
-\ .31 \\
\hline
87.31
\end{array}
$$

$$
\begin{array}{r}
99.4 \\
-27.86 \\
\hline
71.66
\end{array}
$$

$$
\begin{array}{r}
200 \\
-\ .65 \\
\hline
200.65
\end{array}
$$

Find out if you determined Les's error pattern by using his procedure to complete Examples D and E.

D.
$$60 - 1.35 = ?$$

E.
$$24.8 - 2.26 = ?$$

What does he actually understand about subtraction? What does he *not* yet understand?

If you completed Examples D and E, run to page 87 and check your responses. How might you help Les or others using such a procedure?

## ■ Planning Instruction

### Error Pattern A-F-1
*(from Robbie's paper on page 71)*

Did you find Robbie's error pattern?

E.
$$\frac{3}{4} + \frac{1}{5} = \frac{4}{9}$$

F.
$$\frac{2}{3} + \frac{5}{6} = \frac{7}{9}$$

Robbie adds the numerators to get the numerator for the sum, then adds the denominators to get the denominator for the sum—an all-too-prevalent practice. It is likely that Robbie has already learned to multiply fractions and he is following a similar procedure for adding fractions.

How would you help Robbie? Are your ideas among the following suggestions?

Note: Because the error pattern is so similar to the multiplication algorithm, Robbie may be a student who tends to carry over one situation into his perception of another. If so, avoid extensive practice on any single procedure at a given time.

1. *Emphasize both "horizontal" and "vertical."* When adding unlike fractions, it is usually best to write the example vertically so the renaming can be recorded more easily. Give the student experience deciding which of the several examples should be written vertically to facilitate computation and which can be computed horizontally.

2. *Use unit regions and parts of unit regions.* Let the student first represent each addend as fractional parts of a unit region. It will be necessary for him to exchange some of the fractional parts so they are all of the same size (same denominator). The fractional parts can then be used to determine the total number of units. This procedure should be related step-by-step to the mechanics of notation in a written algorithm, probably as an example written vertically so the renaming can be noted more easily.

3. *Contrast ratio situations.* The algorithm used by Robbie is appropriate when adding win-loss ratios for different sets of games. (If he wins six of eight games, then he wins three of four more games, altogether he has won nine of 12 games.) Describe fraction (ratio) situations for the student, and have him decide which ones require a common denominator for addition.

4. *Discuss counting as a strategy.* Show how counting is appropriate when the denominators are the same and how it is not appropriate when denominators are different.

5. *Estimate answers before computing.* This may require some practice locating fractions on a number line and ordering fractions written on cards. Use phrases like "almost a half" and "a little less than one" when discussing problems. In Example F, more than a half is added to a little less than one. The result should be about one and a half.

> At the heart of flexibility in working with rational numbers is a solid understanding of different representations for fractions, decimals, and percents.
>
> *Principles and Standards for School Mathematics*, NCTM[1]

## Error Pattern A-F-2

*(from Dave's paper on page 72)*

Did you find the error pattern Dave is using?

$$\text{E. } \frac{1}{3} + \frac{3}{5} = \frac{4}{15} \qquad \text{F. } \frac{3}{8} + \frac{4}{5} = \frac{7}{40}$$

Dave may remember that you often have to multiply when adding fractions like these, although he does not apply any understanding of common denominators or renaming fractions. He merely adds the numerators to get the numerator for the sum, and multiplies the denominators to get the denominator for the sum.

How would you help a student such as Dave who uses the error pattern illustrated? Are your suggestions included among the activities described?

1. *Estimate answers before computing.* Consider each fraction. Is it closest to zero, to one half, or to one? (The student may need to check a number line for reference at first.) In Example E, one number is a bit less than one half, while the other number is a bit more than one half. Their sum should be about one rather than $\frac{4}{15}$.

2. *Stress that adding requires common denominators.* It makes sense to add the numerators only if the denominators are *already* the same. Explain that the reason we sometimes multiply denominators is to find a number we can use as the denominator for both fractions. Focus on these two questions:
   • What number can I use for both denominators?
   • What equivalent fractions use that denominator?

3. *Use a number line to focus on equivalent fractions.* Prepare a number line from zero to one, with rows of labels for halves, thirds, fourths, and so on. Have the student find and state the many fractions for the same point. State that each point shows a number, and that the fractions are different names for the same number. When we find an equivalent fraction, we are finding a different name for the same number.

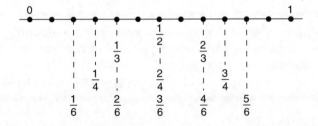

## Error Pattern A-F-3

*(from Robin's paper on page 73)*

Did you find Robin's procedure?

D. $\dfrac{3}{4} = \dfrac{3}{4}$

$+ \dfrac{1}{2} = \dfrac{1}{4}$

$\dfrac{4}{4}$

E. $\dfrac{4}{5} = \dfrac{4}{20}$

$+ \dfrac{1}{4} = \dfrac{1}{20}$

$\dfrac{5}{20}$

Robin is able to determine the least common denominator, and she uses it when changing two fractions so they will have the same denominator. However, she merely copies the original numerator. Robin is able to add like fractions correctly.

How would you help Robin with her difficulty? Are your ideas among those listed here?

**Note:** Corrective instruction should focus on the specific process of changing a fraction to higher terms with a designated denominator; e.g., $\frac{3}{4} = \frac{7}{20}$.

1. *Show that two fractions are or are not equal.*  The equals sign tells us that numerals or numerical expressions on either side are names for the same number (the same fractional part, the same point on a number line). Help Robin find ways to determine if two different fractions name the same number, and have her show in *more than one way* that both fractions show the same amount. Examples of varied procedures that can be used include stacking fractional parts of a unit region, using a number line that is labeled with different fractions (halves, thirds, fourths, and so on), finding a name for one $\left(\frac{n}{n}\right)$ that could be used to change one of the fractions to the other, and for $\frac{a}{b} = \frac{c}{d}$ showing that $ad = bc$.

2. *Use the multiplicative identity.*  Emphasize the role of one by outlining $\frac{n}{n}$ with the numeral "1" as illustrated. Make sure the student observes that both terms of a fraction are multiplied and, therefore, *both* terms in the new fraction are different than the original fraction.

$$\frac{3}{4} = \frac{3 \times \boxed{2}}{4 \times \boxed{2}} = \frac{6}{8}$$

3. *Use games involving equivalent fractions.* Let the student play games in which equivalent fractions are matched, possibly adaptations of rummy or dominoes. Such games provide an excellent context for discussing how to determine if two fractions name the same number.

4. *Use a shield.* Within the algorithm, use a shield as illustrated to help focus on the task of changing a fraction to higher terms. Make sure the student understands that the procedure for changing a fraction is the same as that used *within* this algorithm.

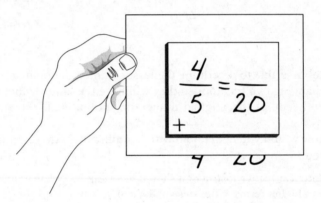

## Error Pattern S-F-1
*(from Andrew's paper on page 155)*

Did you find Andrew's error pattern?

E.
$$5\tfrac{1}{5}$$
$$-3\tfrac{3}{5}$$
$$\overline{\quad 2\tfrac{2}{5}}$$

F.
$$3$$
$$-1\tfrac{1}{3}$$
$$\overline{\quad 2\tfrac{1}{3}}$$

In every case, the whole numbers are subtracted as simple subtraction problems, perhaps even before attention is given to the column of common fractions.

Where only one fraction appears in the problem (Example F), the fraction is simply "brought down." If two fractions appear, Andrew records the difference between them, ignoring whether the subtrahend or the minuend is the greater of the two.

How would you help Andrew correct his erroneous procedure? Are your ideas included among those that follow?

Note: You will want to interview this student and have him think out loud as he works similar examples. Does he question the reasonableness of his answers?

1. *Use fractional parts of a unit region.* Interpret the example as "take-away" subtraction and use fractional parts to show *only* the sum. If the student subtracts the whole numbers first, demonstrate that not enough remains so the fraction can be subtracted. Conclude that the fraction must be subtracted before the whole number. Let the student exchange one of the units for an equivalent set of fractional parts in order to take away the quantity indicated by the subtrahend.

2. *Record the renaming.* Record the exchange of fractional parts (suggested above) as a renaming of the sum. The sum is renamed so the fraction can be subtracted easily.

$$\begin{array}{r} 4\,\frac{6}{5} \\ \cancel{5}\,\cancel{\frac{1}{5}} \\ -\,3\,\frac{3}{5} \\ \hline 1\,\frac{3}{5} \end{array}$$

3. *Practice specific prerequisite skills.* Without computing, the student can decide which examples require renaming and which do not. The skill of renaming a mixed number in order to subtract can also be practiced.

## Error Pattern S-F-2

*(from Chuck's paper on page 75)*

Did you find Chuck's error pattern?

E.

$$6\,\frac{2}{3} - 3\,\frac{1}{6} = 3\,\frac{1}{3}$$

F.

$$4\,\frac{5}{8} - 1\,\frac{3}{4} = 3\,\frac{2}{4}$$

Chuck is subtracting by first finding the difference between the two whole numbers and recording that difference as the new whole number. He then finds the difference between the two numerators and records that difference as the new numerator. Finally, he finds the difference between the two denominators and records that number as the new denominator. The procedure is similar to addition as seen in Error Pattern A-F-1. However, students using this procedure for subtraction necessarily ignore the order of the minuend and the subtrahend.

Someone needs to come to Chuck's aid. How would you help him? Are your suggestions among those that follow?

**Note:** Extended diagnosis is probably wise. Most of the subordinate skills you may have identified for addition with fractions apply equally to subtraction.

1. *Distinguish between horizontal and vertical.* When subtracting with unlike fractions and with mixed numerals, it is usually best to write the example vertically so the renaming can be recorded more easily. Let the student practice deciding which of several examples should be written vertically to facilitate computation and which can be computed horizontally.

2. *Use fractional parts of a unit region.* As you work with the student, or a group of students, let them use fractional parts to show *only* the sum, then set apart the amount indicated by the known addend. Soon students will discover that it is necessary to deal with the fraction before the whole number. They will often need to exchange in order to set apart the amount required. This task can help students relate problems more adequately to the operation of subtraction. However, it can become a cumbersome procedure, so choose examples carefully. (An appropriate example might be $3\frac{1}{6} - 1\frac{2}{3}$.) Step by step, relate the activity with fractional parts to the vertical algorithm.

## Error Pattern S-F-3

*(from Ann's paper on page 76)*

Did you find the pattern?

$$
\text{D.} \quad \begin{array}{r} 5\frac{3}{8} = 5\frac{43}{8} \\ -2\frac{1}{2} = 2\frac{5}{8} \\ \hline 3\frac{38}{8} \end{array}
\qquad\qquad
\text{E.} \quad \begin{array}{r} 4\frac{1}{3} = 4\frac{13}{15} \\ -1\frac{4}{5} = 1\frac{9}{15} \\ \hline 3\frac{4}{15} \end{array}
$$

Ann has difficulty changing mixed numbers to equivalent mixed numbers that have a common denominator. She does determine a common denominator, but she computes each new numerator by multiplying the original denominator by the whole number and adding the original numerator. She merely copies the given whole number.

You probably recognize part of the procedure as the way to find the new numerator when changing a mixed number to a fraction, but doing this makes no sense when changing a mixed number to an equivalent mixed number with a specified denominator.

How would you help Ann subtract correctly when she encounters examples such as these? Are your ideas among the following activities?

**Note:** Corrective instruction should focus on changing a mixed number to an equivalent mixed number, one in which the fraction has a specified denominator.

1. *Prove that mixed numbers are or are not equal.* Emphasize that the whole number and fraction together are one number, and that "equals" written between two mixed numbers says that they name the same number (show the same amount, name the same point on a number line). Two mixed numbers can be shown to be equal with unit regions and fractional parts or with an appropriately labeled number line.

2. *Make many names for a mixed number.* With the help of an aid such as unit regions and fractional parts, let the student generate as many names as possible for a given mixed number. For example, given $3\frac{1}{3}$:

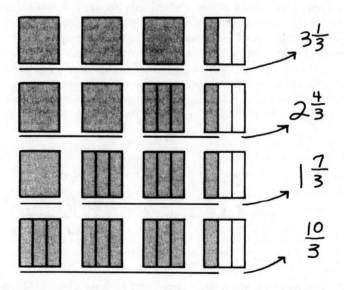

Then, for an example like $3\frac{1}{3} - 1\frac{2}{3} = ?$ ask, "Which is the *most* useful name for $3\frac{1}{3}$ in this example?"

## Error Pattern A-D-1
*(from Harold's paper on page 77)*

Did you find Harold's error pattern?

$$
\begin{array}{cc}
\text{E.} & \text{F.} \\
\begin{array}{r} .3 \\ +.5 \\ \hline .8 \end{array} &
\begin{array}{r} .7 \\ +.7 \\ \hline .14 \end{array}
\end{array}
$$

Harold seemingly adds these decimals as we would add whole numbers, but the placement of the decimal point in the sum is a problem. In every case, he merely places the decimal point at the left of the sum. Or perhaps he thinks something like, "Apples added to apples are apples, and tenths added to tenths are tenths." So in Example F, the 14 is "crowded" into tenths. He might even explain, "Seven tenths plus seven tenths is 14 tenths."

We ought to be able to help Harold with a problem of this sort. How would *you* help him? Are your suggestions among those listed?

**Note:** Some teachers will be tempted to simply tell the student that in problems like Example F, the decimal point should go between the two digits in the sum. However, such directions only compound the problem. This student needs a greater understanding of decimal numeration and the ability to apply such knowledge. Tell students to "line up place values" when they compute with decimals. Do not tell them to "line up decimal points"—that is just a result of lining up place values. Further diagnosis is probably wise. When the addends also include units, does the student regroup tenths as units (as in the first example) or does he think of two separate problems—one to the right of the point and one to the left of the point (as in the second example)?

$$
\begin{array}{ccc}
\begin{array}{r} 6.7 \\ +8.5 \\ \hline 15.2 \end{array} &
\begin{array}{c} \text{or} \\ ? \end{array} &
\begin{array}{r} 6.7 \\ +8.5 \\ \hline 14.12 \end{array}
\end{array}
$$

1. *Use base ten materials.* These can be base blocks, Montessori Golden Beads, or similar materials. Define one size as a unit. Then let the student show tenths in each addend with materials one tenth as large as the unit. After he combines the two sets, he can exchange tenths for a unit, if possible, so he will have "as few blocks as possible for this much wood" (or a

similar expression for the particular materials used). He should compare the results of this activity with his erroneous procedure.

2. *Use a number line.* Mark units and tenths clearly on a number line and show addition with arrows. Compare the sum indicated on the number line with the sum resulting from computation.

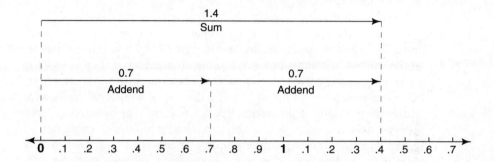

3. *Use vertically lined or cross-sectioned paper.* Theme paper can be turned 90° to use as vertically lined paper. Let the student compute with only one digit placed in a column. If cross-sectioned paper is used, only one digit should be written within each square.

## Error Pattern S-D-1

*(from Les's paper on page 78)*

Did you determine the procedure Les is using?

D.
$$60 - 1.35 = ?$$

E.
$$24.8 - 2.26 = ?$$

$$\begin{array}{r} 60 \\ -\ 1.35 \\ \hline 59.35 \end{array}$$

$$\begin{array}{r} 24.8 \\ -\ 2.26 \\ \hline 22.66 \end{array}$$

When presented with "ragged" decimals such as these, Les simply brings down the extra digits at the right. Apparently, when there are no ragged decimals, he is able to subtract correctly.

What would you do to help Les or other students who subtract as illustrated when they encounter ragged decimals? Are your ideas among those listed?

**Note:** Usually the need to add or subtract decimals arises from measurement situations, and measurements should always be expressed in the same units and with the same precision if they are to be added or subtracted. Ragged decimals are inappropriate. At the same time, ragged decimals sometimes occur in situations with money (e.g., $4 – $.35). They also appear on some standardized tests, and many teachers believe students need to be taught a procedure for computing with them, even if examples are somewhat contrived.

1. *Use a place-value chart.* A place-value chart can be relabeled for use with decimals (e.g., tens, ones, tenths, and hundredths). For a given example, let the student first show the sum (minuend) and then work through the regrouping necessary to subtract as would be done with whole numbers. Point out that the regrouping is being done *as if* additional zeros were written to the right of the decimal point. Suggest that by affixing zeros appropriately, the examples can be computed without the confusion of ragged decimals. If it will simplify things, encourage the student to affix zeros when adding as well as when subtracting. (Be sure students *affix* zeros; they do not add them.)

2. *Use base-ten blocks.* For use with decimals, the unit must be defined differently from the way it is used with whole numbers, so you may choose to use blocks that are not lined. Use them as the place-value chart is used.

3. *Use money.* Use pennies, dimes, dollar bills, and ten-dollar bills much as you would use a place-value chart. Stress the fact that the dollar bill is the unit; the dimes and pennies are tenths and hundredths of one dollar, respectively.

## CONCLUSION

Students with deficient fraction concepts who are introduced to addition and subtraction procedures too soon commonly develop inadequate procedures. The fact that operations with fractions are difficult for students worldwide combined with the fact that they are used less frequently are reasons some educators are beginning to argue that we no longer need to include fractions within the curriculum.[2] However, other educators wisely point to their value in preparation for learning algebra.

Teach computational procedures so that they make sense to students. Those students who tend toward the use of rote procedures sometimes use part of one learned procedure within a procedure they are creating. For example, they may use parts of the procedure for multiplying fractions when they add fractions. Always be on the alert for similar patterns during instructional activities, and keep emphasizing the need for reasonable answers.

Sometimes students create procedures in which they state that one quantity is equal to an entirely different quantity. Keep emphasizing the fact that two equivalent fractions or mixed numbers are names for *the same number*. If the two are shown at different points on a number line, they are not the same.

When students add and subtract with decimals, stress that place values must be aligned. Also remind students that only one digit appears in each place.

Vary instruction as much as possible. Build on each student's strengths, and watch students gain confidence.

## FURTHER REFLECTION

Consider the following questions:

1. How will you know that your students are ready to learn procedures for adding and subtracting with fractions and with decimals? Consider the prior knowledge and skills they will need. How can you assess these?
2. We want our students to connect what they are learning with what they learned earlier. But if the prior learning is incorrect, or if it is applied in an inappropriate context, the new learning will likely be incorrect. Think of specific situations in which this has happened.
3. Teachers sometimes say things that are intended to help students, but students apply it inappropriately and adopt a misconception or an error pattern. Examples include: "take the smallest into the biggest" and "bring down the number." Think of other examples.

## ADDITIONAL PRACTICE

Can you describe the error pattern in each of the following papers? A key is provided on page 233.

Paper 5

A.  $\frac{1}{3} + \frac{2}{9} = \frac{3}{9}$

B.  $\frac{3}{4} + \frac{3}{2} = \frac{6}{4}$

C.  $\frac{5}{6} + \frac{1}{2} = \frac{6}{6}$

Paper 6

A.
$$1\frac{3}{5} = 1\frac{8}{15}$$
$$+ 2\frac{1}{3} = 2\frac{7}{15}$$
$$\overline{\phantom{+2}3\frac{15}{15}}$$

B.
$$4\frac{2}{4} = 4\frac{18}{4}$$
$$+ 1\frac{1}{2} = 1\frac{3}{4}$$
$$\overline{\phantom{+1}5\frac{21}{4}}$$

C.
$$6\frac{2}{3} = 6\frac{20}{6}$$
$$+ 3\frac{1}{6} = 3\frac{19}{6}$$
$$\overline{\phantom{+3}9\frac{39}{6}}$$

PAPER 7

A.

$$.4 + .3 = \underline{.07}$$

B.
$$\begin{array}{r} 1.32 \\ + 3.46 \\ \hline .04\,78 \end{array}$$

C.
$$\begin{array}{r} 27.5 \\ + 8.9 \\ \hline 3.64 \end{array}$$

## REFERENCES

1. National Council of Teachers of Mathematics. (2000). *Principles and standards for school mathematics*. Reston, VA: The Council, p. 215.
2. Groff, P. (1996). It is time to question fraction teaching. *Mathematics Teaching in the Middle School* 1(8), 604–607.

# CHAPTER 6

# Error Patterns:
# Multiplication and Division
## with Fractions and Decimals

It is challenging to teach multiplication and division with fractions and decimals so that the algorithms make sense to students—especially procedures with fractions. Troublesome misconceptions frequently intervene. For instance, students often believe that if you multiply, your answer will be greater, and if you divide your answer will be less. But instruction *can* focus on making sense of procedures by using manipulatives and by applying mathematical ideas understood earlier with whole numbers.

The multiplication and division papers in this chapter involve many misconceptions and incorrect answers. Can you find the patterns in each student's responses? Check each pattern by using the erroneous procedure yourself, then read about the student's procedure. Consider needed instruction; compare your ideas with those in this book.

As you plan instruction, keep the meanings of the two operations in mind along with their relationship to one another. Also remember the varied two- and three-dimensional representations available for teaching about fractions and decimals.

Each error pattern has been labeled to facilitate discussion: M-F for multiplication with fractions, D-F for division with fractions, M-D for multiplication with decimals, and D-D for division with decimals.

## ■ Identifying Patterns
### Error Pattern M-F-1

*Four fifths of the bushes are azaleas. Three fourths of the azaleas are pink. What part of the bushes are pink azaleas?*

If Dan were using good number sense and estimating skills, he would know that his products are not at all reasonable.

Name *Dan*

A.
$$\frac{4}{5} \times \frac{3}{4} = 166$$

B.
$$\frac{1}{2} \times \frac{3}{8} = 68$$

C.
$$\frac{2}{9} \times \frac{1}{5} = 100$$

D.
$$\frac{2}{3} \times \frac{4}{6} = 132$$

Dan appears to be using a procedure he constructed from phrases he heard and parts of procedures he observed. Can you determine what procedure he is using?

Make sure you found Dan's procedure by using it to compute these examples.

E.
$$\frac{3}{4} \times \frac{2}{3} =$$

F.
$$\frac{4}{9} \times \frac{2}{5} =$$

What does Dan actually understand? What does he *not* yet understand?

Turn to page 97 and see if you identified the pattern. Why might Dan be using such a procedure?

## Error Pattern M-F-2

Do you think Lynn is using estimating skills? Does she understand that multiplication with fractions is commutative?

In Example D, two times almost-one ($\frac{4}{3}$) is likely to be almost-two. The product will certainly be *more* than one, and her product is less than one. Most of her products are not reasonable.

Can you find the procedure she is following?

Name *Lynn*

A. $\frac{1}{8} \times 1 = \frac{1}{8}$    B. $\frac{2}{3} \times 3 = \frac{6}{9}$

C. $\frac{1}{4} \times 6 = \frac{6}{24}$    D. $\frac{4}{5} \times 2 = \frac{8}{10}$

Lynn may be confusing this situation with something else she has learned. Can you find the procedure she used? Check yourself by using her error pattern to compute these examples.

E. $\frac{3}{8} \times 4 =$    F. $\frac{5}{6} \times 2 =$

Now that you have completed Examples E and F, turn to page 98 and see if you identified the procedure.

## Error Pattern D-F-1

When Linda divides with fractions, her answers are sometimes correct, but frequently they are not.

She does not appear to be using good number sense and estimating skills. If she were, she might think, for Example C, "How many halves $(\frac{2}{4})$ are in about one half $(\frac{6}{10})$? There should be about one, not one and one half $(\frac{3}{2})$."

Can you find the procedure she is following?

Name *Linda*

A. $\dfrac{4}{6} \div \dfrac{2}{2} = \dfrac{2}{3}$     B. $\dfrac{6}{8} \div \dfrac{2}{8} = \dfrac{3}{1}$

C. $\dfrac{6}{10} \div \dfrac{2}{4} = \dfrac{3}{2}$     D. $\dfrac{7}{5} \div \dfrac{3}{2} = \dfrac{2}{2}$

Linda may be confusing this situation with something else she learned.

See if you found her procedure. Use her error pattern to compute these examples.

E. $\dfrac{4}{12} \div \dfrac{4}{4} =$     F. $\dfrac{13}{20} \div \dfrac{5}{6} =$

Next, turn to page 100 and see if you identified the procedure.

Next, turn to page 100 and see if you identified the procedure.

---

## Have students write problems to assess understanding of division by a fraction.

See Barlow, A. T., & Drake, J. M. (February 2008). Assessing understanding through problem writing: Division by a fraction. *Mathematics Teaching in the Middle School* 13(6), 326–332.

---

## Error Pattern D-F-2

Does Joyce understand the operation of division?

Is she using good number sense and estimating skills? If she is, she might think, for Example A, "Is there less than one half $\left(\frac{3}{8}\right)$ in more-than-a-half $\left(\frac{2}{3}\right)$? Yes, so the answer should be at least one; but my answer $\left(\frac{9}{10}\right)$ is less than one."

Can you find the error pattern she is using?

Name — *Joyce*

A. $\dfrac{2}{3} \div \dfrac{3}{8} = \dfrac{3}{2} \times \dfrac{3}{8} = \dfrac{9}{16}$

B. $\dfrac{2}{5} \div \dfrac{1}{3} = \dfrac{5}{2} \times \dfrac{1}{3} = \dfrac{5}{6}$

C. $\dfrac{3}{4} \div \dfrac{1}{5} = \dfrac{4}{3} \times \dfrac{1}{5} = \dfrac{4}{15}$

See if you found her error pattern. Use her procedure to compute these examples.

D. $\dfrac{5}{8} \div \dfrac{2}{3} =$

E. $\dfrac{1}{2} \div \dfrac{1}{4} =$

When you complete Examples D and E, turn to page 100.

## Error Pattern M-D-1

*Dried fruit costs $6.45 a pound. How much do 3 pounds of dried fruit cost?*

Marsha seems to have difficulty with some multiplication problems involving decimals, but she solves other examples correctly.

If she were estimating Example C, she might think, "A number less than one times 21 has to be less than 21. But my answer is much more than 21."

Can you find her pattern of errors?

---

Name __*Marsha*__

A.
$$\$ 6.45$$
$$\underline{\times \quad 3}$$
$$\$19.35$$

B.
$$3\,2.7$$
$$\underline{\times \quad .5}$$
$$1\,6.35$$

C.
$$21.8$$
$$\underline{\times .4}$$
$$87.2$$

D.
$$4.35$$
$$\underline{\times 2.3}$$
$$1305$$
$$\underline{870}$$
$$100.05$$

---

See if you found Marsha's error pattern. Use her procedure to compute these examples.

E.
$$40.5$$
$$\underline{\times \quad .6}$$

F.
$$6.7$$
$$\underline{\times \quad 3}$$

When you complete Examples E and F, turn to page 102. How might you help Marsha or any other student using such a procedure?

## Error Pattern D-D-1

When Ted started dividing decimals, his answers were usually correct. But now he frequently gets the wrong quotient. Can you find his pattern of errors?

Name __Ted__

A.
$$
\begin{array}{r}
3.91 \\
6\overline{)23.5} \\
18 \\
\hline
5\ 5 \\
5\ 4 \\
\hline
1
\end{array}
$$

B.
$$
\begin{array}{r}
9.62 \\
4\overline{)3\ 8.6} \\
3\ 6 \\
\hline
2\ 6 \\
2\ 4 \\
\hline
2
\end{array}
$$

C.
$$
\begin{array}{r}
1.644 \\
5\overline{)8.24} \\
5 \\
\hline
3\ 2 \\
3\ 0 \\
\hline
24 \\
20 \\
\hline
4
\end{array}
$$

How much does Ted understand about decimal place values? What does he understand about remainders in division examples?

Use Ted's procedure with these examples to see if you found his error pattern.

D. $3\overline{)2.57}$          E. $.7\overline{)9.35}$

Now turn to page 102 and see if you identified the procedure. How might you help Ted or any other student using this error pattern?

## ■ Planning Instruction

### Error Pattern M-F-1
(*from Dan's paper on page 92*)

Did you find Dan's error pattern?

E. $\dfrac{3}{4} \times \dfrac{2}{3} = 89$          F. $\dfrac{4}{9} \times \dfrac{2}{5} = 200$

Dan begins by multiplying the first numerator and the second denominator and recording the units digit of this product. If there is a tens digit, he remembers it to add later (as in multiplication of whole numbers). He then multiplies the first denominator and the second numerator, adds the number of tens remembered, and records this as the number of tens in the answer. The procedure involves a sort of cross multiplication and the multiply-then-add sequence from multiplication of whole numbers.

Dan uses this error pattern consistently. He has somehow learned to multiply fractions this way. How would you help him learn the correct procedure? Are your instructional ideas among the following activities?

**Note:** The student's products are most unreasonable, and continued diagnosis is wise. Does this student understand the equals sign as meaning "the same as"? What kind of meaning does he associate with common fractions? Does he believe that products are *always* greater numbers?

1. *Estimate before computing.* Students often assume that the result of multiplying will be a larger number. Ask if $\frac{2}{3}$ is less than one or more than one. Is $\frac{1}{4}$ of $\frac{2}{3}$ less than one or more than one? $\frac{2}{4}$ of $\frac{2}{3}$? $\frac{3}{4}$ of $\frac{2}{3}$? Will $\frac{3}{4}$ of $\frac{2}{3}$ be less than $\frac{2}{3}$ or more than $\frac{2}{3}$? It will be helpful if the student expects his answer to be less than $\frac{2}{3}$. Of course, a student must understand fraction concepts before he can be expected to learn to estimate.

2. *Use fractional parts of unit regions.* When interpreting an example like $\frac{3}{4} \times \frac{2}{3} = ?$ as $\frac{3}{4}$ of $\frac{2}{3} = ?$, picture a rectangular region partitioned into thirds and shade two of them. This represents $\frac{2}{3}$ of one. Next, partition the unit so the student can see $\frac{3}{4}$ of the $\frac{2}{3}$. What part of the unit is shown as $\frac{3}{4}$ of $\frac{2}{3}$? Be sure he relates the answer to the unit rather than just the $\frac{2}{3}$. Record the fact that $\frac{3}{4}$ of $\frac{2}{3} = \frac{6}{12}$ and solve other problems with drawings. Then redevelop the rule for multiplying fractions by observing a pattern among several examples completed with fractional parts of unit regions.

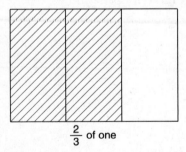

$\frac{2}{3}$ of one

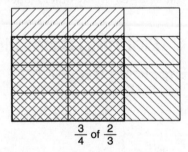

$\frac{3}{4}$ of $\frac{2}{3}$

# Error Pattern M-F-2

*(from Lynn's paper on page 93)*

Did you find the procedure Lynn is using?

E. $\frac{3}{8} \times 4 = \frac{12}{32}$    F. $\frac{5}{6} \times 2 = \frac{10}{12}$

Lynn has learned that when you are multiplying and you have a fraction, you have to multiply *both* the numerator and the denominator of the fraction. Of course, when she multiplies both terms by the same number, she is actually multiplying the fraction by *one* rather than by the whole number in the example. It may be that she multiplied both numerator and denominator by the same number when she practiced changing a fraction to higher terms, and she uses that familiar pattern.

How would you help Lynn correct the pattern illustrated? Are your ideas similar to those listed?

1. *Make the whole number a fraction.* Show the student that when multiplying both terms by the same number, she is multiplying by one (in the form $\frac{n}{n}$) and not by the number given. Have her put 1 under the whole number. Both numbers will be fractions and she can then use the procedure for multiplying fractions; e.g., $\frac{3}{8} \times \frac{4}{1} = \frac{12}{8}$.

2. *Use a number line.* On a number line that is labeled appropriately, have the student draw arrows to show the multiplication. Emphasize that the product tells how many sixths (or whatever denominator is being used). For $2 \times \frac{5}{6}$ or for $\frac{5}{6} \times 2$:

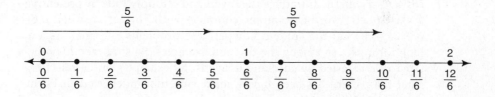

3. *Use addition.* Reverse the factors and have the student solve the addition problem suggested.

$$\frac{3}{8} \times 4 = 4 \times \frac{3}{8}$$

$$4 \times \frac{3}{8} = \frac{3}{8} + \frac{3}{8} + \frac{3}{8} + \frac{3}{8} = \frac{12}{8}$$

## Error Pattern D-F-1

*(from Linda's paper on page 94)*

Did you find the error pattern Linda is using?

$$\text{E.}\quad \frac{4}{12} \div \frac{4}{4} = \frac{1}{3} \qquad\qquad \text{F.}\quad \frac{13}{20} \div \frac{5}{6} = \frac{2}{3}$$

Linda divides the first numerator by the second numerator and records the result as the numerator for the answer. She then determines the denominator for the answer by dividing the first denominator by the second denominator. In both divisions, she ignores remainders. Note that Examples A, B, and E are correct. It may be that she learned her procedure while the class was working with such examples. The common denominator method of dividing fractions may be part of the background because her procedure is similar; however, she fails to change the fractions to equivalent fractions with the same denominator before dividing.

This is a tricky error pattern, producing both correct answers and absurd answers with zero numerators and denominators. Linda obviously needs help. What instructional activities do you suggest to help her correct the error pattern illustrated? See if your ideas are among those described.

**Note:** Selection of appropriate activities will depend somewhat on which algorithm for division with fractions the student was taught originally.

1. *Discover a pattern.* Introduce the Invert and Multiply Rule by presenting a varied selection of examples complete with correct answers: e.g., $\frac{7}{12} \div \frac{3}{5} = \frac{35}{36}$. Let the student compare the problems and answers and look for a pattern among the division examples. Be sure each hypothesized rule is tested by checking it against all examples in the selection. After the pattern has been found, make sure the student verbalizes the rule and makes up a few examples to solve.
2. *Estimate answers with paper strips and a number line.* Using a number line and the measurement model for division, make a strip of paper about as long as the dividend and another about as long as the divisor. Ask how many strips the length of the divisor strip can be made from the dividend strip. For $\frac{5}{8} \div \frac{2}{5} = ?$, the answer might be about one and one half.

## Error Pattern D-F-2

*(from Joyce's paper on page 95)*

Did you find the procedure Joyce is using?

D.

$$\frac{5}{8} \div \frac{2}{3} = \frac{8}{5} \times \frac{2}{3} = \frac{16}{15}$$

E.

$$\frac{1}{2} \div \frac{1}{4} = \frac{2}{1} \times \frac{1}{4} = \frac{2}{4}$$

Joyce knows to invert and multiply, but she inverts the dividend (or product) instead of the divisor. It *does* make a difference.

Dividing fractions seems to involve such an arbitrary rule. How would *you* help Joyce or any other student who uses the error pattern illustrated? Are your ideas among the instructional activities described?

**Note:** Determine whether the student consistently inverts the dividend or alternates between the divisor and the dividend. You may also want to make sure the student has no difficulty distinguishing between right and left.

1. *Use parts of a unit region.* Because inverting the dividend and inverting the divisor produce different answers, the student can use a manipulative aid to determine which result is correct. Parts of a unit region may be appropriate if the example is interpreted as measurement division. For $\frac{1}{2} \div \frac{1}{4} = ?$ have the student first place $\frac{1}{2}$ of a unit on top of a unit region. This shows the dividend or product. Then explain that just as $6 \div 2 = ?$ asks, "How many 2s are in 6?" so $\frac{1}{2} \div \frac{1}{4} = ?$ asks, "How many $\frac{1}{4}$s are in $\frac{1}{2}$?" Have the student cover the $\frac{1}{2}$ of a unit with $\frac{1}{4}$s of a unit. In all, exactly *two* $\frac{1}{4}$s are equal to $\frac{1}{2}$. The correct result is two, not $\frac{2}{4}$; it is the result obtained by inverting the divisor on the right.

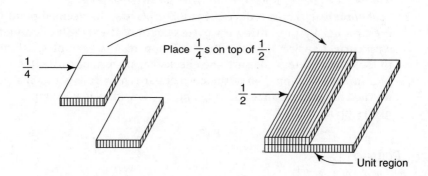

Place $\frac{1}{4}$s on top of $\frac{1}{2}$.

$\frac{1}{4}$

$\frac{1}{2}$

Unit region

2. *Use paper strips and a number line.* These can be used as described in the previous error pattern, but used in this case to determine which fraction should be inverted for the correct result.

## Error Pattern M-D-1

*(from Marsha's paper on page 96)*

If you used Marsha's error pattern, you completed Examples E and F as they are shown.

E.

$$
\begin{array}{r}
4\,0.5 \\
\times \quad\; .6 \\
\hline
2\,4.30
\end{array}
$$

F.

$$
\begin{array}{r}
6.7 \\
\times \quad 3 \\
\hline
2.01
\end{array}
$$

In her answer, Marsha places the decimal point by counting over from the left instead of from the right in the product. She frequently gets the correct answer (as in Examples A, B, and E), but much of the time her answer is not the correct product.

If you were Marsha's teacher, what corrective procedures might you follow? Are your ideas for instruction among those described?

1. *Estimate before computing.* Use concepts like less than and more than in estimating the product before computing. For Example E, a bit more than 40 is being multiplied by about a half. The product should be a bit more than 20. There is only one place where the decimal point could go if the answer is to be a bit more than 20. Similarly, in Example F, 6.7 is between 6 and 7; therefore, the answer should be between 18 and 21. Again, there is only one place the decimal point can be written for the answer to be reasonable. For $3.452 \times 4.845$, it can easily be seen that the product must be between 12 (i.e., $3 \times 4$) and 20 (i.e., $4 \times 5$), and there will be only one sensible place to write the decimal point.
2. *Look for a pattern.* Introduce the rule for placing the decimal point in the product by presenting a varied selection of examples complete with correct answers. As the student compares the examples, ask her to look for a pattern. Be sure she checks her pattern against all examples in the selection. When the correct pattern or rule is established, let the student verbalize the rule and use it with a few examples she makes up herself.

## Error Pattern D-D-1

*(from Ted's paper on page 97)*

If you found Ted's error pattern, your results are the same as the erroneous computations shown.

D.

$$3 \overline{)2.57} \;\; .852$$

$$\begin{array}{r} .852 \\ 3\overline{)2.57} \\ \underline{24} \\ 17 \\ \underline{15} \\ 2 \end{array}$$

E.

$$\begin{array}{r} 13.34 \\ .7\overline{)9.35} \\ \underline{7} \\ 23 \\ \underline{21} \\ 25 \\ \underline{21} \\ 4 \end{array}$$

Ted has incorrect quotients because of the way he handles remainders. If division does not "come out even" when taken as far as digits given in the dividend, Ted writes the remainder as an extension of the quotient. He may believe this is the same as writing R2 after the quotient for a division problem with whole numbers. Some students, having studied division with decimals, use a procedure similar to Ted's when dividing whole numbers. For example, 600 divided by 7 is computed as 85.5.

How would you help Ted? Are your ideas among the suggested instructional activities?

1. *Label columns on lined paper.* Turn theme paper 90 degrees and write each column of digits between two vertical lines. Then label each column with the appropriate place value. This may help discourage moving digits around mechanically. In Example D, 2 hundredths is not the same as 2 thousandths.
2. *Study alternatives for handling remainders.* By using simple examples and story problems, first show that for division of *whole* numbers, there are at least three different ways to handle remainders:
   a. As the amount remaining after distributing. Either a measurement or partitioning model for division can be used.

ANSWER: 64 (GROUPS, OR IN EACH GROUP)

WITH 3 LEFT OVER

$$\begin{array}{r} 64 \\ 6\overline{)387} \\ \underline{36} \\ 27 \\ \underline{24} \\ 3 \end{array}$$

b. As a fraction within the quotient expressed as a mixed number. A partitioning model for division is usually used here.

Answer: $93\frac{1}{4}$ for each of the 4

$$
\begin{array}{r}
9\ 3^1\!/_4 \\
4\overline{)3\ 7\ 3} \\
\underline{3\ 6}\phantom{00} \\
1\ 3 \\
\underline{1\ 2} \\
1
\end{array}
$$

c. As an indicator that the quotient should be rounded up by one, often in relation to the cost of an item. For example, items priced at 3 for 29¢ would sell for 10¢ each.

Answer: 10¢ each

$$
\begin{array}{r}
9\phantom{0} \\
3\overline{)2\ 9} \\
\underline{2\ 7} \\
2
\end{array}
$$

Next, consider remainders for division of decimals similarly. If the remainder in Example D is viewed as the amount leftover after distributing, 0.02 would remain. If it is viewed as a common fraction within the quotient, the quotient would be $0.85\frac{2}{3}$ or 0.857.

## CONCLUSION

As you emphasize multiplication and division meanings, you may find it helpful to review those meanings with whole numbers before talking about fractions and decimals. For 8 divided by 2, we can think, "How many 2s in 8?" And for $\frac{1}{2}$ divided by $\frac{1}{3}$ we can think, "How many $\frac{1}{3}$s in $\frac{1}{2}$?"

Before letting students practice procedures for multiplying and dividing with fractions, take time for them to estimate many of the products and quotients. "Will almost one times one half be greater than a half or less than a half? Why?" Students can discuss several examples and describe answers that are reasonable.

Be alert for any student who believes that a product must be a greater number. Frequently students infer this from their work with whole numbers.

Make sure students use what they know about the relationship between multiplication and division as they estimate reasonable quotients, and verify the results of their computation. Ask questions like, "Will the number be greater than one or less than one? Why?"

## FURTHER REFLECTION

Consider the following questions:

1. Why do students often believe a product should be equal to or greater than either factor? How can we deal with this when teaching multiplication with fractions?
2. Sometimes students use procedures or patterns they learned previously in new situations where they are not appropriate, as Linda did in Error Pattern D-F-1. How can we teach new material so this does not happen?
3. Why does invert and multiply work?

## ADDITIONAL PRACTICE

Can you describe the error pattern in each of the following papers? A key is provided on page 233.

PAPER 8

A.

$$\frac{7}{8} \times \frac{3}{4} = \frac{7}{8} \times \frac{6}{8} = \frac{42}{8}$$

B.

$$\frac{1}{6} \times \frac{2}{3} = \frac{1}{6} \times \frac{4}{6} = \frac{4}{6}$$

C.

$$\frac{5}{12} \times \frac{1}{4} = \frac{5}{12} \times \frac{3}{12} = \frac{15}{12}$$

PAPER 9

A.

$$5\frac{1}{3} \times 6\frac{3}{4} = 30\frac{3}{12}$$

B.

$$7\frac{2}{5} \times 2\frac{1}{8} = 14\frac{2}{40}$$

C.

$$1\frac{7}{8} \times 4\frac{2}{3} = 4\frac{14}{24}$$

A.

$$0.5\overline{)60} \longrightarrow 0.5\overline{)\begin{array}{c}12\phantom{0}\\60\\5\phantom{0}\\\hline10\\10\\\hline\end{array}}$$

B.

$$60\overline{)2.4} \longrightarrow 60\overline{)\begin{array}{c}0.04\\2.40\\\underline{2.40}\end{array}}$$

C.

$$0.4\overline{)18} \longrightarrow 0.4\overline{)\begin{array}{c}4.5\phantom{0}\\18.0\\\underline{16\phantom{0}}\\20\\\underline{20}\end{array}}$$

# CHAPTER 7

# Introduction to Misconceptions and Error Patterns:
# Geometry and Measurement

Learning computational procedures involves looking for patterns, but so does much of learning in other areas of mathematics. Each student paper in this chapter contains examples focusing on a particular aspect of geometry or measurement.

In some cases, a student has inferred an erroneous concept, possibly over-generalizing from limited experiences. In other cases, the student may have created a procedure that uses bits and pieces of information heard from time to time; the procedure gives the student an answer, but it does not make mathematical sense and it does not always provide correct answers.

While you are identifying the misconception or pattern, be sure to consider each example given. Respond as the student did to complete the additional examples.

As you think of instructional activities that might help the student, remember the resources that are available for teaching geometry and measurement— materials like geoboards, dot paper, and cutout shapes. Then compare your ideas for activities with those presented in this text.

Each error pattern has been labeled simply G-M to identify it with geometry or measurement.

## ■ Identifying Patterns

### Error Pattern G-M-1

Sometimes Martha names geometric figures correctly, but she often seems confused. Look carefully at her written work. Can you find the error pattern she is following?

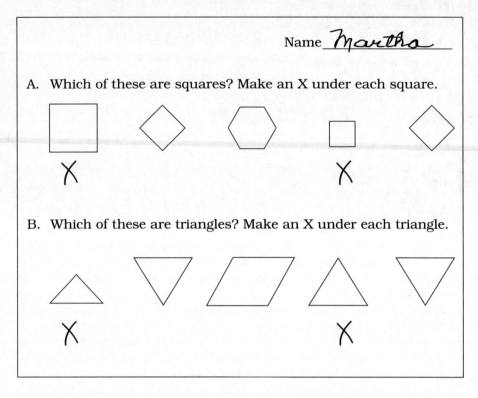

Clearly, Martha is experiencing difficulty. In constructing her own understanding of these figures, has she inferred something that is not actually true?

Make sure you found Martha's misconception by using her error pattern for the following exercise.

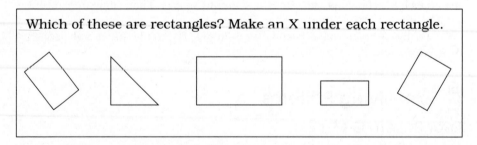

Why might Martha be responding this way? Turn to Error Pattern G-M-1 on page 117 and see if you identified her misconception. Can you think of a way to help Martha?

## Error Pattern G-M-2

Oliver seems confused when right angles are discussed in class. Look carefully at his written work. Can you identify his misconception?

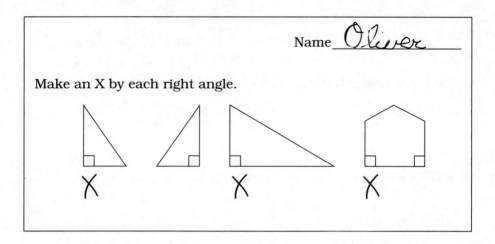

Did you determine what he is doing? In Oliver's thinking, what distinguishes a right angle? Why might he have come to that conclusion?

Make sure you found Oliver's misconception by using his thinking to respond to this exercise.

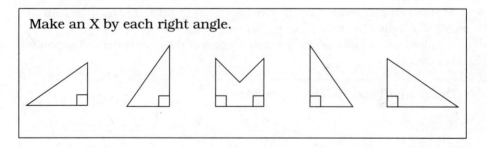

Now turn to Error Pattern G-M-2 on page 118 and compare your response. Can you think of a way to help Oliver?

## Error Pattern G-M-3

Charlene is confident she knows how to determine the altitude of a triangle. Does she really?

Look carefully at her written work. Can you determine the procedure she used when responding in this exercise?

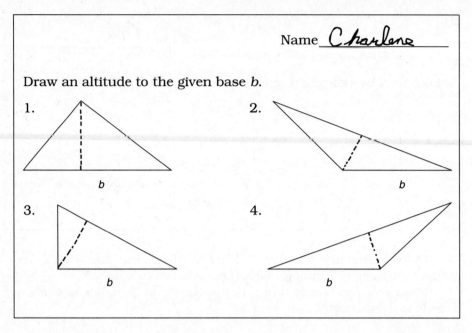

Name _Charlene_

Draw an altitude to the given base *b*.

1.

2.

*b*                                    *b*

3.                                    4.

*b*                                    *b*

Did you determine what Charlene is doing? In her thinking, what is an altitude? Why might she have come to that conclusion?

Make sure you found her procedure by using the error pattern to respond to this exercise.

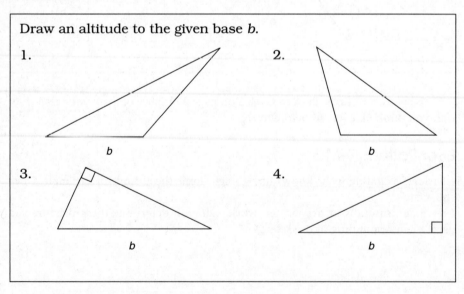

Draw an altitude to the given base *b*.

1.

2.

*b*                                    *b*

3.                                    4.

*b*                                    *b*

Now turn to Error Pattern G-M-3 on page 119 and compare your response. Can you think of a way to help Charlene or other students with a similar misconception?

## Error Pattern G-M-4

Denny quickly determines the perimeter for a given figure. Sometimes he is correct, but other times he is not.

Look carefully at his written work. Can you determine the procedure he used in this exercise?

---

Name _Denny_

Determine the perimeter of each of these rectangular regions:

1.

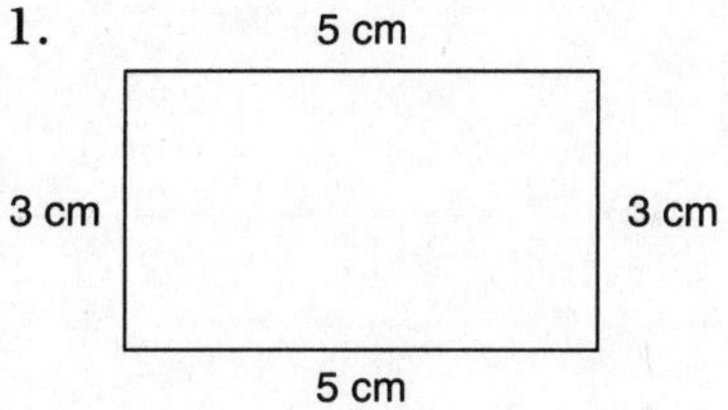

5 cm

3 cm        3 cm

5 cm

Answer ___ **16 cm** ___

2.

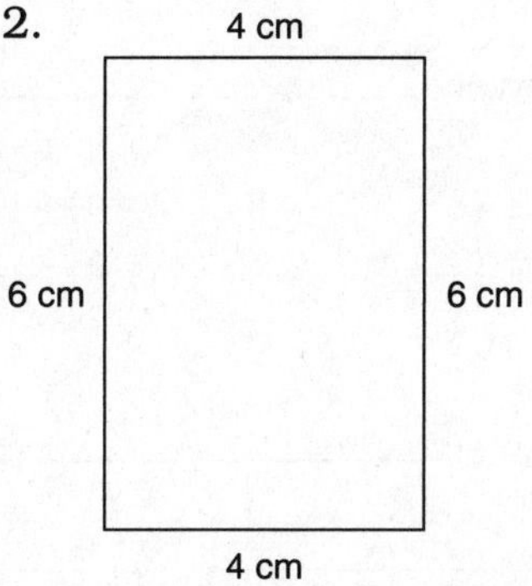

4 cm

6 cm        6 cm

4 cm

Answer ___ **20 cm** ___

3.

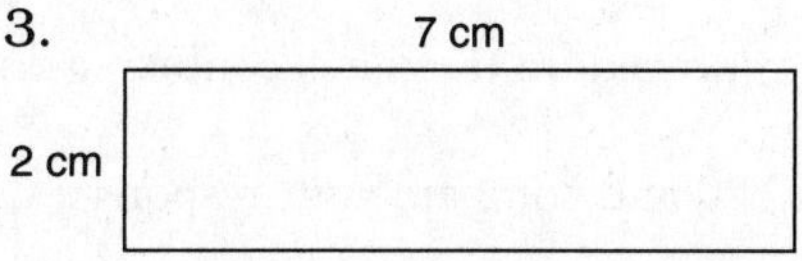

7 cm

2 cm

Answer ___ **14 cm** ___

4.

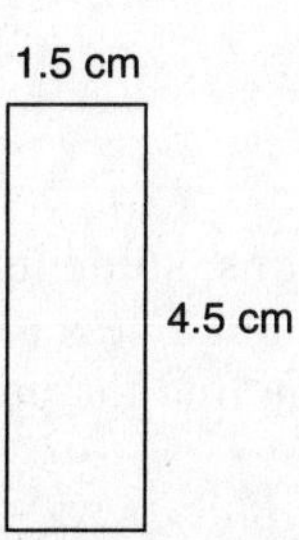

1.5 cm

4.5 cm

Answer ___ **6.75 cm** ___

Did you determine what Denny is doing? What does he understand about perimeter? What does he not yet understand?

Make sure you found his procedure by using the error pattern to respond to the following exercise.

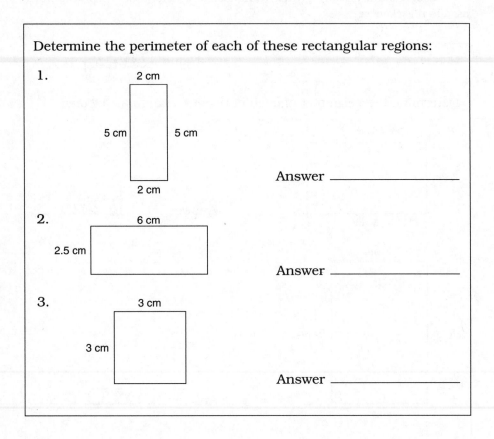

Determine the perimeter of each of these rectangular regions:

1.

2 cm

5 cm        5 cm

2 cm

Answer _____

2.

6 cm

2.5 cm

Answer _____

3.

3 cm

3 cm

Answer _____

Has Denny learned another concept or procedure that he is confusing with this situation?

Turn to Error Pattern G-M-4 on page 120 and compare your response. Can you think of a way to help Denny?

## Error Pattern G-M-5

The teacher hoped that after studying ratios and proportions, students would apply what they had learned to the study of similar figures, but Teresa is experiencing difficulty. Look carefully at her written work. Can you find the procedure she is following?

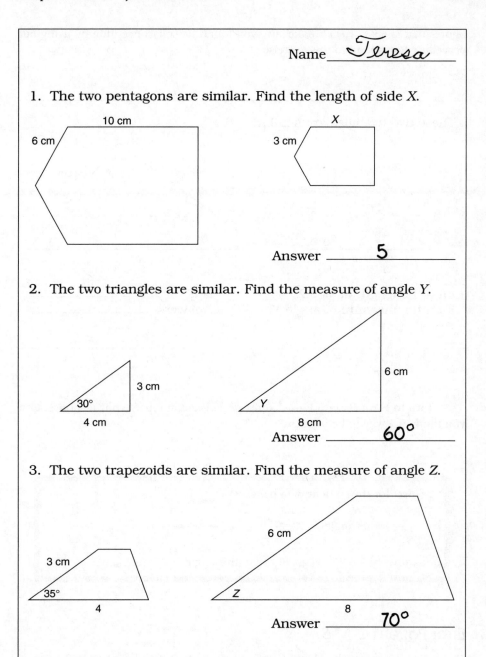

Name _Teresa_

1. The two pentagons are similar. Find the length of side X.

10 cm

6 cm

X

3 cm

Answer _____5_____

2. The two triangles are similar. Find the measure of angle Y.

3 cm

30°

4 cm

6 cm

Y

8 cm

Answer _____60°_____

3. The two trapezoids are similar. Find the measure of angle Z.

6 cm

3 cm

35°

4

Z

8

Answer _____70°_____

Did you determine what Teresa is doing? What does she understand about similar figures that is correct? What does she believe to be true about similar figures that is *not* correct? Make sure you found her misconception by using her procedure to respond to this exercise.

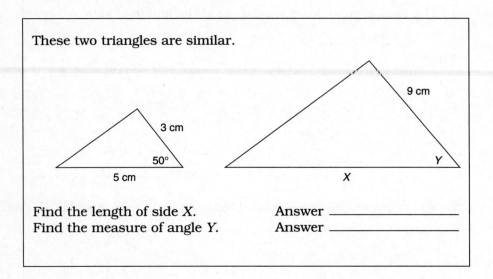

These two triangles are similar.

3 cm

9 cm

50°

5 cm

X

Y

Find the length of side *X*.          Answer _____

Find the measure of angle *Y*.        Answer _____

Turn to Error Pattern G-M-5 on page 121 and compare your response. Can you think of a way to help Teresa?

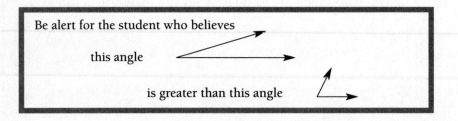

Be alert for the student who believes

this angle

is greater than this angle

## Error Pattern G-M-6

Even though the teacher hoped students would apply what they had learned about ratios and proportions to the study of similar figures, Nick developed his own procedure to respond to the exercises. Look carefully at his written work. Can you find his pattern?

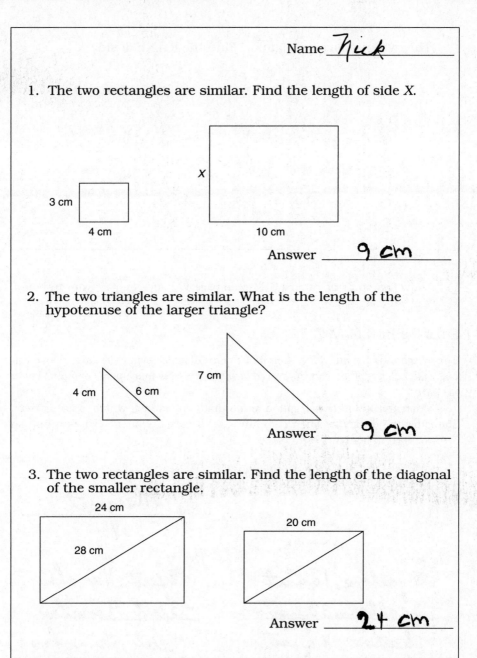

Name _Nick_

1. The two rectangles are similar. Find the length of side X.

3 cm

4 cm

X

10 cm

Answer ___9 cm___

2. The two triangles are similar. What is the length of the hypotenuse of the larger triangle?

4 cm    6 cm

7 cm

Answer ___9 cm___

3. The two rectangles are similar. Find the length of the diagonal of the smaller rectangle.

24 cm

28 cm

20 cm

Answer ___24 cm___

Did you determine what Nick is doing? Make sure you found his error pattern by using his procedure to respond to this exercise.

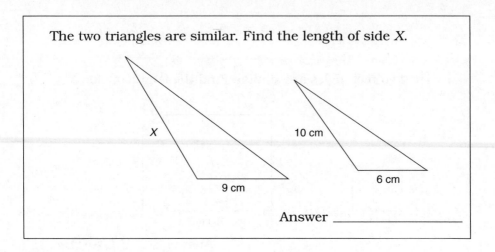

The two triangles are similar. Find the length of side X.

X

10 cm

9 cm

6 cm

Answer _____

Now turn to Error Pattern G-M-6 on page 122 and compare your response. How can you help Nick?

## Error Pattern G-M-7

*The refrigerator contained 5 gallons and 1 quart of punch before the party. Three gallons and 3 quarts of punch were served at the party. How much punch remained after the party?*

Margaret found that 1 gallon and 8 quarts remained, which is not correct. She is having difficulty when computing with measurements. Can you find an error pattern in her work?

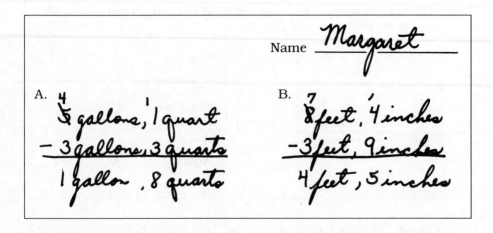

Name *Margaret*

A.
```
    4
    5 gallons, 1 quart
  - 3 gallons, 3 quarts
    1 gallon , 8 quarts
```

B.
```
    7
    8 feet, 4 inches
  - 3 feet, 9 inches
    4 feet, 5 inches
```

Check yourself by using Margaret's erroneous pattern to complete these examples.

C.
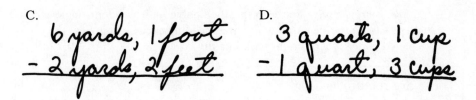

D.

Why is Margaret computing this way? What does she not yet understand?

After you finish Examples C and D, turn to page 123 to see if you accurately identified Margaret's error pattern.

## ■ Planning Instruction

### Error Pattern G-M-1
*(from Martha's paper on page 108)*

If you discovered what Martha was doing, you probably completed the exercise as shown.

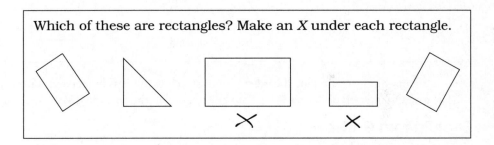

Martha's understanding of what a square is, what a triangle is, and what a rectangle is, includes a specific orientation. It is as if she said, "If you turn a square and make a diamond, it's not a square anymore."

Students often see examples of squares, triangles, and rectangles with one particular orientation (often with a horizontal base). Martha probably associated the name of each figure with that configuration. She does not appear to have been taught the name of each figure while observing examples with different orientations.

If you were Martha's teacher, what help would you provide? Are your ideas among those that follow?

1. *Turn the figure.* Let the student make a rectangle on a geoboard, copy it on geoboard dot paper, then turn the geoboard and copy the rectangle again. This can be done several times. Emphasize that this is the same rectangle turned different ways.

2. *Make concept cards.* For each specified polygon, let students make a concept card. Provide cards with three headings. For rectangles, the completed concept card might look like this:

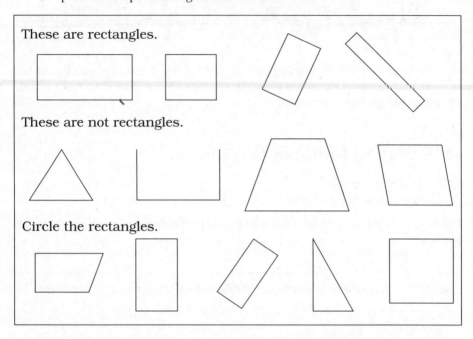

Students can give completed cards to other students to identify rectangles in
the last row. Orientation of figures is likely to be included in the ensuing discussion.

## Error Pattern G-M-2
*(from Oliver's paper on page 109)*

If you discovered Oliver's misconception, you probably completed the exercise as
shown.

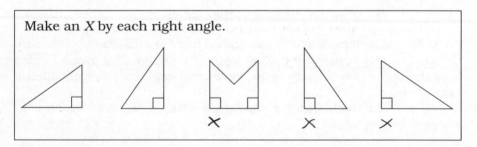

To Oliver, a *right angle* goes to the right. (It is possible he also believes that
some angles are *left angles*.)

It may be that when the term *right angle* was introduced, the examples that
he observed actually did have a horizontal leg going to the right. He assumed that
this was part of what makes a right angle.

If you were Oliver's teacher, how would you help him correct his understanding? Are any of the instructional activities you suggest similar to these?

1. *Use a square corner.* Let the student use the (square) corner of an object to find right angles. Emphasize that *any* triangle with a square corner is a right triangle; it does not make any difference how the triangle is turned.
2. *Make a tesselation.* Will a right triangle tesselate? Let the student repeatedly trace around a cutout right triangle to make a tesselation if he can. Emphasize the need to turn the right triangle different directions. Then let the student mark the right angle in each right triangle.
3. *Make a concept card.* Let the student make a concept card for the concept *right triangle,* as described for Error Pattern G-M-1.
4. *Relate the right angle to the hypotenuse.* Show the student several right triangles with varied configurations and orientations. For each triangle, let the student identify the right angle and the hypotenuse. Then the student can write a sentence that describes the relationship between the right angle and the hypotenuse.

## Error Pattern G-M-3
*(from Charlene's paper on page 110)*

If you discovered what Charlene is doing, you probably completed the exercise as shown.

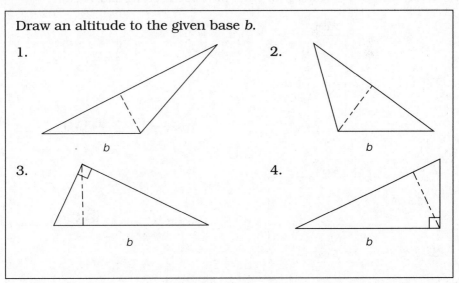

Charlene appears to believe that an altitude is a line segment from the angle opposite the longest leg of the triangle *to* the longest leg, and that line segment is perpendicular to the longest leg. (This often works with altitudes presented in examples.)

She does not appear to consider "to the given base" in the direction for the exercise; she just draws the altitude as she understands it. Sometimes she draws it correctly.

How would you help Charlene understand what an altitude is and be able to draw altitudes correctly? Your suggestions will probably focus, in part, on the idea of "the base of a triangle." Are your suggestions among those listed?

1. *Investigate.* Let the student investigate these questions:
   - How many altitudes does a triangle have?
   - Do all triangles have the same number of altitudes? Why?

   The student can write about what she found and draw triangles and altitudes to illustrate her paragraph.
2. *Use cutouts of triangles.* For each specified triangle cutout, let the student trace around the shape three times, with three different orientations, so that each of the legs serves as the base. Then the student can construct an altitude for each triangle. Note that three different altitudes can be drawn from the same cutout triangle.

## Error Pattern G-M-4

*(from Denny's paper on page 112)*

If you discovered what Denny is doing, you probably completed the exercise as shown.

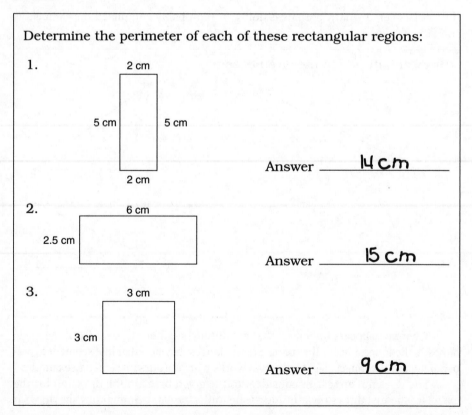

Determine the perimeter of each of these rectangular regions:

1.
2 cm
5 cm     5 cm
2 cm
Answer ____ 14 cm ____

2.
6 cm
2.5 cm
Answer ____ 15 cm ____

3.
3 cm
3 cm
Answer ____ 9 cm ____

Denny appears to have constructed his own procedural definition for finding perimeters, something like: "If all four sides have numbers, add; if only two sides have numbers, multiply." He may be confusing this situation with a procedure he used when finding the area of a rectangle.

How would you help Denny more adequately understand what a perimeter is and be able to determine the length of each perimeter more accurately? Are any of your suggestions similar to these?

1. *Trace around the figure.* Let the student trace around the figure with his finger and say the measure (the length) of each side as he does. He can then add to find the total perimeter.
2. *Relate to a fence.* Let the student determine how long a fence is that goes around the figure. He will need to make sure he has a measurement for each side before finding the total length.
3. *Copy and label.* Let the student copy or trace the figure, then label every side. If some measurements are not given, he will have to think about what he already knows about figures like these.
4. *Study regular polygons with only one side labeled.* Let the student write out how to find the perimeter of any regular polygon. If he can, he should describe more than one way.

## Error Pattern G-M-5
*(from Teresa's paper on page 114)*

If you discovered Teresa's error pattern, you probably completed the exercise as shown.

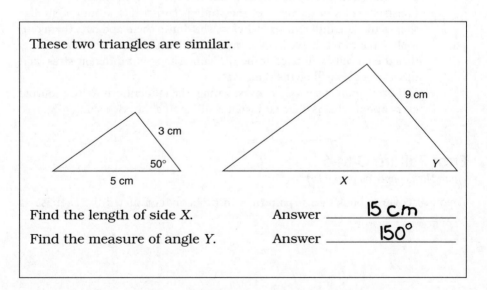

These two triangles are similar.

3 cm

9 cm

50°

5 cm

X

Y

Find the length of side X.        Answer _____15 cm_____

Find the measure of angle Y.      Answer _____150°_____

Teresa appears to have overgeneralized as she constructed her own rule for exercises involving similar figures. She thinks something like: "Do the same thing to everything. If one thing is twice as much, everything is twice as much." She does not seem to distinguish between comparing sides of similar triangles and comparing angles in similar triangles.

How would you help Teresa more adequately understand similar figures and be able to complete such exercises correctly? Are the instructional activities you suggest among those that follow?

1. *Use a geoboard.* Can the student make this triangle on her geoboard?

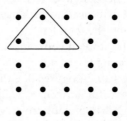

   Challenge her to make a second triangle in which all three sides are two times as long. The triangles should be the same shape but different sizes. The two triangles can be copied on geoboard dot paper and cut out, and the student can compare the angles.
2. *Compare what is alike and different.* Examine cutout shapes of pairs of similar polygons. Place one on top of the other to determine what is the same (angle measure) and what is different (lengths of sides).
3. *Construct pairs of shapes.* Let the student construct cutouts of similar shapes that are different sizes. Before she draws them and cuts them out, is she able to tell how she will know that her shapes are similar? Stress that the cutouts will need to be the same shape but different sizes, and that the angles will be the same size.
4. *Make a journal entry.* After investigating, the student can write a journal entry about what is alike and what is different about two similar figures.

## Error Pattern G-M-6
*(from Nick's paper on page 116)*

If you discovered Nick's error pattern, you probably completed the exercise as shown.

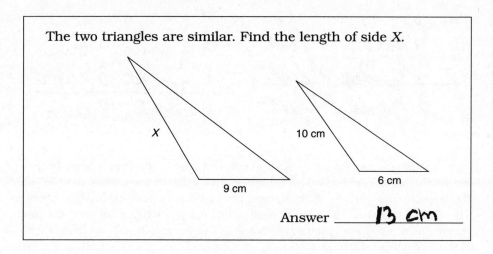

The two triangles are similar. Find the length of side X.

X          10 cm

9 cm                6 cm

Answer _____ 13 cm

Nick appears to believe that measures of related sides of similar figures differ by the same number. Therefore, if the difference between two related sides is known, addition or subtraction can often be used to determine missing lengths. Clearly, his understanding of similar figures and equivalent ratios (proportions) is not satisfactory.

How would you help Nick more adequately understand relationships in similar figures and be able to complete correctly exercises such as these? Are your ideas among these?

1. *A group investigation.* Let students examine many pairs of carefully selected similar figures and measure and record measurements for corresponding sides. They can reflect on the relationship between corresponding sides. Is it an addition-subtraction relationship? Is it a multiplication-division relationship? Students can write about what they did and what they decided.

2. *Relate to equivalent ratios.* Do the measures of corresponding sides form equivalent ratios? That is, do the ratios of two pairs of corresponding sides make a proportion? Why? The student can measure examples of similar figures to investigate.

## Error Pattern G-M-7

*(from Margaret's paper on page 117)*

Using Margaret's error pattern, Examples C and D would be completed as shown.

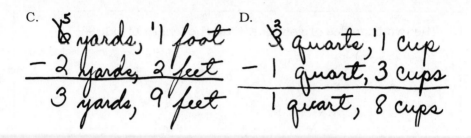

C.
$$\begin{array}{r}{}^5\!\!\!\!\!/\!\!6 \text{ yards, } {}^{\backprime}1 \text{ foot} \\ -\ 2 \text{ yards, } 2 \text{ feet} \\ \hline 3 \text{ yards, } 9 \text{ feet}\end{array}$$

D.
$$\begin{array}{r}{}^2\!\!\!\!\!/\!\!3 \text{ quarts, } {}^{\backprime}1 \text{ cup} \\ -\ 1 \text{ quart, } 3 \text{ cups} \\ \hline 1 \text{ quart, } 8 \text{ cups}\end{array}$$

Margaret is regrouping in order to subtract, just as she does when subtracting whole numbers expressed with base-ten numeration. She crosses out the left figure and writes one less above it, then places a one in front of the right figure. This technique produces a correct result when the relationship between the two measurement units is a base-ten relationship, but the results are incorrect whenever other relationships exist.

How would you help Margaret? What instructional activities would make it possible for Margaret to subtract correctly in measurement situations? Are your ideas similar to any of these?

1. *Use measuring devices.* First, let the student show the minuend with measuring devices. In Example C, it could be shown with yardsticks and foot rules. Let the student see if she can take away as much length (volume, and so on) as is suggested by the subtrahend. In the process, it will be necessary to exchange. Be sure to point out that exchanges are not always a ten for ten ones: many other kinds of exchanges occur with measurement situations.

2. *Regroup in many different number bases.* Use multibase blocks, chip trading activities, place-value charts, or sticks and bundles of sticks to learn to regroup in different number bases. A game-rule orientation in which the rule for exchanging changes from game to game may help the student generalize the regrouping pattern. For base-4 games and activities, the rule would be "Exchange a 4 for ones"; in base-12 games, the rule would be "Exchange a 12 for ones," and so on. Follow such activities with computation that involves measurement. Help students connect regrouping within computation with exchanges that were encountered when working in other number bases.

## CONCLUSION

Many students learn misconceptions and develop error patterns as they study geometry or measurement. They think about some of the examples (they may actually observe *only part* of the representations presented by the teacher or text); they may also make invalid assumptions or overgeneralize.

This suggests a need to provide varied instructional experiences during which students reflect on and sometimes write about what they are observing. Many useful manipulatives and diagrams are available for modeling geometric concepts, including drawings, cutout shapes, geoboards. and dot paper. Frequently it is helpful to provide both examples and non-examples of a concept.

Sometimes students can be challenged to create models of what they are studying. For example: "How could you show subtraction of these measurements? Could you use base-ten blocks? Why?"

Geometry and measurement are areas where making an investigation is a particularly useful instructional strategy. "What is the relationship between two similar triangles? Between their sides? Between their angles?"

Throughout the study of geometry and measurement, be alert for students who overgeneralize.

## FURTHER REFLECTION

Consider the following questions:

1. How are the concepts *ratio* and *proportion* related to similar polygons?
2. Why should a teacher vary the orientation of geometric figures when teaching about particular polygons, and when teaching about concepts such as right triangles and altitude?
3. In Error Pattern G-M-4, Denny multiplied the two given numbers when he determined the perimeter of a rectangle. Should this error be discussed with students when teaching perimeter and its application in the world around us? Explain your answer.

# CHAPTER 8

# Introduction to Misconceptions and Error Patterns:
# Percent, Proportion, Integers, and Algebra

This chapter contains selected examples of papers with percent problems solved by students using procedures they assumed to be correct, papers in which students practiced adding and subtracting with integers, and papers in which students practiced working with variables while simplifying and evaluating expressions.

As you look for misconceptions and error patterns, remember that students sometimes overgeneralize—they remember what was true in a limited number of situations and apply it more generally.

Misconceptions are common about the way symbols are typically used. For example, students often assume that if two variables are different, they cannot be replaced by the same number: the solution for $x + y = 6$ could not be $3 + 3 = 6$; and yet, by convention we allow the same number to be substituted for different variables. Among the papers are evidences of purely mechanical procedures with symbols. Operations are misunderstood. These students actually practiced applying concepts and procedures that are not correct.

After you find misconceptions and identify error patterns, verify your hypotheses by completing the additional examples. As you suggest instructional activities to help the student, remember that when you are thinking about percent, you are thinking about hundredths, or parts per 100. Also recall that a proportion is a statement that two ratios name the same number. Keep in mind the relation of subtraction to addition, and different models for addition of integers such as number-line models and counting models.

After you suggest at least two instructional activities for an error pattern, compare your suggestions with those provided in this book.

To facilitate discussion, each pattern is arbitrarily labeled by a code: P-P for percent problems and proportion, A-I for addition with integers, S-I for subtraction with integers, and ALG for algebra.

## ■ Identifying Patterns

### Error Pattern P-P-1

Sara correctly solves some percent problems, but many answers are incorrect. Can you find an error pattern?

---

Name *Sara*

A. On a test with 30 items, Mary worked 24 items correctly. What percent did she have correct?

$$\frac{24}{30} = \frac{X}{100}$$

Answer: *80 %*

B. Twelve students had perfect scores on a quiz. This is 40% of the class. How many students are in the class.

$$\frac{12}{40} = \frac{X}{100}$$

Answer: *30 students*

C. Jim correctly solved 88% of 50 test items. How many items did he have correct?

$$\frac{50}{88} = \frac{X}{100}$$

Answer: *57 items*

---

When you think you have found Sara's error pattern, use it to solve these problems.

D. Brad earned $400 during the summer and saved $240 from his earnings. What percent of his earnings did he save?

ANSWER: _____

E. Barbara received a gift of money on her birthday. She spent 80% of the money on a watch. The watch cost her $20. How much money did she receive as a birthday gift?

ANSWER: _____

F. The taffy sale brought in a total of $750, but 78% of this was used for expenses. How much money was used for expenses?

ANSWER: _____

Next, turn to page 132 to see if you identified the pattern. Why might Sara or any student adopt such a procedure?

## Error Pattern P-P-2

Steve is having difficulty solving percent questions. Can you find an error pattern in his paper?

---

Name *Steve*

A. What number is 30% of 180?

$$
\begin{array}{r}
1\,8\,0 \\
\times\ .3\,0 \\
\hline
0\,0\,0 \\
5\,4\,0 \\
\hline
5\,4.0\,0
\end{array}
$$

Answer: _54_

B. Fifteen percent of what number is 240?

$$
\begin{array}{r}
2\,4\,0 \\
\times\ .1\,5 \\
\hline
1\,2\,0\,0 \\
2\,4\,0 \\
\hline
3\,6.0\,0
\end{array}
$$

Answer: _36_

C. What percent of 40 is 28?

$$
\begin{array}{r}
4\,0 \\
\times .2\,8 \\
\hline
3\,2\,0 \\
8\,0 \\
\hline
1\,1.2\,0
\end{array}
$$

Answer: _11.2_

---

When you find Steve's error pattern, use it to solve these examples.

D. What number is 80% of 54?

ANSWER: _____

E. Seventy is 14% of what number?

ANSWER: _____

F. What percent of 125 is 25?

ANSWER: _____

Now, turn to page 134 to learn if you found Steve's procedure. How would you help a student who computes in this way?

## Error Pattern A-I-1

*Acme stock decreased in value 8 points on Monday, then increased in value 6 points on Tuesday. What was the total change in value for the two days?*

Karl is enjoying some success when adding with integers. However, he frequently gets incorrect sums that are not even reasonable. Can you determine the error pattern he is using?

Name **Karl**

A. $^-8 + 6 =$ **-2**    C. $7 + {}^-2 =$ **5**
B. $5 + {}^-9 =$ **4**    D. $^-4 + 10 =$ **-6**

Karl may have constructed his procedure while working with examples that have a common characteristic. Make sure you found his error pattern by using his procedure to complete these examples.

E. $10 + {}^-6 =$ _____    F. $10 + {}^-14 =$ _____

Would it help Karl if he estimated before adding? Turn to page 136 and see if you identified his procedure.

## Error Pattern A-I-2

Daphne gets some correct sums. Even so, many of her sums are incorrect.

She constructed her own rule for adding integers, but it is not an easy error pattern to determine. Can you find her procedure?

---

Name __Daphne__

Write the sum.

A. $^-6 + ^-8 =$ __2__     C. $4 + ^-3 =$ __7__

B. $^-8 + ^-3 =$ __-5__     D. $^-2 + ^-5 =$ __3__

---

Make sure you found her error pattern by using her procedure to complete these examples.

E. $^-6 + 10 =$ _____     F. $10 + ^-6 =$ _____

Turn to page 137 and see if you identified her procedure. How would you help Daphne or any student with this kind of error pattern?

## Error Pattern S-I-1

From time to time, Nicole subtracts integers and gets the correct difference. Very frequently, however, her answer is incorrect.

She appears to have learned a phrase or rule in another context, and she is applying it inappropriately. Can you find her error pattern?

---

Name __Nicole__

Write the sum.

A. $3 - (^-4) =$ __7__     C. $7 + ^-2 =$ __5__

B. $^-6 + 2 =$ __8__     D. $^-5 - 4 =$ __9__

---

Make sure you found Nicole's procedure by using it to subtract these examples.

E. $^-6 - 3 =$ _____     F. $^-2 - ^-5 =$ _____

What phrase (or "rule") has Nicole learned that she appears to be applying inappropriately? Turn to page 139 and see if you identified Nicole's procedure.

## Error Pattern ALG-1

The error pattern in Ivette's paper is all too common. Can you find it?

Name _Ivette_

1. $(a^2)^2 =$ $a^4$
2. $(b^2)^3 =$ $b^5$
3. $(a^3b^4)^2 =$ $a^5 b^6$

Did you find Ivette's procedure? Check yourself by using her procedure to complete Examples 4 and 5.

4. $(x^3)^2 =$ _____
5. $(xy^2)^2 =$ _____

Turn to page 140 to see if you identified the procedure. Why might Ivette be using such a procedure?

## Error Pattern ALG-2

Can you find Juan's error pattern?

Name _Juan_

1. $6(1+4x)+2 =$ $6(5x)+2$
   $= 30x+2$

2. $7+5(2+3x) =$ $7+5(5x)$
   $= 7+25x$

Did you find Juan's procedure? Check yourself by using his procedure to complete Examples 3 and 4.

3. $3(2x+1) =$ _____
4. $2(3+2x)+4 =$ _____

Turn to page 141 to see if you identified the procedure. Turn to page 141 to see if you identified the procedure. Why might Juan be doing this?

## Error Pattern ALG-3

Can you find the error pattern in Booker's paper?

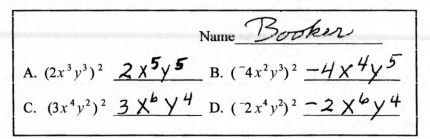

Name *Booker*

A. $(2x^3y^3)^2$  $2x^5y^5$    B. $(^-4x^2y^3)^2$  $-4x^4y^5$

C. $(3x^4y^2)^2$  $3x^6y^4$    D. $(^-2x^4y^2)^2$  $-2x^6y^4$

Did you find Booker's procedure? Check yourself by using his procedure to complete Examples E and F.

E.  $(2x^2y^2)^2$ _____      F.  $(-3x^2y^3)^2$ _____

Now turn to page 142 to see if you identified the procedure. Why might Booker be doing this?

## ■ Planning Instruction

### Error Pattern P-P-1
*(from Sara's paper on page 128)*

If you used Sara's error pattern, you completed the three percent problems as shown.

D.  Brad earned $400 during the summer and saved $240 from his earnings. What percent of his earnings did he save?

$$\frac{240}{400} = \frac{X}{100}$$

Answer: $60\%$

E.  Barbara received a gift of money on her birthday. She spent 80% of the money on a watch. The watch cost $20. How much money did she receive as a birthday gift?

$$\frac{20}{80} = \frac{X}{100}$$

Answer: $\$25$

F. The taffy sale brought in a total of $750, but 78% of this was used for expenses. How much money was used for expenses?

$$\frac{78}{750} = \frac{X}{100}$$

Answer: **$10.40**

Sara successfully solved percent problems when the class first solved them, but as different types of problems were encountered, she began to have difficulty.

Sara is solving correctly the proportion she writes for the problem. However, she uses a procedure that often does not accurately represent the ratios described in the problem. She is using the following proportion for every problem encountered:

$$\frac{\text{lesser number in the problem}}{\text{greater number in the problem}} = \frac{x}{100}$$

She may have created her procedure from initial experiences with problems like A and D, although the procedure also seems to work with problems of the type illustrated by B and E. The procedure does not provide a correct solution with problems of the type illustrated by C and F.

How would you help Sara correctly solve percent problems? Are your ideas among those listed?

**Note:** When you assign percent problems, ask to see all of the work done on each problem. You need to see what ratios are derived from the problem, and whether the proportion itself is correctly developed. This particular student is correctly processing the proportion once it is determined and does *not* need instruction concerning cross multiplication. For this student, corrective instruction should focus on the concepts of percent, relating data in a problem to ratios (to fractions), and possibly equal ratios.

1. *Use 10 × 10 squares of graph paper.* Redevelop the meaning of percent as "per 100." Therefore, n% is always $\frac{n}{100}$. For example:

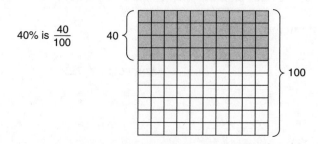

40% is $\frac{40}{100}$      40 $\{$      100

2. *Use base-ten blocks.* To redevelop the meaning of percent, a flat block for 100 can be partially covered with long blocks for 10 and with unit

blocks. But if this is done, it must be emphasized that the flat block (for 100) now represents *one*, and part of that whole (a certain percent of it) has been covered.

3. *Identify what is being "counted."* Ask, "Do we know how many there are in the whole set? Do we know how many are in part of the set?" Show these numbers with a fraction:

$$\frac{\text{number in part of the set}}{\text{number in the whole set}}$$

In Problem B, for example, we are counting students. We know there are 12 students in part of the class, but we do not know how many students are in the whole class. Therefore, the fraction is:

$$\frac{12}{n}$$

4. *Use number lines to show equivalent ratios.* Sketch a number line for the fraction in which both numbers are known.

$40\% = \dfrac{40}{100}$ $\longrightarrow$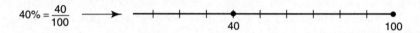

Then sketch another number line just below it for the other fraction. Because the two fractions are equal, you can align the terms of one fraction with the counterparts in the other fraction. See if the student can estimate the unknown number.

$\dfrac{12}{n}$ $\longrightarrow$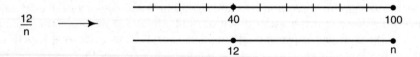

## Error Pattern P-P-2

*(from Steve's paper on page 129)*

If you found Steve's error pattern, your results are as follows.

D. What number is 80% of 54?

$$
\begin{array}{r}
5\,4 \\
\times\ \ .8\,0 \\
\hline
0\,0 \\
4\,3\,2\ \ \\
\hline
4\,3.2\,0
\end{array}
$$

Answer: __43.2__

E.  Seventy is 14% of what number?

$$
\begin{array}{r}
70 \\
\times .14 \\
\hline
280 \\
70 \phantom{0} \\
\hline
9.80
\end{array}
$$

Answer: _____9.8_____

F.  What percent of 125 is 25?

$$
\begin{array}{r}
125 \\
\times .25 \\
\hline
625 \\
250 \phantom{0} \\
\hline
31.25
\end{array}
$$

Answer: _31.25_

Steve's solutions are correct when he is finding the percent of a specified number (Problems A and D). However, his solutions are incorrect when the percent is known and he needs to find a number (Problems B and E) or when he needs to find what percent one number is of a specified number (Problems C and F).

Usually, the first percent problems a student encounters involve finding the percent of a number. Steve probably developed his procedure while solving such problems, and he is using a version of it when he attempts to solve other types of percent problems. When the percent is given, he changes it to a decimal then multiplies this number times the other number given. When the percent is not given, he treats the lesser of the two given numbers as if it were a decimal and proceeds similarly.

How would you help Steve correctly solve percent problems? Are your ideas among those that follow?

**Note:** Emphasizing a rule like "percent times a number equals percentage" is not likely to be helpful because this is actually the rule Steve is attempting to apply. Many students find it difficult to identify the three types of percent problems; they also confuse the terms *percent* and *percentage*. Instead, it may be helpful to develop a strategy that is basically the same for all three types of percent problems—possibly the proportion method.

See if your suggestions are among those that follow.

1.  *Show equal fractions.* Write a proportion for each problem with one fraction equal to another. With one fraction, show what the problem tells about percent, and with the other, show what the problem tells about the number of things. Use *n* whenever you are not told a number. For example:

Seventy is 14% of what number? (That is, 14 is part of 100 in the same way that 70 is part of some amount.)

$$\text{percent} \begin{cases} \dfrac{14}{100} = \dfrac{70}{n} & \leftarrow \text{part of the amount} \\ & \leftarrow \text{the whole amount} \end{cases}$$

2. *Cross multiply.* When the student is able to write a correct proportion for a percent problem, suggest that there is a pattern that can help us find the unknown number. Have the student supply several pairs of fractions known to be equal, fraction pairs like $\frac{1}{2} = \frac{2}{4}$. Then, as illustrated, lightly draw an X on each pair and ask the student to compare the products of the two numbers within each line of an X. For $\frac{1}{2} = \frac{2}{4}$, compare the product of 1 and 4 with the product of 2 and 2. When something like "their products are equal" is noted, have the student test the observation with other pairs of fractions. Then apply cross multiplication to percent problems.

$$\frac{1}{2} = \frac{4}{8} \qquad \begin{array}{l} 1 \times 8 = 2 \times 4 \\ 8 = 8 \end{array} \qquad \frac{14}{100} = \frac{70}{n} \qquad \begin{array}{l} 14\,n = 100 \times 70 \\ 14\,n = 7000 \\ n = 500 \end{array}$$

## Error Pattern A-I-1
*(from Karl's paper on page 129).*

If you discovered Karl's error pattern, you probably completed the exercise as shown below.

E. $10 + {}^{-}6 = \underline{\quad 4 \quad}$        F. $10 + {}^{-}14 = \underline{\quad 4 \quad}$

As Karl was considering addition and subtraction of integers—with all the negative and minus signs as well as plus signs—he apparently concluded that in order to add, you find the difference between what we would call the absolute values of the two integers. But where does he get the sign he attaches to his sum? He seems to use the sign of the first addend.

Karl's procedure does produce the correct sum at times, thereby reinforcing his conviction that he is adding integers.

How would you help Karl more adequately understand positive and negative integers and addition of integers? Are your ideas included in these activities?

1. *Use checkers.* Discrete objects such as black and red checkers can be used to show addition of integers. Let each black checker represent a positive one and each red checker a negative one. Given an addition example, have the student show the two integers by creating a set for each. To show addition, put the two sets together; that is, match the two sets one-to-one. A black-and-red combination is worth zero, and it is ignored or discarded because $(+1) + (-1) = 0$; they cancel each other. The number and color of nonmatching checkers shows the sum.

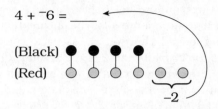

$$4 + \,^-6 = \underline{\qquad}$$

2. *Use a number line.* Arrows for integers are drawn on the number line as follows:
   - Length is determined by the absolute value of the number.
   - Direction is determined by the sign of the number:
     Arrows for positive numbers go to the right.
     Arrows for negative numbers go to the left.
   *To add*, start at zero, and draw the arrow for the first addend.

   $$^-3 + \,^+2 = \underline{\qquad}$$

   Begin the arrow for the second addend at the tip of the first arrow.

   $$^-3 + \,^+2 = \underline{\,^-1\,}$$

   The sum is indicated by the tip of the second arrow.

   **Note:** A more accurate modeling for *equals* is suggested by letting the sum be shown by another arrow going from zero to the tip of the second arrow. That is, addition with the two addend arrows produces the same number as the sum arrow.

3. *Focus on the sign of the sum.* For a set of examples, do not have the student compute sums. Instead, have the student determine *only* the sign of each sum. She may want to use checkers to help her decide.
4. *Write a rule.* Have the student write out his own rule for adding two integers. He then needs to test his rule to see if it always produces the correct sum, possibly by using checkers.

## Error Pattern A-I-2

*(from Daphne's paper on page 130)*

If you discovered Daphne's error pattern, you probably completed the exercise as shown.

E. $^-6 + 10 = \underline{\quad 4 \quad}$          F. $10 + \,^-6 = \underline{\quad 16 \quad}$

Daphne may picture a number line in her mind and begin at the place where the first addend is located. In order to add, she apparently moves to the right as indicated by the second addend. However, she seems to ignore the sign of the second addend. She uses the absolute value of the second addend, with the effect that she uses the second addend as a positive number, even when it is negative.

How would you help Daphne more adequately understand positive and negative integers, and addition of integers? Are your suggestions among these?

1. *Focus on the four possible combinations.* Let the student examine the four possible combinations, those with like signs and those with unlike signs. Provide examples of each combination and let the student use checkers (see Error Pattern A-I-1) to determine correct sums. What patterns does the student observe?

$$3 + 5 = ? \qquad {}^-3 + {}^-5 = ?$$
$$3 + {}^-5 = ? \qquad {}^-3 + 5 = ?$$

2. *Focus on the sign of the sum.* Instead of computing sums, let the student determine the sign of each sum for a set of examples you provide. She may want to use checkers to help decide.

3. *Use cutout arrows.* Cutout arrows can be used in a manner similar to the way a number line is used in Error Pattern A-I-1. Prepare a set of cutout arrows varying in length from one unit to five units long. Also prepare a mat to use with the arrows.

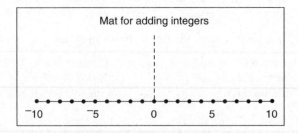

Arrows are selected for each integer as follows:
- Choose an arrow of the length suggested by the absolute value of the integer.
- Turn the arrow as suggested by the sign of the integer by placing the point to the right if it is positive and by placing the point to the left if it is negative.

*To add,* place the heel of the first arrow at zero. Then place the heel of the second arrow at the tip of the first arrow.

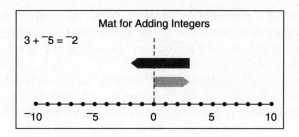

The sum is indicated by the tip of the second arrow. (See the note in Error Pattern A-I-1.)

4. *Make a journal entry.* Let the student describe her experiences adding integers. She should illustrate her journal entry with examples and include any patterns or rules she has observed. Make sure she tests any rule to see if it always produces the correct sum, possibly by using checkers.

## Error Pattern S-I-1

*(from Nicole's paper on page 130)*

If you discovered Nicole's error pattern, you probably completed the exercise as shown below.

E. $^-6 - 3 = $ _____ 9 _____          F. $^-2 - {}^-5 = $ _____ 3 _____

Nicole is confusing signs of operations and signs of numbers. She is also inappropriately applying something she must have learned by rote: "Two negatives make a positive."

She counts the plus/positive and minus/negative symbols (symbols for operations and for numbers). If there are two minus/negative symbols, she adds the absolute values. If the number of minus/negative symbols is odd, she subtracts the absolute values. Surprisingly, Nicole's procedure *does* produce the correct difference at times.

How would you help Nicole more adequately understand positive and negative integers and operations on integers—including subtraction? Are your ideas included among these?

1. *Distinguish numbers and operations.* For several examples, let the student circle the sign of the operation, then tell you the two numbers that are to be added. Emphasize that the word *negative* is used with numbers; a *minus* sign indicates subtraction.

2. *Make equivalent expressions.* Explain how to show the same as $^-5 - 7$ by changing it to an equivalent addition expression: $^-5 + {}^-7$. Add the

inverse (or opposite) of the addend (the second number). Let the student make equivalent addition expressions for many subtraction expressions, including examples of all four combinations of positive and negative numbers. Are any patterns observed?

3. *Subtract by adding.* Remind the student that an open number sentence (usually an equation) asks a question, and there are different ways of asking the same question. A question using subtraction can be changed into an equivalent question using addition. Checkers and arrows and number lines are most useful for adding, and they can be used for subtraction if we change the subtraction example into an equivalent addition example. Provide subtraction examples and have the student change each into an equivalent addition example, then find each sum using whatever method makes most sense to the student.

## Error Pattern ALG-1

*(from Ivette's paper on page 131)*

Did you find Ivette's error pattern?

$$4.\ (x^3)^2 = \underline{\ x^5\ }$$

$$5.\ (xy^2)^2 = \underline{\ x^3y^4\ }$$

When simplifying such expressions, Ivette adds the exponents as the parentheses are removed. Sometimes students verify a procedure by substituting a particular number and making sure the two expressions are equal, but apparently Ivette has not done this.

What *does* Ivette understand? What does she *not* yet understand? Ivette should not continue to practice her procedure. How would you help her? Are your suggestions among those listed?

1. *Focus on the total number of factors.* Explain that such an expression involves multiplying; for example, $(b^2)^3$ means $b^2 \times b^2 \times b^2$, which includes three sets of two factors: $(b \times b) \times (b \times b) \times (b \times b)$. Altogether, $b$ is a factor *six* times. Ask, "How can we find the total number of factors (the product in this case) without so much writing?" (You multiply exponents.)

2. *Substitute a small number and compute the amount.* Substitute a number like 4 or 5, and compute the amount. Begin within the parentheses, then continue. Have the student examine the written work and reflect on what was done. For $(b^2)^3$, three pairs of factors are six factors, so $(b^2)^3$ is

$(b)^6$ and the exponents 2 and 3 can be multiplied. Would this also be true if a different number were substituted for $b$?

## Error Pattern ALG-2

*(from Juan's paper on page 131)*

Did you find Juan's error pattern?

$$3.\ 3(2x+1) = 3(3x)$$
$$= 9x$$
$$4.\ 2(3+2x)+4 = 2(5x)+4$$
$$= 10x + 4$$

When simplifying such expressions, Juan adds (incorrectly) before he removes parentheses. He does not distinguish between numbers that are and are not coefficients.

What *does* Juan understand? What does he *not* yet understand? How could you help Juan so he does not continue to practice such a procedure? How would you help him? Are your ideas included in the activities described?

1. *Use an array to represent the product.* For a product like $3(2z + 1)$, you may want to let a rectangle suggest the array.

$$
\begin{array}{c}
\phantom{3}\quad 2z+1 \\
3\ \boxed{\phantom{xxxxxxxxxx}}
\end{array}
$$

Then partition the array much as you would for multiplication with whole numbers.

For $3 \times 14$:

$$
\begin{array}{c}
\phantom{3}\quad 10+4 \\
3\ \boxed{\ 3\times10\ \mid\ 3\times4\ } \longrightarrow 30+12 \longrightarrow 42
\end{array}
$$

Similarly:

$$
\begin{array}{c}
\phantom{3}\quad 2z+1 \\
3\ \boxed{\ 3\times2z\ \mid\ 3\times1\ } \longrightarrow 6z+3
\end{array}
$$

Have Juan compare the result with his error pattern and discuss (possibly write out) a procedure that produces the correct product.

2. *Substitute a small number and compute the amount.* For instance, for $3(2z + 1)$, assume that $z = 4$. Then $3(2z + 1) = 3(8 + 1)$. But $8 + 1$ is 9, and $3 \times 9$ is 27. (Using the erroneous pattern with $z = 4$, the result is 36.) Compare the procedures and note that there are not three $z$'s; there are only two $z$'s before multiplication by 3.

## Error Pattern ALG-3

*(from Booker's paper on page 132)*

Did you find Booker's error pattern?

E. $(2x^2y^2)^2 \underset{=}{\cdot} 2x^4y^4$    F. $(^-3x^2y^3)^2 \underset{=}{\cdot} -3x^4y^5$

When Booker simplifies expressions like these, he makes two errors. First, he does not square the numerical coefficient. Second, he adds exponents when he should multiply them.

How would you help Booker? How might you help him correct his error pattern? Are your ideas included in the following activities?

1. *Write out all factors and rearrange them.* An expression like $(2a^2b^3)^2$ represents one number named by a long string of factors multiplied together, so rewrite the number as a string of factors, then rearrange the factors by like terms.

$$
\begin{aligned}
(2a^2b^3)^2 &= (2a^2b^3) \times (2a^2b^3) \\
&= (2 \times a \times a \times b \times b \times b) \times (2 \times a \times a \times b \times b \times b) \\
&= (2 \times 2) \times (a \times a \times a \times a) \times (b \times b \times b \times b \times b \times b) \\
&= 4 \times a^4 \times b^6
\end{aligned}
$$

Have the student examine the result and reflect, "How can the result be obtained without writing out all of the factors?"

2. *Determine the frequency of each term as a factor.* Altogether, how many times is 2 a factor? How many times is $a$ a factor? And $b$?

## CONCLUSION

If students are taught and then practice specific procedures when they lack sufficient understanding of related concepts, they are apt to acquire misunderstandings and adopt error patterns similar to those encountered in this chapter. Before your students practice solving percent problems, make sure they can relate percents to other expressions for rational numbers (fractions and decimals). Make sure they also understand equivalent fractions and proportions. You may want to determine whether they understand the equivalence of two special products within a proportion: if $a/b = c/d$, then $a \times d = b \times c$.

Symbols are often a source of confusion when students work with integers. Help them distinguish between symbols or signs for numbers, and symbols for operations. Numbers can be represented with sets or locations on a number line, while operations are represented in other ways.

The meaning of the equals sign is very important for students to understand. For example, an expression indicating addition of two numbers (e.g., $2 + {}^-3$) is itself a name for a number, and their sum (${}^-1$) is a name for a number; they are names for the same number, and that is what the equals sign indicates. This is as true for integers as it is for whole numbers and rational numbers.

Algebra is a powerful system that uses symbols, but you need to be alert to error patterns in students' early work with symbols. Do not focus only on procedures and getting correct answers. As students learn algebra, they need a well-developed number sense and knowledge of the properties of operations on numbers. It is often helpful for students to be reminded that a particular expression is simply a name for a number. Sometimes that name is itself a sum or a difference; at other times, it is a product and it can be broken down into a string of factors.

Students experiencing difficulty may profit from being part of a group of students who create representations to illustrate problems and their solutions. Graphic representations often help students estimate a reasonable answer.

Diagnosis is a continuous process. It continues even during instructional activities as you observe students at work. Keep looking for patterns.

## FURTHER REFLECTION

Consider the following questions:

1. How can the concept *percent* be taught so that students think of percent as "per hundred"? List several instructional activities.
2. How can percent problems be expressed as proportions? Can you illustrate three different types of percent problems that can be expressed as a proportion? What procedure can be used for solving all three types?
3. How can you help your students distinguish between the sign of a number and the sign of an operation? Show how each can be represented differently.
4. Your students are simplifying expressions with exponents. How can you help them distinguish between when it makes sense to add exponents and when it makes sense to multiply exponents?

## ADDITIONAL PRACTICE

Can you describe the error pattern in each of the following papers? A key is provided on page 233.

PAPER 11

1. $-8 + 6 =$ ___$-2$___ 　　　 3. $7 + -2 =$ ___$5$___
2. $5 + -9 =$ ___$4$___ 　　　 4. $-4 + 10 =$ ___$-6$___

PAPER 12

1. $3 - (-4) =$ ___$7$___ 　　　 3. $7 + -2 =$ ___$5$___
2. $-6 - 2 =$ ___$8$___ 　　　 4. $-5 - 4 =$ ___$9$___

PAPER 13

a. $\sqrt{3} + \sqrt{20} =$ ___$\sqrt{23}$___ 　　　 b. $\sqrt{5} + \sqrt{8} =$ ___$\sqrt{13}$___

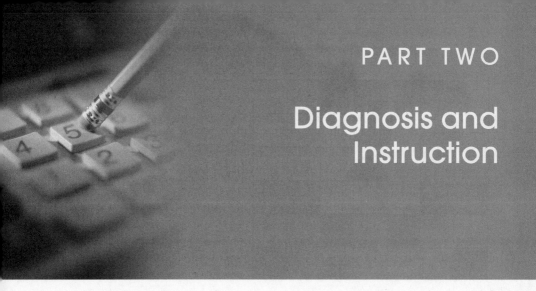

# Diagnosis and Instruction

In Part Two, you will read about specific things you can do to find out what each of your students already knows and can do, and what is yet to be learned. Tools for diagnosis are described in Chapter 9. Diagnostic teaching involves careful observation; it attempts to determine the concepts that individuals are truly learning and the procedures they are really employing—whether correct or not.

As we learn more about a particular student, we tailor our instruction to that student; we observe and learn more and adjust instruction again. We repeat this diagnosis-instruction cycle as often as necessary.

Chapters 10 and 11 present many ideas to help us design instruction to meet the specific needs of our students. Concepts and procedures that help us plan instruction in computation are the focus of Chapter 10, while Chapter 11 describes more general strategies that are useful as we plan instruction in mathematics.

# CHAPTER 9

# Diagnosing Misconceptions and Error Patterns in Computation and in Other Mathematical Topics

*I cannot teach students well*
*if I do not know them well.*

Theodore Sizer[1]

As Sizer reminds us, before we can teach our students, we need to know them well. Each of our students is unique, and learning is a very personal process.

Before we plan lessons and attempt to teach, we need to know what each of our students already understands and what each does not yet understand. Have any of our students learned misconceptions? What is the disposition of each student toward mathematics and toward learning mathematics? As we plan lessons and teach, we will need to make many professional judgments for which there are no tidy rules, so the more information we have the better.

We expect *all* students to learn, and for many of our students, we will need to go beyond careful examination of their work. We will need to probe deeply for information about their learning.

## The Equity Principle

Excellence in mathematics education requires equity—high expectations and strong support for all students.[2]

## The Assessment Principle

Assessment should support the learning of important mathematics and furnish useful information to both teachers and students.[3]

We collect data about each student as we observe, interview, probe, and gather data in a variety of ways. It is like letting a bucket down to get water from a deep well: We need to go deep to get what we need to know about each child.

146

Many students seem to view arithmetic (and possibly all of mathematics) as an either-or sort of thing. The answer is correct and arithmetic is enjoyable and life is rosy, or the answer is not correct and arithmetic and life are frustrating. We may wonder why such students are so answer-oriented. Yet we *do* need to face the question of why *some* students do not seem to be able to get the correct answers they need. This chapter is designed to help you find out.

Misconceptions and error patterns should not be the only focus of data gathering. We must get at the thinking of students by also collecting evidence regarding concepts understood and skills attained; then we can plan instruction that builds on each student's prior attainments. This is emphasized in the Assessment Principle in *Principles and Standards for School Mathematics* by the National Council of Teachers of Mathematics (NCTM) (2000):

> **To maximize the instructional value of assessment, teachers need to move beyond a superficial "right or wrong" analysis of tasks to a focus on how students are thinking about the tasks. Efforts should be made to identify valuable student insights on which further progress can be based rather than to concentrate solely on errors or misconceptions.[4]**

Assessment is the process of gathering information about student learning and the use of that information to plan instruction. Assessment must be aligned with our curricular goals; even specific assessment tasks should be planned with these goals in mind. As we teach mathematics, we need to be *continually* assessing.

Though we need to be continually assessing, we do *not* need to be continually testing. We should also collect evidence of student learning from projects and from various writings and tasks—many of which are described in this chapter. By gathering data from a variety of sources, we are more likely to obtain an accurate picture of each student's knowledge, skills, and learning processes.

Some educators believe that we as teachers do not know how to teach, or even what specifics to teach, unless we know *how* we will assess it—the particular evidences of learning we will collect.

# ■ Assessing for Varied Purposes

Teachers assess for various reasons, but information gathered should monitor student progress, improve programs, and guide instruction. The overall purpose of mathematics assessment must be to improve student learning.

External assessments help us know the extent to which our students are meeting established standards. These typically focus on state or provincial standards, but they may focus on regional or national standards. Insights gained from these large-scale tests may help us improve our programs, for example, by better aligning our instruction with our curriculum. However, teachers are best able to assess the learning of individual students from day to day.

*Summative* assessments occur *after* completion of a particular lesson or unit of instruction, enabling us to make judgments about student learning. They may involve tests, completion of projects, or even culminating performance tasks. Summative evaluations can point to the effectiveness of the lesson or unit itself.

*Formative* assessments occur when data are gathered *before* completion of a particular lesson or unit of instruction. Data gathered enables teachers to decide how they should alter instruction from what was planned.

We are primarily concerned with formative assessment in this book. Diagnosis can be used to help us design specific instructional alternatives for *individual* students—students for whom our regular instruction may not be adequate.

## ■ Using Formative Assessment: Diagnosing

*Failure in learning, just like learning itself,
is an individual affair.*[5]

Although we teach a group of students, learning is done by individuals. Our assessment tasks should help us teach *individual* students.

We observe (and collect data in other ways) to determine what students know and how individuals are thinking. Then we use what we learn to adjust our plans for teaching particular students. This is assessment during the instructional process—assessment used to shape or form ongoing instruction. It is *formative* assessment. Formative assessment should be an integral part of the instructional process, with assessment and instruction cycling continuously—sometimes rapidly. Formative assessment and instruction should be woven together seamlessly.

Formative assessment helps clarify what students are expected to know and be able to do. Students are more apt to take ownership of their own learning when individuals begin to understand what *specific* concepts, principles, and procedures they need to learn. Formative assessment can enable us as teachers to create more effective classroom activities; it may also enable our students to become learning resources for one another.

While we are teaching, we sometimes use the process we call diagnosis as a type of formative assessment: we collect data about rather specific areas of instruction. For example, after posing a problem for your students, have groups of students discuss possible solutions. Listen to their conversations; you may realize that you need to alter your instructional plan. Sometimes you will want to collect data *before* you begin teaching a lesson or unit of instruction in order to tailor instruction to particular students.

The specific areas of instruction that are the focus of diagnosis can be broad topics (measurement, for example), or more narrow topics (linear metric measurement). On the other hand, the focus of diagnosis can be specific concepts and principles (*equals* means the same as; the order of factors does not affect the product), or they can be specific procedures (renaming a fraction so it has greater terms). A diagnostic interview administered to an individual often focuses on specific concepts, principles, and procedures.

# ■ Using Open-Ended Assessment

When you are teaching mathematics, do you assume students understand what they are doing whenever they produce correct responses? Do some of your students think procedural skills are the only really important thing in mathematics? If so, you probably need to dig a little deeper and get at their thinking; provide students with tasks or problems that will show the assumptions they are making and how they are reasoning.

One way to get at their thinking is to use open-ended assessment items in conjunction with instruction. An assessment item is open-ended if it has multiple correct answers and a variety of strategies can be used to solve the problem. Correct answers for the problem should vary in complexity and sophistication.

So-called broken calculator problems are examples of open-ended assessment items: "How could you make your calculator show the number 65 if the 5 key is broken?"[6] When you use open-ended items, make sure your students share their responses and explain how they got their answers.

Creating open-ended assessment items can be challenging, but it is sometimes possible to create new items by varying known items. For example, the broken calculator problem cited above can be varied by having the 5 key *and* the plus sign broken, or having all the odd-numbered keys broken.

If your students have no experience with open-ended items, they may find it difficult to explain their thinking; they can do computations but have difficulty explaining why they do what they do. Tell students that the open-ended problems are a special type of problem; with these problems, the goal is to explain your thinking so well that another student can follow it.[7]

You may want to have students work in pairs or in small groups you can monitor. In addition to letting you observe how well they understand particular concepts (such as numeration concepts), students working with open-ended tasks gain experience with NCTM process standards: problem solving, reasoning, and communication.

# ■ Encouraging Self-Assessment

As teachers, we have an important role in the diagnosis of areas where our students need instruction, but each student also has a significant role in diagnosis. Self-assessment is a powerful tool for teaching and learning, and it may be the most important aspect of the assessment process.

> **The most effective assessment of all is that of one's own learning. One of the most valuable lifelong skills students can acquire is the ability to look back and reflect on what they have done and what they still need to do. Students who develop a habit of self-assessment will also develop their potential for continued learning.**[8]

After our students complete an assignment, we may want to hold a debriefing session to help them reflect on what they did. A debriefing can take the form of large or small-group discussions, or individual interviews. Questions can be posed that will help our students evaluate their experiences. Although specific questions may help students make judgments about relevant data, we need to include open-ended questions like:

- How do you think you did with this assignment?
- What does someone need to know to be able to do this assignment?
- What was easy for you in this assignment?
- What was difficult for you?

Self-assessment can also be facilitated if each student has a mathematics portfolio. (See "Using Portfolios to Monitor and Encourage Progress" in Chapter 11 for specific suggestions.)

Another way we can help our students acquire the habits of mind needed for self-assessment is to provide experiences with checklists. Students can use checklists as they reflect upon and comment about their own written work. Figure 9.1 is an example of a brief checklist completed after an assignment with paper-and-pencil computation; Figure 9.2 is an example of a longer checklist to be completed by students and turned in with a division assignment when completed.

We can also involve our students in self-assessment by using a questionnaire designed to follow up a particular assignment. Figure 9.3 is an example of a questionnaire for students to use after they have solved a set of nonroutine problems.

Self-assessment is involved when students score written work with the help of a rubric *that focuses on more than correct answers.* Figure 9.4 is an example of a rubric used with a practice assignment for division by a one-digit number. After students complete the assignment, they score it twice: Students determine the number of correct answers first, then they determine a rubric score.

**FIGURE 9.1** Sample checklist for self-assessment.

```
Turn in this checklist with your assignment.

                                                    Name _____
                                                    Date _____

1. My digits are written in place-value columns.        Y    ?    N
2. Others can read my numerals.                         Y    ?    N
3. Sometimes I was stuck.                               Y    ?    N
4. I checked my answers.                                Y    ?    N
5. Describe a situation in which this computation could be used.

   _____

   _____


Comments
```

Less-structured comments like those written in student journals often involve self-assessment. Journals, along with selected student written work, can be filed in individual assessment portfolios. Include in assessment portfolios any checklists, questionnaires, or rubrics students have completed. Later, have students examine these papers and reflect on what they find. Have they grown in their ability to assess themselves?

**FIGURE 9.2** Checklist for self-assessment with a division lesson.

```
Turn this in with your assignment.

                                                         Name _____
                                                         Date _____

 1. My digits are written in place-value columns.            Y     ?     N
 2. Others will be able to read my numerals and my writing.  Y     ?     N
 3. I checked my work to learn which answers are correct.    Y     ?     N
 4. Sometimes I don't know how to start or what to do.       Y     ?     N
 5. I think I will be able to really use division.           Y     ?     N
 6. Sometimes I give up if the problem is hard.              Y     ?     N
 7. I like to do division problems.                          Y     ?     N
 8. I used multiplication to check my work.                  Y     ?     N
 9. Dividing is often easy for me.                           Y     ?     N
10. I like to work alone on problems like these.             Y     ?     N

Comments
```

**FIGURE 9.3** Questionnaire for self-assessment.

Turn in this questionnaire with your assignment.

Name _____
Date _____

1. What mathematics did you use to solve these problems?

2. Did you use drawings or manipulatives to help you solve the problems? If so, describe how you used them.

3. Did you use a calculator? If so, how did you use it?

4. Explain how you solved Problem 3.

5. Did you get stuck at any place with Problem 3? If so, tell about it.

6. How do you know your answer to Problem 3 is correct?

7. Are there other correct answers for Problem 3?

Comments

**FIGURE 9.4** Rubric for division by a one-digit number.

Turn in this rubic with your assignment.

Name _____
Date _____

Look at all of the examples in the assignment. Next, read all five paragraphs. Then decide which paragraph you think *best* describes what you have done. Finally, circle the number of points in front of that paragraph.

1. I did a few examples, but I did not complete all of them.

2. I did all of the examples. Several do not have correct answers. Digits are not always in place-value columns.

3. I did all of the examples. One or two do not have correct answers. Digits are written in place-value columns.

4. All examples have correct answers. Digits are written in place-value columns.

5. All examples are correct, and I can show why they are correct with base ten blocks. I can also write a story problem for examples like these.

# ◼ Interviewing

Interviews done sensitively and with demonstrated interest in the student are an effective way to collect information about a student's mathematical concepts, skills, and dispositions. They are a way to gain both quantitative and qualitative data about an individual.

Consider the following vignette of the first part of an interview. It is October, and Ms. Barnes is interviewing Dexter while other students are working individually and in groups. Dexter was recently assigned to Ms. Barnes's third-grade class. Dexter and Ms. Barnes are seated at a table in a corner of the class-room; Ms. Barnes faces the center of the classroom and Dexter faces her.

The class is learning to add with regrouping. Dexter computes as follows:

A. 
$$\begin{array}{r} 43 \\ +75 \\ \hline 118 \end{array}$$
B. 
$$\begin{array}{r} 87 \\ +49 \\ \hline 1216 \end{array}$$

| | |
|---|---|
| MS. BARNES: | I need to find out more about how you add so we can plan our work together. (*She shows him his paper and points to Example A.*) Tell me, how did you add this example? The sum is correct, but I need to know *how* you added. I'll write the problem and you can add. Think out loud so I can learn how you added. |
| DEXTER: | Three and five is eight. (*He writes "8" below the line.*) Four tens and 7 tens is eleven tens. (*He writes "11" below the line.*) |
| MS. BARNES: | And what is the sum? What is the total amount? |
| DEXTER: | Eleven tens and 8 ones. |
| MS. BARNES: | (*She encircles the "118" with her finger.*) Can you read this number for me a different way? |
| DEXTER: | One, one, eight . . .? |
| MS. BARNES: | Thank you. That's very helpful. (*She points to Example B.*) Tell me, how did you add this example? I'll write the problem here, and you can add. Again, think out loud so I can learn how you added. |
| DEXTER: | Seven and nine is 16. (*He writes "16" below the line.*) Eight tens and four tens is twelve tens. (*He writes "12" below the line.*) |
| MS. BARNES: | What is the sum? What is the total amount? |
| DEXTER: | Twelve tens and 16 ones. |
| MS. BARNES: | (*She encircles the "1216" with her finger.*) Can you read this number for me a different way? |
| DEXTER: | One, two, one, six . . .? |

| MS. BARNES: | (*She reaches for a set of base-ten blocks from a nearby shelf.*) Dexter, have you ever worked with blocks like these? |
| DEXTER: | We had them in our class at my old school. |
| MS. BARNES: | (*She writes the numeral "1216" on a separate sheet of paper, then holds up a unit block.*) This is one. (*She points to the numeral.*) I want you to show me this much with the blocks. |
| DEXTER: | (*He counts out 12 longs or tens blocks, and 16 unit blocks.*) |
| MS. BARNES: | And how much is that altogether? |
| DEXTER: | Twelve tens and 16 ones. |
| MS. BARNES: | Could you show me that much using fewer pieces of wood? |
| DEXTER: | (*He studies awhile, but is not sure how to proceed.*) |

Interviews are worth the time they take because they enable teachers to:

- Gain insights into the student's understanding of concepts and proce-
  dures and identify any misconceptions or error patterns,
- Observe how he or she reasons,
- Learn how well the student can communicate mathematical ideas, and
- Discover the student's disposition toward mathematics.

An interview is not just oral testing to determine whether a student can do a task. When we interview a student, we need to think like an assessor and ask ourselves questions like these listed by Wiggins and McTighe:

- What would be sufficient and revealing evidence of understanding?
- How will I be able to distinguish between those who really understand and those who don't (though they may seem to)?
- What misunderstandings are likely? How will I check for these?[9]

An interview is not a time for expressing our opinions or asking questions prompted by mere curiosity. Rather, it is a time to observe the student carefully and a time to *listen*. We need to avoid giving clues or asking leading questions. It has been said that we are all born with two ears and one mouth, and we probably should use them in that proportion. This applies quite specifically to us as teachers because we sometimes want to talk and explain when we should listen.

The pace of the interview should be adapted so the student will respond comfortably.

## Getting at a Student's Thinking

Interviews can vary widely in regard to the way we ask a student to respond, but generally we want to encourage students to respond with as much detail as possible. When we ask a student to choose among alternatives that we present, we can ask *why* the particular choice was made.

If we are to get at a student's thinking, we need to have the student comment on his or her own thought process. This can be accomplished through either introspection or retrospection.

When eliciting *introspection*, ask the student to comment on thoughts as the task is being done; have the student think out loud while doing the task. For example, ask, "What do you say to yourself as you do this? Say it out loud so I can understand, too." But when using introspection, the very process of commenting aloud can influence the thinking a student does.

On the other hand, when eliciting *retrospection*, do not ask the student to comment on thoughts until after the task is completed. Then have the student explain the problem situation in his or her own words: Ask how the task was done, and why it was completed the way it was. Try to determine the reasoning used. But when using retrospection, remember that the student may forget wrong turns that were taken.

It is probably best to elicit introspection part of the time and retrospection part of the time.

Following is a transcript of part of an interview I had with a fourth grader. We were discussing what she had written:

$$\frac{1}{3} = \frac{4}{12}$$
$$+$$
$$\frac{1}{4} = \frac{3}{12} \quad \frac{7}{12}$$

| | |
|---|---|
| TEACHER: | What do the equals signs tell us? |
| STUDENT: | They tell us . . . that you just do the answer. |
| TEACHER: | Which is more, one third or four twelfths? |
| STUDENT: | (*Pause*) One third? . . . No . . . . |

This student knows a procedure, but her understanding of the concept *equals* is inadequate. The interview may even help her evaluate her own thinking.

Many mathematics educators believe that what a student knows about herself as a learner and doer of mathematics—and how she regulates her own thinking and doing while working through problems—can affect her performance significantly.

Some of the questions we ask while interviewing a student will help the student become more aware of her own cognitive processes. For example:

- How did you get your answer? I may have missed something.
- Why is your answer correct?
- If someone said your answer is not correct, how would you explain that it *is* correct? Could you explain it another way?

- Can you make a drawing to show that your answer is correct?
- If you had to teach your brother to do this, how would you do it? What would you say to him?

Garofalo lists other questions that can help students become more aware of their cognitive processes:

- What kinds of errors do you usually make? Why do you think you make these errors? What can you do about them?
- What do you do when you see an unfamiliar problem? Why?
- What kinds of problems are you best at? Why?
- What kinds of problems are you worst at? Why? What can you do to get better at these?[10]

In addition to interview questions, we can use written responses (such as journal entries) to increase awareness of cognitive processes.

> **By requiring students to examine the processes carefully that they are going through and to verbalize them on paper, the teacher (or other students) can follow the students' algorithms and find the hidden bugs in their thought processes.[11]**

When students derive answers to problems, we not only need to get at their thinking in order to understand how they obtained those answers, we also need to learn how they *justify* their answers—how they prove they are correct in their own thinking. We can look for the three kinds of justification schemes identified by Sowder and Harel[12] and illustrated by Flores.[13]

- *Schemes that are externally based*, in which a textbook or authority figure is cited as justification.
- *Schemes that are empirically based*, in which students use perception or concrete objects to show that their answer is correct.
- *Schemes that use analysis*, in which students use counting strategies or cite mathematical relations to justify their answer.

As a student's thinking develops over time, we expect to see fewer uses of justification schemes that are externally based. We even hope to see use of empirically based schemes eventually give way to schemes that employ analysis, for such thinking is distinctly mathematical.

## Observing Student Behavior

As we interview our students, we observe their behaviors. Here the term *observe* refers not only to seeing but also to listening attentively. Observing a student is more complex than it sounds because students often develop defense mechanisms to cover their confusion and make us believe they understand even when they do not. Observations may be quite informal, interactive, or more structured.

*Informal Observations.*    Informal observations take place wherever we have opportunities to observe students. These observations can be a source of information, whether the student is engaged in a classroom lesson, participating in a group, working at a learning center, or playing on the playground.

Students bring informal mathematical knowledge to school settings. Note how your students get the mathematical information they need as you watch them play games, plan bulletin boards, or do other activities. Listen to their conversations, and pose a diagnostic question from time to time.

*Interactive Observational Assessment.*    Diagnosis and instruction are both involved in this interactive approach to teaching.

> Students are engaged in a mathematical problem while the teacher circulates among them to observe and make note of their work. Rather than nod and say, "Yes, you have it" or tell the students that they "have not found the solution yet," the teacher responds to them by writing questions that challenge their thinking and mathematical reasoning.[14]

When we use this approach with students in our classes, we observe their behavior as they work and also observe their responses to the written questions we give them to ponder.

*Structured Observations.*    Interviews that involve more structured observations take place within contexts as varied as clinical settings and one-on-one interaction between a student and classroom teacher or aide.

The *structure* in a structured observation comes from a script for the interviewer. The actual words used in the interview may or may not vary from the script, depending upon the purpose of the interview. (Research studies are more apt to require strict adherence to a planned script.) Even when we use a script of some kind, we must remember that we are involved in structured *observation*. Remember to keep your eyes and ears open as the student responds, and make appropriate records!

Here is an example of a simple script; it was used to diagnose a student who is experiencing difficulty solving verbal problems.

- Read me the problem, please.
- What is the question asking you to do?
- How are you going to find the answer?

- Do the work to get the answer and tell me about your thinking as you work.
- Write down the answer to the question.[15]

## Recording Student Behavior

A record of responses needs to be made during an interview. This can be done by writing notes and/or by audio or video recording. (Do not rely on your memory to make a record at a later time.) Even when a recording is made, it may be wise to supplement the recording with written notations that describe only those things that will *not* appear on the recording. We may also want to write our judgments about the student's level of understanding.

Written responses can take different forms, but regardless of the form they should end up in some kind of student assessment folder so we can look for patterns across different kinds of responses.

Notes can be written on three-by-five-inch cards. Cards such as the one shown in Figure 9.5 are useful for making records of brief interviews during instruction. Or we can keep an observation sheet for each student, similar to Figure 9.6. An advantage of an observation sheet is that it gives us a single record over time, a record we can easily share with parents. A disadvantage is that a particular student's sheet is not likely to be readily available when we want it; we may have to make a quick note and later transfer it to the observation sheet.

When conducting a more structured interview, we may want to write notes in a space provided at the side of our planned question. Our script can be on a sheet of paper or on a set of cards. Figure 9.7 shows what one card might look like.

We need to plan ahead so we will be able to make records of pertinent observations. Forms such as the examples in Figures 9.5 through 9.7 can be adapted to fit our own situations.

**FIGURE 9.5** A simple observation form for general use.

| Name _____ Date _____ |||
| Observation/Interview |||
| **Activity** | **Observed Behavior** | **Suggestion for Instruction** |
| | | |

**FIGURE 9.6**   An observation sheet for an individual.

| OBSERVATION SHEET Name _____ | | | |
|---|---|---|---|
| **Date** | **Activity** | **Observed Behavior** | **Program Suggestions** |
|  |  |  |  |

*Source*: Adapted from J. K. Stenmark (Ed.). *(1991). Mathematics assessment: Myths, models, good questions, and practical suggestions* (p. 33). Reston, VA: National Council of Teachers of Mathematics.

**FIGURE 9.7**   Card for question and record of observation.

| QUESTION/TASK | OBSERVED BEHAVIOR |
|---|---|
| **Show:**   Numeral "243"<br>             Set of base ten blocks<br><br>**Ask:**   How would you show this<br>          number using as *few* blocks<br>          as possible? |  |

# Watching Language: Ours and Theirs

Usually, written and oral language in mathematics is grammatically simple, but sometimes it is more complex linguistically. Even with young children, an expression as simple as 2 + 3 is interpreted in varied ways.

- two and three
- two plus three
- two and three more
- three more than two

As adults we know that these expressions are equivalent, but young students are confused by such a diversity of interpretations.

What we say is sometimes complex linguistically because we tend to use pre- and post-modifiers. Needlessly complex expressions abound and include sentences like:

- Find the pair of numbers whose product is greater than 100.
- The value of this digit's place is one tenth of the value of what place?

It is also true that we verbally interpret in different ways the question asked by an open number sentence. For example, $N - 28 = 52$ might be expressed as "28 less than what number is 52?" or as "What number less 28 is 52?" Sometimes our students do not know what we mean because of the way we say it.

How might a particular student say it? We may be able to gain insight into his or her use of language by having the student read or interpret an expression with the same structure but with single-digit numbers. For example, before asking the question posed by $N - 28 = 52$, show $N - 3 = 5$ and ask, "What question does this ask?"

The way we use language is crucial not only as we assess, but *whenever* we teach. When we teach second-language students, we need to remember that they may think in different categories and make different associations. The way we use language is also crucial as we teach people with disabilities. What we say may enhance their dignity or it may reflect stereotypes. Furthermore, language is constantly changing, and we need to be sensitive to current usage.

## Probing for Key Understandings

When we need to learn what a particular student understands about *specific* ideas, we can solicit evidence of understanding by asking a question or presenting a carefully designed task for the student to do; then observe the student's response.

Likely, we will need to present follow-up questions or related tasks before we can make appropriate inferences regarding what the student understands. Think how the particulars in the task could be changed a bit to create a related task.

Rather than always focusing on computation skills per se, we frequently need to focus on concepts related to number sense and on understanding the operations of arithmetic—concepts that enable students to know which operation to use when solving problems.

During such interviews, how might we get at a student's understanding of each of the following stated key ideas? What evidence of understanding might we elicit? What could we say or do? Possibilities are illustrated for each statement: A question that could be asked or a task that could be presented follows the statement. (If you try these with your students, you may have to adapt them to the appropriate grade level.)

- A digit's value in a numeral is determined by the place where it is written.

> With base-ten blocks at hand, show the numeral "243" and say: "Can you show this much with the blocks? Try it." Then, "How do you know which blocks to use for the 2?"

- The values of places within a numeral are powers of ten in sequence.

> Show a numeral for a whole number (as great as appropriate) and say, "Start at this end, and tell me the values of each place within the numeral." Then, "Can you do it if you start at the other end? Try it." Then, "Is there some kind of pattern? Can you tell me about it?"

- The value of a numeral for a whole number is the sum of all the products (face value × place value) for each digit.

> Lay out a collection of base-ten blocks and show the numeral "2453" saying, "Show me this much with the base-ten blocks." Then repeat the procedure with a place-value chart or an abacus. Next say, "How do you know how much the numeral shows?" After the student responds, you may want to ask, "As you decide what the number is, do you add? . . . Or subtract? . . . Or multiply? . . . Or divide? Think about it."

- Equals means "the same as."

> Show the equation 25 + 12 = □ and ask, "Can you tell me the sum?" Then point to the equals sign and ask, "What does this mean?" (If the student responds, "Equals," ask, "What does that mean?") Then present the equation □ = 13 + 22 and ask, "Can you tell me the sum?" Again, point to the equals sign and ask, "What does this mean?"

The student who thinks equals means "results in" rather than "is the same as" may respond to the second equation: "You can't do that."

- Addition tells the sum if you know both addends.

> Show the equation $\Box - 3,278 = 5,190$ and ask, "How would you find the missing number?" Then ask, "Why would you do that?"

- Division tells the missing factor if you know the product and only one factor.

> Show the equation $\Box \times 624 = 1,872$ and ask, "How would you find the missing number?" Then ask, "Why. would you do that?"

- A fraction in which the numerator and denominator name the same number is a name for 1.

> Show a number line for whole numbers 0 to 100, then also show the numeral $\frac{3}{3}$. Point to the fraction and say, "Can you point to where this amount is on the number line?" Then, "Can you write other fractions for 1?"

## Designing Questions and Tasks

When we present a question or a task to a student during an interview, we actually provide a stimulus situation to which the student responds. Stimulus situations can be presented in varied modes.

| Mode | Examples |
|---|---|
| Verbal | Words, oral and written |
| Written symbols | Numerals |
| Two-dimensional representations | Paper-and-pencil diagrams, photographs |
| Three-dimensional representations | Base-ten blocks, match balance, place-value chart with sticks |

Each stimulus calls for a response; responses for a given stimulus can be similarly varied among modes. We increase our confidence in what we learn about a student when we use a variety of questions and tasks to elicit evidences of understanding.

Make sure directions clearly indicate what is expected. Tasks should engage students and elicit their best performances.

Following are things we can do that may help us obtain information we will get no other way.

1. Say, "This time I'll hold the pencil and you tell me what to do."
2. Have students describe to other students how they solved a problem, or have them write their descriptions on paper.
3. Provide a slightly different context, and ask students to use the idea.
4. Sometimes we can have a student explain a graphic organizer she has made: a number line, a cognitive map, a flowchart, etc.
5. We may want to ask the student to tell how he would explain the idea or procedure to a younger sibling, or have him make a poster that explains what he did.
6. At different times, it may be helpful to say, "Your answer is different from mine. I could be wrong and you could be correct. Show me that yours is correct." Or "Can you show me another way?"
7. We can often get useful information about what a student understands by asking questions like:
   "How do you know that $4/9 \times 60$ is $< 30$?"
   "How do you know that $1/4 > 1/5$?"

An interview typically involves rather focused questions and tasks designed to gain information regarding specific concepts and skills the student may or may not possess. But we can often gain a more complete understanding of a student's mathematical thinking by including items that are more open-ended. Examples like these are sometimes used as warmups or as homework.

- Instead of presenting $\boxed{4 \times 17 = ?}$ ask the student to find two numbers with 108 as their product: a one-digit number and a two-digit number.
- Instead of presenting diagrams and asking which diagrams represent 3/4, ask the student to draw several diagrams or pictures that show 3/4.

Furthermore, as we design our questions and tasks, we need to remember:

- We may need to diagnose a student's ability to estimate; instruction may need to focus on this important skill and the concepts involved.
- Realistic contexts in assessment as well as instruction can help to engage and motivate students.
- Students with learning disabilities often communicate information that is incorrect, yet it is what they actually see.

A procedure for planning, conducting, and reporting a diagnostic interview is described in Appendix G. A rubric is provided for instructors who use it as an assignment.

When you conduct a diagnostic interview:

**Be sure to**

- Find a place with few distractions or interruptions, and have the student face you with his or her back toward potential distractions.
- Start with easier tasks, and very gradually present more difficult material.
- Accept the student's responses without judging. Use neutral feedback such as a nod of the head.
- Ask probing questions in response to both correct *and* incorrect answers. Keep your tone of voice the same, whether the response is correct or not.
- Encourage the student to think out loud to solve problems in different ways and to verify answers.

**But do not**

- Tell the student that errors have been made.
- Interrupt the student, or begin to teach what is "correct."
- Give praise as feedback. You may want to say, "Thank you" or "That was helpful."

# ■ Using Graphic Organizers for Diagnosis

We want students with different intelligences and learning styles to be able to show us what they actually do understand and are able to do; and for this to happen we need to use assessment tasks that are varied in format. Tasks incorporating graphic organizers often provide a format that focuses on relationships while requiring fewer verbal skills.

Graphic organizers that have been used during instruction are especially useful for diagnosis. When numeration has been related to number lines, for example, a number line task can be used to help determine what the student understands about numeration (see Figure 9.8).

### Draw Number Lines Carefully!

In one research study, uniform length of units within number lines did not seem important to teachers, but *it had important consequences for student learning!*[16]

**FIGURE 9.8**   A number line used for assessing numeration concepts.

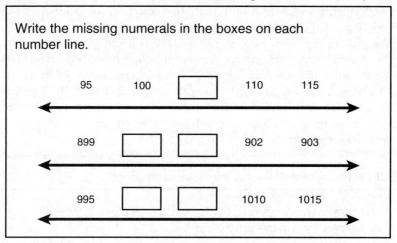

Write the missing numerals in the boxes on each number line.

95     100     [   ]     110     115

899     [   ]  [   ]     902     903

995     [   ]  [   ]     1010     1015

**FIGURE 9.9**   A teacher-made item using a concept map.

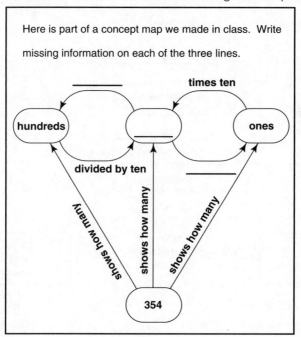

Here is part of a concept map we made in class.  Write missing information on each of the three lines.

_____     **times ten**

**hundreds**     _____     **ones**

**divided by ten**     _____

shows how many     shows how many     shows how many

**354**

Figure 9.9 is another assessment item incorporating a graphic organizer. It uses a cognitive map that focuses on numeration concepts.

If our students have had experiences interpreting flowcharts, we can construct performance items from flowcharts they used or from similar flowcharts. Figures 9.10 and 9.11 are examples of items based on flowcharts.

We may also want to have students make concept maps to communicate what they know about mathematics. A concept is written on paper, then relationships are shown with lines. Linking words (usually verbs) also can be added, It is important that students put *their* thoughts on paper. Figure 9.12 points to a fourth-grade boy's *very* limited understanding of "subtraction." And Figure 9.13 shows how another fourth grader responded to "fractions." She associated fractions with drawings, which she labeled incorrectly.

**FIGURE 9.10**  A teacher-made item using a flowchart.

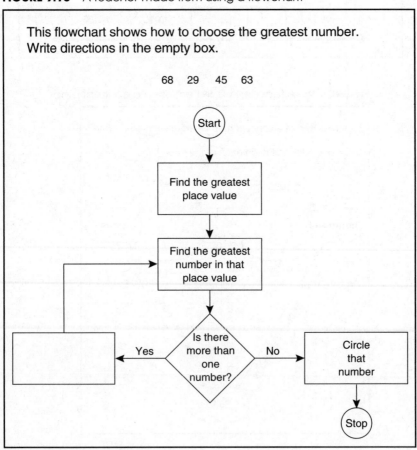

**FIGURE 9.11**    A teacher-made item focusing on procedural knowledge for adding fractions.

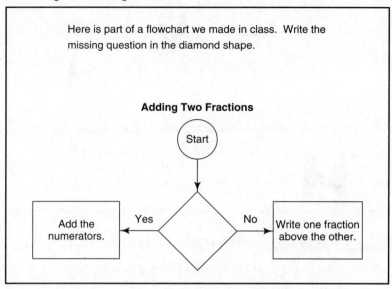

**FIGURE 9.12**    Cognitive map for subtraction by a fourth-grade boy.

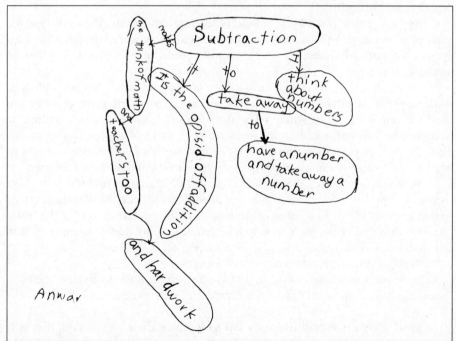

**FIGURE 9.13**   Cognitive map for fractions by a fourth-grade girl.

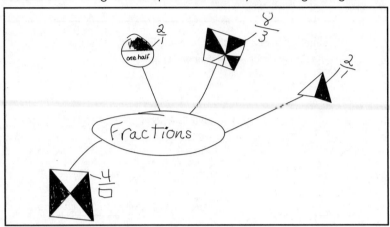

## ■ Using Tests for Diagnosis

Although effective assessment is integrated with teaching day by day, there are times when a more focused and complete look at student performance is helpful. For example, we may administer a diagnostic test when we begin working with a new class of students, when a new student is assigned to us, or when a student is experiencing difficulty.

Any diagnostic test we use should be curriculum-based. Within the *specific* areas of mathematics that constitute our curriculum is where we need to learn about a student's strengths. We may then plan needed instruction that will build on those strengths.

As we diagnose what students understand about mathematics and their skills in problem solving and computation, part of what we learn comes from their written work. Even when calculators are used in assessment, arithmetic computation is often tested on a *non*calculator portion of an assessment procedure. Student papers shown in earlier chapters in this book illustrate some of what we can learn by examining paper-and-pencil assignments very carefully.

When appropriate, diagnostic data gathering may include a test—a sequence of performance tasks—to be completed by individuals. Whether administered individually or to a group of students, a diagnostic test is one of the many forms of data gathering that can help us learn about individual strengths within selected areas of mathematics. After we administer a diagnostic test, we must actually adjust instruction for individual learners.

State accountability tests usually provide very limited diagnostic feedback regarding the instructional needs of individuals. Popham notes:

> **Most state accountability tests fail to produce the kinds of data that will improve teaching and learning. Teachers can get the data they need from classroom assessments—if they know how to design instructionally useful tests.**[17]

Standardized *achievement* tests have limited value for diagnostic purposes. They can help identify broad areas of strength and weakness, thereby serving as a springboard to further assessment. For example, they might show a student performing at grade level in one operation but not in another. However, they usually sample such a broad range of content that we are not likely to learn what we need to know about specific concept and skill categories. Achievement tests sometimes emphasize lower-order thinking and can result in misleading information.

Commercial *diagnostic* tests are available; examples include Early Math Diagnostic Assessment (EMDA)[18] for PreK through Grade 3 students and the KeyMath 3 Diagnostic Assessment.[19] Such commercial diagnostic tests are designed to help us identify and plan appropriate instruction for individual students.

As we interpret diagnostic test performances, especially in the area of computation, we must try to distinguish between a student's lack of conceptual understanding and his not knowing a correct procedure. For example, among those students who are learning to add with renaming, one student may understand that a two-digit number consists of tens and ones, but he records the two-digit sum at the bottom in the ones column. That student needs to be taught that only one digit can be written in each place. On the other hand, another student may write "1" at the top of the tens column (correct procedure) but not actually understand that the sum for the ones column is one ten and so many ones.

Frequently we do not have time to interview *each* student to determine his or her knowledge and skill related to a particular concept or procedure; from time to time we probably need to prepare our own test items for a specific concept or skill category. For instance, we may need a short test to administer to those students who have experienced difficulty subtracting when regrouping is involved.

Error patterns suggest distractors we can use for diagnostic test items. For example, the following multiple-choice item was built from error pattern responses in Chapter 2: Each distractor is an answer a student might choose if she has learned an erroneous procedure. When you use items like this, try to ask individual students *why* they chose their answers.

$$\begin{array}{r} 4372 \\ -2858 \\ \hline \end{array}$$

The answer is:
a.  2526
b.  1514
c.   524
d.  2524

# ■ Using Problem Writing for Diagnosis

What do your students understand about particular operations? One way to assess what each student knows is to have your students write word problems that incorporate conditions you state in prompts.

Drake and Barlow list the following as sample prompts for students who are to write word problems.[20]

- The answer is 32 cents. Create the word problem.
- Create a word problem that involves subtraction and division.
- Write a word problem that involves averaging.
- Examine the graph provided. Write at least four different word problems that can be answered using the graph.

Determine whether their problems contain the mathematics you called for in your prompts. Is the mathematics represented correctly? Varied levels of understanding may be in evidence after providing a prompt like "Write a word problem that can be represented with $3 \times 4 = \square$."

After your students write word problems, you may want to gather additional data from some of the students before planning needed instruction.

# ■ Assessing Dispositions

*There is little value in telling students how exciting*
*mathematics is if they are not actively engaged*
*in doing mathematics themselves.*[21]

When we assess dispositions toward mathematics, we need to assess more than a student's interest in mathematics—how the student feels about it. We need to consider the student's disposition *to do* mathematics. This requires that we actually involve the student in mathematical tasks—problems to solve.

When a particular student undertakes mathematical tasks, does the student demonstrate these characteristics?

- Confidence: engages the tasks with assurance
- Curiosity: raises questions for the teacher and for students
- Flexibility: invents different ways to complete tasks
- Perseverance: does not give up easily

The presence or absence of these characteristics should enable us to make a judgment about a student's disposition *to do* mathematics. If we find a positive disposition to do mathematics, we are likely also to find a positive attitude toward mathematics.

However, attitudes—or how students feel about mathematics—can be assessed in other ways. While interviewing an individual, we are likely to observe many evidences of either positive or negative attitudes toward mathematics.

Here are two ways we can assess how each student feels about mathematics while we are working with a group of students:

- Students complete a survey.[22]
  Provide a survey form for each student that lists incomplete sentences similar to these:
  To be good in math you need to . . . because . . .
  Math is hard when . . .
- Students complete faces and thought bubbles.[23]
  Provide a drawing of a student working a math problem; the face is empty, and there is a thought bubble. Ask students to draw what the face looks like and, in the bubble, write what the student is thinking.

## ■ Guiding Diagnosis in Computation

A student's work not only must be scored, it must be analyzed if it is to provide useful information. Whenever someone else marks examples correct or incorrect (students or a paraprofessional), we can spend more of our time analyzing student work and planning needed instruction.

Observe what a particular student does and also what the student does not do; note computation with a correct answer and also computation that has an incorrect answer, and look for those procedures that might be called mature and those that appear less mature. Distinguish between situations in which the student uses an incorrect procedure and situations in which he does not know how to proceed at all.

Following are principles to keep in mind as we diagnose the work of students who are having difficulty with computation.

1. *Be accepting.* Diagnosis is a highly personal process. Before a student will cooperate with us in a manner that may lead to fewer difficulties with computation, he must perceive that we are interested in and respect him as a person, that we are genuinely interested in helping him, and that we are quite willing to accept a response—even when that response is not correct. We must exhibit something of an attitude of a good physician toward his patient. As Tournier, a Swiss physician and author noted many years ago, "What antagonizes a patient is not the truth, but the tone of scorn, pity, criticism, or reproof which so often colors the statement of the truth by those around him."[24]
2. *Focus on collecting data.* It is true that assessment is a continuous process; even during instruction we need to keep alert for evidence that a student does not understand or has learned a misconception or an error pattern.

Even so, there are times when we need to make a focused diagnosis, and at those times, we must differentiate between the role of collecting data and the role of teaching—we need to collect data, but not instruct. Diagnosing involves gathering as much useful data as possible and making judgments on the basis of data collected; in general, the more data, the more adequate the judgments that follow. A student is apt to provide many samples of incorrect and immature procedures if he sees that we are merely collecting information that will be used to help him overcome his difficulties. However, if we point out errors, label responses as "wrong," and offer instruction while collecting data, he is far less likely to expose his own inadequate performance. Many teachers tend to offer help as soon as they see incorrect or immature performance. When those teachers begin to distinguish between collecting data and instruction, they are often delighted with the way students begin to open up and lay bare their thinking.

3. *Be thorough*. A single diagnosis is rarely thorough enough to provide direction for ongoing instruction. If we are alert during instruction following a diagnosis, we may pick up cues that suggest additional diagnostic activities. Keep in mind the fact that we need to use varied types of assessment tasks if we are to observe each individual at his or her best.

4. *Examine specific understandings and skills*. More formal assessments, published tests, or computer-generated tests may help to identify broad areas of strength and weakness. Let them serve as springboards for further assessment in which more specific concepts and skill performances are examined—often through an interview.

5. *Look for patterns*. Data should be evaluated in terms of patterns, not isolated events. A decision about corrective instruction can hardly be based upon collected bits of unrelated information. As we look for patterns, we look for elements common to several examples of a student's work—a kind of problem-solving activity. We try to find repeated applications of erroneous definitions and consistent use of incorrect or immature procedures. The importance of looking for patterns can hardly be overstressed. Many erroneous procedures are practiced by students, while teachers and parents assume they are merely careless or "don't know their facts."

6. *Discuss progress with parents*. Be sure to help parents understand the full scope of the mathematics curriculum and what their child is learning and will be learning. For areas of difficulty, be sure to discuss the student's progress. Our conversations with parents often give us additional clues that help us plan instruction.

## CONCLUSION

As we teach mathematics we need to be continually gathering and using information about student learning. This is no less true when we teach concepts and skills related to computation. As we examine students' papers diagnostically, we look for patterns, hypothesize possible causes, and verify our ideas.

Checklists, rubrics, and questionnaires can sometimes facilitate self-assessment, which is to be encouraged. Published tests may help identify areas of strength and weakness, but interviews are likely to be needed from time to time to get at students' thinking and probe for specific understandings and skills. We may have to design performance tasks, possibly using manipulatives or graphic organizers, to examine specific concepts.

Serious students of diagnosis will want to examine many of the resources listed at the end of this book. Diagnosis of misconceptions and error patterns in computation is a continuing process; it interacts with instruction in computation—which is the focus of the next two chapters.

## FURTHER REFLECTION

Consider the following questions:

1. As teachers, why do we need to be *continually* assessing?
2. While interviewing a student, it is usually best *not* to interrupt and begin to teach what is correct. Why?
3. Describe means of gathering data that can help us discover very specific misconceptions of a student.
4. How can you determine if a particular student understands the *concepts* of equivalence and area? Keep in mind the fact that students sometimes make computations and get correct answers, even though they do not understand the underlying concepts.

## REFERENCES

1. Sizer, T. R. (1999). No two are quite alike. *Educational Leadership* 57(1), 6–11.
2. National Council of Teachers of Mathematics. (2000). *Principles and standards for school mathematics* (p. 12). Reston, VA: The Council.
3. National Council of Teachers of Mathematics. (2000). *Principles and standards for school mathematics* (p. 22). Reston, VA: The Council.
4. National Council of Teachers of Mathematics. (2000). *Principles and standards for school mathematics* (p. 24). Reston, VA: The Council.
5. Ben-Yehuda, M., Lavy, I., Linchevski, L., & Sfard, A. (2005). Doing wrong with words: What bars students' access to arithmetical discourses. *Journal for Research in Mathematics Education* 36(3), 179.
6. Leatham, K. R., Lawrence, K., & Mewborn, D. S. (2005). Getting started with open-ended assessment. *Teaching Children Mathematics* 11(8), 413.
7. Leatham, K. R., Lawrence, K., & Mewborn, D. S. (2005). Getting started with open-ended assessment. *Teaching Children Mathematics* 11(8), 415.
8. Stenmark, J. K. (Ed.). (1991). *Mathematics assessment: Myths, models, good questions, and practical suggestions* (p. 6). Reston, VA: National Council of Teachers of Mathematics.

 9. Wiggins, G, & McTighe, J. (1998). *Understanding by design* (p. 68). Alexandria, VA: Association for Supervision and Curriculum Development.
10. Garofalo, J. (1987). Metacognition and school mathematics. *The Arithmetic Teacher* 34(9), 22–23.
11. Mingus,T., & Grassl, R. (1998). Algorithmic and recursive thinking: Current beliefs and their implications for the future. In L. Morrow & M. Kennedy (Eds.). *The teaching and learning of algorithms in school mathematics* (p. 38). Reston, VA: National Council of Teachers of Mathematics.
12. Sowder, L., & Harel, G. (1998). Types of students' justifications. *Mathematics Teacher* 91(8), 670–675.
13. Floras, A. (2002). How do children know that what they learn in mathematics is true? *Teaching Children Mathematics* 8(5), 269–274.
14. Albert, L. R., Mayotte, G., & Cutlersohn, S. (2002). Making observations interactive. *Mathematics Teaching in the Middle School* 7(7), 396–401.
15. Clarke, D. (1991). Assessment alternatives in mathematics. In J. K. Stenmark (Ed.). *Mathematics assessment: Myths, models, good questions, and practical suggestions* (p. 30). Reston, VA: National Council of Teachers of Mathematics.
16. Izsak, A., Tillema, E., & Tunc-Pekkan, Z. (2008). Teaching and learning fraction addition on number lines. *Journal for Research in Mathematics Education* 39(1), 33–62.
17. Popham, J. W. (2003). The seductive allure of data. *Educational Leadership* 60(5), 48.
18. Pearson (see www.pearsonschool.com).
19. Pearson (see www.pearsonschool.com).
20. Drake, J. M., & Barlow, A. T. (December 2007/January 2008). Assessing students' levels of understanding multiplication through problem writing. *Teaching Children Mathematics* 14(5), 272–277.
21. National Council of Teachers of Mathematics. (1991). *Professional Standards for Teaching Mathematics* (p. 104). Reston, VA: The Council.
22. Whitin, P. E. (2007). The mathematics survey: A tool for assessing attitudes and dispositions. *Teaching Children Mathematics* 13(8), 426–431.
23. Zambo, D., & Azmbo, R. (2006). Using thought bubble pictures to assess students' feelings about mathematics. *Mathematics Teaching in the Middle School* 12(1), 14–21.
24. Tournier, P. (1965). *The healing of persons* (p. 243). New York: Harper and Row.

# Providing Data-Driven Instruction in Computation

> ## The Teaching Principle
> Effective mathematics teaching requires understanding what students know and need to learn and then challenging and supporting them to learn it well.[1]
>
> ## The Learning Principle
> Students must learn mathematics with understanding, actively building new knowledge from experience and prior knowledge.[2]

Instruction in computation that really helps students learn must be based on data we collect from *each* of our students. Chapter 10 is designed to help you provide that instruction. We are urged to make sure each student makes sense out of numerals *before* we teach him or her how to compute. Then, as we teach, we are urged to emphasize important mathematical ideas and make connections. Varied manipulatives and instructional activities are described that can help your students understand and recall basic facts. Teaching paper-and-pencil procedures is addressed; teaching other methods of computation is emphasized also.

The previous chapter focused on diagnosis because it is important to collect varied forms of data and make thoughtful inferences about student learning. But diagnosis must serve instruction. We need diagnostic teaching in which diagnosis is *continuous* throughout instruction. We can interweave instruction and diagnosis as we teach computational procedures—always alert to what each student is actually doing and eager to probe deeper. We can be willing to change our plans as soon as what we see or hear suggests that an alternative would be more fruitful in the long run. Diagnostic teaching is, first of all, an attitude of caring very much about *each* student's learning.

Diagnostic teaching is also cyclical. After an initial diagnosis, we plan and conduct a lesson, but what we see and hear during the lesson prompts us to modify our previous judgments and seek more information before planning the next lesson. Sometimes we move through a cycle very rapidly several times in the course of a single lesson. At other times, one cycle occurs over a span of several lessons.

The instruction we plan should focus on our students' mathematical thinking—including their thinking about procedures and algorithms. Do students know when and why a particular procedure is used, or if an algorithm always provides correct answers, or why it does?

Our students learn various computational procedures and the concepts and principles that underlie the different forms of computation; as they learn, they observe patterns and construct knowledge—but more is needed. If our students are to understand and actually use what they are learning, they must *reflect* on what they observe and connect it with other mathematical ideas they already know. We must help students not only learn concepts, principles, and procedures, but also help students *understand how these are related*.

As we teach, we ourselves inevitably model a disposition toward mathematics and learning mathematics. We need to demonstrate an approach to mathematical situations and to learning mathematics that is confident, flexible, curious, and inventive.

## ■ Developing Number Sense

When students develop a good foundation, including required number concepts and principles, they are ready to learn about operations and computation. What we sometimes call *number sense* is the most basic component of that foundation.

> **During the early years teachers must help students strengthen their sense of number, moving from the initial development of basic counting techniques to more sophisticated understandings of the size of numbers, number relationships, patterns, operations, and place value.[3]**

The following NCTM expectations for pre-K through second grade suggest what is meant by number sense:

- count with understanding and recognize "how many" in sets of objects;
- use multiple models to develop initial understandings of place value and the base-ten number system;
- develop understanding of the relative position and magnitude of whole numbers and of ordinal and cardinal numbers and their connections;
- develop a sense of whole numbers and represent and use them in flexible ways, including relating, composing, and decomposing numbers;
- connect number words and numerals to the quantities they represent, using various physical models and representations;
- understand and represent commonly used fractions, such as $\frac{1}{4}$, $\frac{1}{3}$, and $\frac{1}{2}$.[4]

These expectations suggest activities for developing number sense in the early grades, instruction that can provide a good foundation for teaching computation. Much of this instruction can take the form of problem solving.

Even in the early grades we must be alert to what each student already knows and can do—then select activities that are appropriate for our particular students. The instruction we plan needs to be driven by data we collect from each of our students.

## ■ Helping Students Understand Big Ideas

Some students have difficulty learning to compute because they do not adequately understand the concepts and principles that underlie algorithms. Their understanding of multi-digit numerals and what the operations mean does not provide the foundation needed to learn procedures that make sense to them. Similarly, when they are introduced to algorithms with fractions, their understanding of fractions and what the operations mean is not adequate for them to make sense of those procedures. Very often, computation procedures that make no sense to a student are not remembered accurately—nor are they used appropriately.

Math resource teacher Mazie Jenkins wrote the following as she thought about students she had interviewed.

> I recently interviewed ten fourth and fifth graders whose mathematics instruction had not focused on big ideas. These children all had been taught procedures that didn't make sense to them, so they didn't remember them. They often pieced together different algorithms in senseless ways. It was painful to watch them solve problems; I could have cried . . . When they were done, many students looked at me and asked, "Did I do it right?" Children who don't have an understanding have to look to the outside for validation. They didn't look inside and think, "I know I did it right." Unless someone teaches them how to learn mathematics with understanding, they will be lost.[5]

Procedural learning should be tied to conceptual learning as noted in Chapter 1. As we teach computation procedures we must encourage our students to think about *why* they are doing what they are doing; they need to *reflect* on what they are doing—to connect what they are learning to what they already know. Our students need to justify procedures rather than merely state procedures.

In our students' minds, symbols need to be connected not only to words, but also to concepts and to principles. Equality is an important idea, and we tend to assume our students understand more than they do when they say, "Equals." The systems we use for creating numerals for whole and rational numbers involve many concepts, some of which are not easy for young children to understand.

A few of these important concepts and principles are discussed in the sections that follow. These are big ideas our students truly need to understand!

## Many Names for a Number

Numbers have many names: oral and written number words (whatever the language), numerals, and numerical expressions are examples. An equation like $2 + 3 = 5$ merely states that a particular numerical expression and a particular numeral name the same number. The "5" is the standard name for that number; the numerical expression "$2 + 3$" names the same number.

Over time students learn many additional names for any given number. Those names include numerical expressions with different operations and other symbols, like exponents. A useful activity for students is to list as many different names as they can for a given number. With younger children this can be as simple as creating as many names for 5 as possible with a math balance and recording each with a number sentence beginning "5 equals . . ."; addition is the only operation used.

## Numeration

Place value is the key to teaching computation with our base-ten numerals, but understanding Hindu-Arabic numerals for whole numbers is *not* just identifying place values. The concept of values assigned to places is important, but it is only part of what students need to know if they are to understand multi-digit numerals and learn computational procedures.

If instruction in numeration is to be data-driven, we must learn what our students already understand about numerals for whole numbers. One thing we can do is write true/false statements such as the following, and ask our students which number sentences are true and which are false. We also need to ask them *how they know* it is true or false.[6]

    a. $56 = 50 + 6$
    b. $87 = 7 + 80$
    c. $93 = 9 + 30$

Consider this principle: "A multi-digit numeral names a number which is the *sum* of the products of each digit's face value and place value."[7] [For example: $398 = (3 \times 100) + (9 \times 10) + (8 \times 1)$.] The terms used in this statement alert us to different ideas that are incorporated within multi-digit numerals. To understand multi-digit numerals a student must first have some understanding of the operations of addition and multiplication, and be able to distinguish between a digit and the complete numeral.

Understanding a digit's face value involves the cardinality of the numbers zero through nine. Place value itself involves assignment of a value to each position within a multi-digit numeral; that is, each place within the numeral is assigned a power of ten. We therefore identify and name the tens place and the thousands place. This rather specific association of value with place is independent of whatever digit may happen to occupy the position within a given numeral.

Occasionally, students associate the ones place with the left position within a given numeral. Their teacher may have referred to the ones as the "first" position. If she did she was probably thinking "on the right," but her students assumed it was "on the left" because they normally proceed left to right—as when they read. We must make sure that our explanations are clear, and solicit feedback (formative assessment) to make sure our students understand correctly.

Sometimes students having difficulty with whole-number computation can identify and name place values, but they cannot get the next step. They have not learned to combine the concepts of face value and place value. It is the *product* of a digit's face value and its place value, sometimes called "total value of the digit" or "product value," that must be used. The *sum* of such products is the value of the numeral. In renaming a number (as we often do when computing) we must consider continually these products of face value and place value; and while considering these things, our students also need to think about the numeral as a whole.

Students do not quickly develop the conceptual structures associated with our place-value system for writing numbers; it takes a long time. We should introduce numerals as a written record of observations made while looking at or manipulating objects. For multi-digit numerals for whole numbers, these observations frequently follow manipulation of materials according to accepted rules in order to obtain the fewest pieces of wood (or the like). We may need to trade ten objects for one object that is equivalent to the ten if we can, or we may be required to exchange chips in a trading game. In this way, representations for the standard or simplest numerical name for a number are obtained.

When students associate a numeral with concrete aids, it is important that they have opportunities to "go both ways." On the one hand, students may be given materials to sort, regroup, trade, and so on, and then record the numeral that shows how much is observed. But they also need to be given a multi-digit numeral to interpret by selecting or constructing materials that show how much the numeral represents. If our students are able to go from objects to symbol and also from symbol to objects, they are coming to understand what multi-digit numerals mean.

 **Be alert!**

**. . . for the student who believes**

- 0.04 > 0.4 because "the numeral 0.04 is longer than 0.4."
- 0.63 < 0.5 because "numbers with hundredths are worth less than numbers without hundredths."

In our base-ten numeration system, the value represented by each digit involves a relationship with the unit This is true not only for numerals for whole numbers that state the number of units, but also for decimals that must be interpreted as part of a unit. We must help our students *focus on the unit.*

Decimals are numerals for rational numbers—but so are fractions and percents. If our students are to use all of these numerals effectively in computation, they need much experience with the varied meanings associated with the numerals—meanings as varied as *part of a whole* and *indicated division*. Furthermore, they need to be able to relate the different kinds of numerals for rational numbers—decimals, fractions, and percents.

---

## Multi-Digit Numerals for Whole Numbers

Which of these ideas do you understand?

Which do your students understand?

☐ Each position or place in the numeral is assigned a value, a *place* value. The place values are powers of ten.

☐ Only *one* digit can be placed within each position or place in a standard multi-digit numeral.
> Answers are sometimes incorrect because students do not understand this. (Admittedly we sometimes crowd a position with more than one digit *within* a computational procedure, but the answer is always the standard numeral.)

☐ Therefore, each digit has *two* uses:
   a. Every digit has a face value, and
   b. Every digit holds a particular position or place—a place assigned a particular power of ten.

☐ Positions are ordered sequentially.
   a. From right to left they are increasingly greater in value; the next place is always ten times as great as the previous place. And conversely,
   b. From left to right they are less in value; the next place is always one tenth as much as the previous place.

☐ *Within* a multi-digit numeral, the value of a particular digit is the *product* of its face value and place value. This number is sometimes called its "product value."

*A multi-digit numeral names a number*
   *that is the sum*
      *of the products*
         *of each digit's face and place values.*

## Equals and Equivalent

When we say *equals,* we mean the *same,* whether we are talking about numbers or not. When two numerical expressions refer to the same number, we say the expressions are *equivalent.* We can express that relationship with the word (or symbol) *equals* because both sides of the equation name the same number.

We say $20 + 4 = 24$ and $8 + 7 = 9 + 6$ and $21 = 15 + 6$. Both $20 + 4$ and 24 are names for the number we call *twenty-four.* There is only one such number (it is one point on the number line) but it can be named many different ways—with different numeration systems, and with mathematical expressions involving various operations. Both symbolic expressions name *the same* number; they are equivalent. Students are taught to say "equals means *is the same as*"; but often it is a rote response that is not applied.

The basic relational concept we call "equals" is difficult for many young students. Early instruction too often encourages students to conceive of equals as a step in a procedure. To them, it actually means *results in*; therefore, $2 + 4 = 6$ becomes "two and (plus) four results in six." Or it is understood to follow a question where it means "do it now," with the answer given next. These students do not think of equals as naming or describing a relationship; instead, they think of equals as an operator indicating a calculation to be done. It is not surprising that the author finds that when presented with an equation like $\square = 7 + 8$, many young students respond, "You can't do that." Or given an equation like $3 + 2 = 4 + 1$ they say, "You can only have one number after equals."

> [M]any children see only examples of number sentences with an operation to the left of the equal sign and the answer on the right, and they overgeneralize from those limited examples. . . . [L]imiting children's exposure to a narrow range of number sentences does appear to contribute to students' misconceptions about the equal sign.[8]

If they are to enjoy success with arithmetic and with all of mathematics, it is extremely important that students come to an accurate understanding of equality. Many mathematics educators view the understanding of equality as a foundation for algebra.

Carpenter, Franke, and Levi suggest benchmarks for us to work toward as each student constructs their own understanding of equals.

- Children describe what they think the equals sign means.
- They accept as true a number sentence not in the form $a + b = c$ (for example: $6 = 2 + 4$, or $5 = 5$).
- Children carry out calculations on both sides of the equals sign and compare; that is, they recognize a relationship.
- They compare without carrying out the calculations.[9]

## Operations

Knowing different ways to compute will be of little value to students if they do not understand what each operation does. As our students solve problems in the world around them, they must understand the *meaning* of each operation if they are to know which operation to compute and which numbers to use within a problem situation.

In *Principles and Standards for School Mathematics,* the National Council of Teachers of Mathematics (NCTM) emphasizes the need for students to understand what the operations mean and how they relate to each other.[10] During the early grades, students encounter subtraction interpreted as "take away" and as "comparison"; they also encounter what are called "missing addend" situations in which the problem situation may be recorded with a plus sign but subtraction is used to solve the problem (e.g., $24 + \square = 53$). They may also encounter what might be called "missing sum" situations in which the problem situation is recorded with a minus sign but addition is used to solve the problem (e.g., $\square - 37 = 28$). Later, students encounter comparable situations involving multiplication and division.

Meanings for the different operations are often described in terms of structures characteristic of problem situations for particular operations, and these structures can be investigated. While studying addition and subtraction situations, students can explore relationships between the numbers for parts and the total amount. Later, when they study multiplication and division situations, they can investigate relationships between the numbers that tell about equivalent parts and the total amount. The structures they learn for each operation are useful, whether problem situations involve whole numbers or rational numbers. One way of summarizing these structures is as *total-and-parts meanings*. Appendix F discusses how they can be introduced to students. A summary of these meanings follows:

- *Addition* tells the total amount (sum) whenever you know the amounts for the two parts (addends).
- *Subtraction* tells the amount in one part (addend) whenever you know the total amount (sum) and the amount in the other part (addend).
- *Multiplication* tells the total amount (product) whenever you know the amount for both numbers that tell about equivalent parts (factors).
- *Division* tells the amount for one number about equivalent parts (factor) whenever you know the total amount (product) and the other number about equivalent parts (factor).[11]

These understandings are very useful when there are equations or problems to solve. Students can reflect on many of these ideas even as they encounter the basic facts of arithmetic. Without such "deep meanings" for the operations, students tend to merely react to the symbols they see and do not make the needed connections conceptually. For example, the student who sees $56 + \square = 83$ may think "56 and 83; it is *plus* so you add the numbers."

## Other Concepts and Principles

Other concepts and principles are incorporated within various computational procedures. Our students need to investigate them while studying algorithms, though they do not need to be able to express them with precise language in order to compute. Initially, they can be described informally, but eventually these powerful principles—these big ideas—will need to be expressed using words and symbols.

For example, our students can reflect on the following compensation principles.

- When adding two numbers, if the same number is added to one number and subtracted from the other number, the sum of the two numbers stays the same. ($398 + 552 = 400 + 550 = 950$)
- When subtracting one number from another number, if the same number is added to both numbers (or subtracted from both), the difference remains the same. ($552 - 398 = 554 - 400 = 154$)

Students can investigate other concepts and principles, too, and they can apply them to computational procedures. Some of these principles are properties of operations on numbers.

- When we add, we can reverse the order of the addends without changing the sum. ($87 + 46 = 46 + 87$)
- When we multiply, we can reverse the order of the factors without changing the product. ($38 \times 6 = 6 \times 38$)
- When we add or subtract zero, the result is the number we started with. ($1,000,000 - 0 = 1,000,000$)
- A number minus that same number equals zero. ($367 - 367 = 0$)
- We can multiply in parts. We can distribute multiplication over addition:

$$4 \times 65 = 4 \times (60 + 5) = (4 \times 60) + (4 \times 5) = 240 + 20 = 260$$

and we can distribute multiplication over subtraction:

$$4 \times 58 = 4 \times (60 - 2) = (4 \times 60) - (4 \times 2) = 240 - 8 = 232$$

Clearly, many of these concepts and principles are involved not only in paper-and-pencil computations, but they can help our students estimate and compute mentally. They can also be applied when calculations are simplified.

## Making Connections

Research makes clear that our instruction will likely help our students develop conceptual understanding if it involves:

- attending explicitly to *connections* among facts, procedures, and ideas; and
- encouraging our students to wrestle with important mathematical ideas in an intentional and conscious way.[12]

How can we make clear the connections among facts, procedures, and ideas? How can we make important relationships explicit? We can have our students compare manipulatives and symbols, and note similarities regarding quantities and operations. We can plan activities that involve patterns—patterns that point to connections. Often, as we have our students justify their solutions to problems, we can discuss connections. At other times we can explain why procedures work as they do, and make connections as we explain.[13]

Teachers sometimes connect mathematical ideas with literature. Basic number concepts in counting books are only one example.[14] Concepts of very great numbers are exemplified in books such as Schwartz's *How Much Is a Million?*[15] Operations on numbers are also represented in children's literature. More complex concepts are sometimes exemplified; for example, the sequence of powers of 2 are encountered in folktales of both India and China.[16]

Often, we can ask students themselves to connect mathematical ideas with other ideas they already know. Questions similar to the following are suggested by O'Connell.[17]

- Does this remind you of anything you have seen before?
- Can you think of examples of this in the world outside school?
- How can you use this idea?

Many topics can be interrelated by planning a unit that emphasizes connections. For example, the unit on multiplication described in Appendix H connects multiplication with several other topics.

A single topic can be taught so that connections are emphasized during instruction. In the next section activities are described that can help students understand and recall the basic facts of arithmetic. Students make many connections; they compare manipulatives and symbols, and note sequences and other patterns.

# ■ Understanding and Recalling Basic Number Facts

Ultimately our students need to understand the basic number facts of arithmetic and be able to recall them. Initially they need to understand the operations, but they eventually need to be able to recall basic facts without resorting to inefficient procedures.

> [S]tudents should know the "basic number facts" because such knowledge is essential for mental computation, estimation, performance of computational procedures, and problem solving.[18]

The basic facts of arithmetic are the simple equations we use when we compute. They involve two one-digit addends if they are addition or subtraction facts, or they involve two one-digit factors if they are multiplication or division facts. Examples include the following:

$$6 + 7 = 13 \qquad 12 - 8 = 4 \qquad 3 \times 5 = 15 \qquad 27 \div 9 = 3$$

Students study basic number facts in the context of learning what the operations of arithmetic mean. Initially we should let younger students approach individual facts as problems to solve, often presented as open number sentences like $5 \times 4 = \square$. When our students are permitted to investigate these problems in cooperative groups, they build on each other's informal knowledge.

We must emphasize thinking during the study of basic facts and help our students make connections between them. Basic facts for different operations are often related (some would say they are "close kin"); for example, $5 \times 7 = 35$ and $35 \div 7 = 5$ both have 5 and 7 as factors, and they have 35 as the total amount or product. Instead of always asking students to find a single number as in $6 + \square = 13$, we should frequently pose more open-ended questions.

> When two numbers are added, the total amount (their sum) is 13. What might the two numbers be? What are the solutions to $\square + \square = 13$? How many of the pairs of numbers include a 6?

For addition facts, students can use patterns to generate new information. Visual patterns, for example, can be constructed with counting cubes or colored rods, and related to sequences of basic facts. For example, basic addition and subtraction facts that have 9 as the sum or total amount can be generated as follows:

| | |
|---|---|
| $9 + 0 = 9$ | $9 - 0 = 9$ |
| $8 + 1 = 9$ | $9 - 1 = 8$ |
| $7 + 2 = 9$ | $9 - 2 = 7$ |
| $6 + 3 = 9$ | $9 - 3 = 6$ |
| $5 + 4 = 9$ | $9 - 4 = 5$ |
| $4 + 5 = 9$ | $9 - 5 = 4$ |
| $3 + 6 = 9$ | $9 - 6 = 3$ |
| $2 + 7 = 9$ | $9 - 7 = 2$ |
| $1 + 8 = 9$ | $9 - 8 = 1$ |
| $0 + 9 = 9$ | $9 - 9 = 0$ |

Other patterns can be related to compensation principles. For example, when one addend is *increased* by a particular number and the other addend is *decreased* by the same number, the sum remains the same. When our students consider this principle—possibly in a learning center—they can select basic fact cards to place above and below relationship indicators.

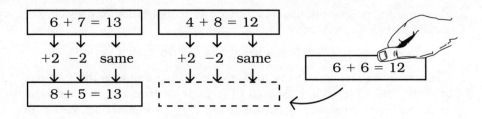

Before mastery activities are introduced, our students need to be taught increasingly mature ways to determine a missing number. Isaacs and Carroll describe strategies that can help students understand and recall the basic facts of arithmetic; they classify strategies in terms of focus: on counting, on parts and wholes, and on derived facts.[19] The following list is an adaptation of categories suggested by Isaacs and Carroll.

### Counting

| | |
|---|---|
| Counting on | addition, subtraction |
| Missing addend[20] | subtraction |
| Skip counting | multiplication, division |
| Repeated addition | multiplication, division |

### Observing Parts and Wholes

| | |
|---|---|
| Make ten, and so many more | addition<br>$6 + 7 = (6 + 4) + 3 = 10 + 3 = 13$ |

### Deriving Basic Facts from Other Basic Facts

| | |
|---|---|
| One/two more/less than | addition, subtraction |
| Ten-based strategies | addition, subtraction |
| Compensation | addition, subtraction |
| Use the related addition fact | subtraction<br>for $13 - 5$ think, $5 + ? = 13$ |
| Use the related multiplication fact | division<br>for $42 \div 6$ think, $6 \times ? = 42$ |
| Same addends or factors (commutative) | addition, multiplication<br>$5 \times 6 = 30$, so $6 \times 5 = 30$ |
| Multiply in parts: rename, multiply, and then add or subtract[21] | multiplication<br>$7 = 5 + 2 \quad 9 = 10 - 1$<br>$5 \times 7 = 5 \times (5 + 2) = (5 \times 5) + (5 \times 2)$<br>$7 \times 9 = 7 \times (10 - 1) = (7 \times 10) - (7 \times 1)$ |

Nines pattern: next        multiplication
  product is one            $5 \times 9 = 45$, so $6 \times 9 = 54$
  more ten, and
  one less unit

Kamii and Lewis state that a child who knows the sum of two single-digit numbers solidly can deduce quickly the part that is unknown when presented with the related subtraction fact, and they argue that "we must deemphasize fluency in subtraction in the first two grades and heavily emphasize addition."[22]

Sometimes when we think a student was merely careless while attempting to recall specific basic facts, the student actually attempted one of the strategies listed above; however, the strategy was incorrectly applied. Perhaps the student attempted to count on, but miscounted. We need to assume that incorrect recall is rarely due to carelessness and attempt to find out what is really going on. Remember: Diagnosis should be continuous.

*Mastery* of the basic facts of arithmetic is the ability to recall missing sums, addends, products, and factors promptly and without hesitation. A student who has mastered $6 + 8 = 14$, when presented with "$6 + 8 = $ ?" either orally or in writing, will recall 14 without counting or figuring it out. When a student attempts to find the product of two whole numbers (such as 36 and 457) by using a paper-and-pencil procedure, lack of mastery of the basic multiplication facts requires time-consuming and distracting ways of finding the product. Lack of mastery of the basic facts also greatly hampers mental computation and the ability to estimate.

If an older student has not mastered the basic facts, she probably persists in using counting or elaborate procedures to find needed numbers. She may understand the operations, yet she continues to require the security of time-consuming procedures when computing. She probably does not feel confident to simply recall the number. If such a student is involved in extensive practice activity, she reinforces use of less-than-adequate procedures. What she needs is practice *recalling* the missing number. How can we provide an instructional environment in which students feel secure enough to try simply recalling missing numbers?

Games provide a safe environment for simple recall. The teacher always seems to want "the correct answer," but in a game it is acceptable to lose at least part of the time. The competition encourages students to try simply recalling the basic fact. Further, games often make possible greater attending behavior because of the materials involved. For instance, a student who rejects a paper-and-pencil problem such as "$6 + 5 = $ ?" because it is a reminder of failure and unpleasantness may attend with interest when the same question is presented with numerals painted on brightly colored cubes that can be moved about.

Obviously, what is intended is *not* an arithmetic game modeled after an old-fashioned spelling bee designed to eliminate less able students; nor is it a game designed to put a student under pressure in front of a large group of peers. The best games will be those involving only a few students, preferably students with rather comparable abilities. In such games a student can feel secure enough to try simple recall. We should choose games that provide immediate or early verification; students need to know if they recalled correctly. Commercial games are available, but games can be made using simple materials—many of which are already in the classroom. Our students are quite capable of making up games and altering rules to suit their fancy when they are encouraged to do so. A homemade game using a mathematical balance would provide immediate verification for each student's response (see Figure 10.1). Kamii and Anderson describe how they made and used games involving basic multiplication facts in a third-grade classroom; they note that some of their games are adaptations of other games or even commercial games.[23] After students have mastered the basic facts, games are useful for retention.

When a particular basic fact is difficult for a student to recall, teachers sometimes use a combination of large visual presentation and muscle movement to help the student. For example, if the basic fact $8 \times 7 = 56$ is difficult for a student, give the student six sheets of paper and a bold marker, and have him or her write one large item on each sheet: 8, 7, 56, $\times$, $\div$, and $=$. The student arranges sheets in order to make true number sentences. See if the student can discover and write horizontally eight number sentences. (The product can be to the left of the equals sign as well as to the right.)

Triangle flash cards can be used to practice recalling basic facts and making connections between facts. Prepare flash cards in the shape of an equilateral triangle, with the total amount (product or sum) in one vertex and the two numbers about parts (factors or addends) in the other two vertices. Use one color for the total amount and a different color for the two numbers about parts. Cover one vertex as you present a card; see if the student can say the missing number (factor or addend)

**FIGURE 10.1**  Verification with a mathematical balance.

and can then say (or write) all four related basic facts (two facts in the case of doubles). Students can work in pairs to present triangle flash cards to each other.[24]

Another way to help a student remember particular multiplication facts is to have the student make drawings that represent those facts. The author of this text has done this by introducing the array and measurement of area, specifically the area of a rectangle. Given a combination like $6 \times 7$ and a ruler, the student draws a 6 cm by 7 cm rectangle and determines the area to be 42 cm². This can be especially effective if the student has strong spatial intelligence.

Calculators can be used to help students learn basic facts. For example, the constant function on a calculator can be used to help students generate products. For the products of 6 and numbers 2 through 9, children press $\boxed{6}$ $\boxed{+}$ $\boxed{6}$ $\boxed{=}$, $\boxed{=}$, $\boxed{=}$, and so on. Students will not lose count if they repeatedly press the equals key and say: 2 sixes is 12, 3 sixes is 18, and so on.

Individuals can also use calculators as they practice recalling basic facts. For example, a student says "six times seven" as he presses $\boxed{6}$ $\times$ $\boxed{7}$. Then, he puts his hand behind his back and says "equals 42" *before* he presses the equals sign. The student receives immediate confirmation that he was correct. If he was incorrect, he should repeat the complete procedure immediately.

Our students need to understand the operations of arithmetic; yet in time they also need to be able to recall the basic facts of arithmetic. They need to make connections among basic facts and acquire thinking strategies for finding missing numbers. Eventually, our students need practice—often in the form of games—to ensure mastery of the basic facts.

# ■ Attaining Computational Fluency

Admittedly, before we teach our students how to find sums, differences, products, or missing factors, we must teach *when* such numbers are needed. Students must understand the meanings of the operations in order to know which button to push on the calculator or which algorithm to use, that is, whether to add, subtract, multiply, or divide.

When a student *does* need to compute, there are actually four different ways to obtain the number: estimation, mental computation, paper-and-pencil algorithm, and calculator (or computer). As adults, we compute in all these ways; we use the method appropriate to the situation. Our students, if they are to be fluent in computation, also need to be able to compute in each of these ways, and they need practice in choosing the appropriate method for particular situations. They need to practice choosing the appropriate form of computation to use while solving varied problems in unfamiliar situations—including real-world contexts. Figure 10.2 illustrates how methods of computation fit within a problem-solving context.

When should each method of computation be used? This is a judgment that must be made in context, but the guidelines in Figure 10.3 may be helpful.

In *Principles and Standards for School Mathematics*, NCTM stresses the need for students at all levels of instruction to be able to use computational tools and

**FIGURE 10.2**   Methods of computation chosen within a problem-solving context.

CONTEXT: Problem Solving

1. Understand the problem.

2. Devise a plan.
    This often involves understanding the meanings of the different operations on numbers.
3. Carry out the plan.
    This often involves choosing the appropriate method of computation.

METHODS OF COMPUTATION

*Approximation*                    *Exact Computation*

• Estimation                       • Mental computation
                                   • Paper-and-pencil algorithm
                                   • Calculator or computer

4. Look back.

*Source:* Based on George Polya, *How to Solve It,* 2d. ed. (Princeton, NJ: Princeton University Press, 1973), xvi–xvii.

**FIGURE 10.3**   Guidelines for selecting the method of computation.

Use

• *estimation* when an approximate answer is sufficient, for example, when the question is: About how many?
• *mental computation* when an exact answer is needed, and it can be readily computed mentally by using known facts and principles, for example, basic facts, multiplying by powers of ten, and distributivity, as in computations like 7 × 604 or 6 × 98.
• *calculator or computer* when an exact answer is needed, a calculator or computer is readily available, and computation would be quicker than using other methods, as in 508,032 ÷ 896.
• *paper-and-pencil* when an exact answer is needed and other methods are not appropriate or available.

strategies fluently and estimate appropriately. The term *computational fluency* reflects the ability to efficiently use different forms of computation as appropriate.[25]

When computation procedures are taught, a balance between conceptual and procedural learning is needed. If instruction focuses exclusively on following procedures and rote memorization, students' habits of mind are likely to become less curious and creative in their approach to solving problems; if students memorize procedures by rote, they are less likely to remember them. When students "have memorized procedures and practiced them a lot, it is difficult for them to go back and understand them later."[26] Students need instruction that is balanced— instruction that involves both conceptual and procedural learning.

That balance *does* include practice. Students need to practice reliable procedures and develop computational fluency if they are to become good problem solvers. As much as possible, our instruction in computation should be within real-world, problem-centered contexts, with isolated drills or games as supplemental instruction when required to enhance specific skills. Keep the focus on problem solving.

## ■ Teaching Mental Computation

Students and adults use mental computation during daily living more often than they use written computation. Truly, mental computation is an important skill for students to learn. It is also a "natural stepping-stone to developing written computation and computational estimation."[27]

Mental computation is concerned with exact answers, but there is no set procedure for computing a particular operation such as addition. Instead, strategies involving known concepts and principles are applied thoughtfully, flexibly, and creatively within particular situations. For example, to mentally compute the sum 98 + 99 an individual may choose to apply knowledge that 98 is also 100 − 2 and 99 is also 100 − 1, and reason that their sum is 200 − 3, or 197. (This is actually easier than doing the paper-and-pencil procedure "in your head.") As our students come to understand an operation like addition and how a number can be renamed as a difference, they should be given opportunities to apply this knowledge by computing mentally. Often mental computation can be practiced in odd moments during the day, for example, while waiting for a teacher to arrive or a bell to ring.

Sometimes mental computation strategies can be learned and practiced as warm-ups before math lessons. We should not wait until after we teach paper-and-pencil algorithms. Mochón and Román conclude from their research that it is "wise to develop strategies of mental computation before or simultaneously with introduction of the formal algorithms."[28]

Instruction in mental computation often applies principles of numeration like place value and properties of operations like commutativity, associativity, and distributivity. Many specific strategies can be taught to facilitate mental computation. Examples include the following:

- Find pairs of numbers that add to one, or to 10, or to 100. For example, think of 45 + 76 + 55 as 45 + 55 + 76, then 100 + 76 is 176.
- Find a more useful name for a number. For example, 28 + 56 is the same as (30 − 2) + 56, which is 86 − 2 or 84.
- Do the operation "in parts." Distributivity can often be used. For example, 4 × 7 is the same as 4 × (5 + 2), and 20 + 8 is 28 (a partitioned array will help).
- Use numbers that are multiples of 10 and 100 and 1000. For example, 4 × 298 is the same as 4 × (300 − 2), and 1200 − 8 is 1192.

Instruction in mental computation can help many of our students develop a flexible approach to computation. They will be less likely to limit a needed computation to a particular procedure.

# ■ Teaching Students to Estimate

Our students need to learn to estimate not only to solve problems that do not require an exact number, but also to make sure results are reasonable when performing exact computations. A proper emphasis on estimation eliminates much of the need for future corrective instruction.

Instruction in estimation must begin early and occur often. Students who estimate well are thoroughly grounded conceptually. But any student who thinks that 27 is closer to 20 than 30 will have difficulty estimating, as will the student who does not understand that $\frac{7}{8}$ is almost 1. Students need a robust number sense in which numeration concepts are understood and applied, the basic facts are easily recalled and used, and compensation principles and other relational understandings are employed.

Attitudes toward estimation are also important. Typically, students believe "there is only one correct answer"; but when estimating, there are only reasonable answers—and some answers are more reasonable than others. Our students must learn to recognize when an estimate is all that is needed, and they must feel free to use terms like *almost, a bit more than, about, a little less than,* and *in the ballpark.*

The ability to estimate incorporates varied mental computation skills, any one of which may require instruction. Included among such skills for whole numbers are:

- Adding a little bit more than one number to a little bit more than another; adding a little bit less than one number to a little bit less than another; and, in general, adding, subtracting, and so on, with a little bit more than or a little bit less than.
- Rounding a whole number to the nearest ten, hundred, and so on.
- Multiplying by ten, and by powers of ten—in one step.
- Multiplying two numbers, each of which is a multiple of a power of ten (e.g., 20 × 300). This should be done as one step, without the use of a written algorithm.

With fractions and decimals less than one, estimation often involves using benchmarks, determining if a particular number is closer to zero, one-half, or one.

When possible, we should teach estimation informally in the context of problem solving. Here are examples:

- Problems involving the total cost of items purchased are reasonable to estimate because the buyer needs to know how much money to have at hand for the cashier.

- The purchase of a discounted item also requires an estimate of actual cost and the amount of money needed for the cashier.

One way to provide practice with estimation is to present students with a problem and several possible answers. Students can then use estimation to choose the answer that is most reasonable. Here is a problem with possible answers:

A $1,495 large-screen television set has been discounted 20%. Which cost is the most reasonable estimate?

$1,000    $1,100    $1,200    $1,300    $1,400

Also, if students are given numerical expressions such as the following, they can be asked to list the expressions in order from least to greatest. For the following expressions, students would list the letters in order from least product to greatest product.

a. $89 \times 102$        c. $48 \times 320$
b. $75 \times 98$         d. $8.9 \times 10.2$

In general, our students will become more and more able to determine when an answer is reasonable as they gain the habit of asking if the answer makes sense, and as they develop a more robust number sense. Students who habitually consider the reasonableness of their answers are not likely to adopt incorrect computational procedures.

# ■ Teaching Students to Use Calculators

When solving a problem, sometimes the sensible choice for computation is a calculator. Occasionally students think that using a calculator is cheating, so we need to make sure our students experience and think about a calculator as a viable choice for computation.

Of course there are times during instruction when calculators should be set aside—when mental computation or estimation is the focus, for example. Usually, when students are being encouraged to invent paper-and-pencil procedures or when they are studying particular conventional algorithms, calculators are not used.

Often, students who are free to use calculators can solve a more extensive range of problems, and they can approach these problems earlier. For example, they can use real-world problems based on situations reported in the local newspaper—even when they have not developed paper-and-pencil procedures for the required computations.

Research suggests that "calculators should be an integral part of mathematics instruction including the development of concepts and computational skills."[29] A meta-analysis of 54 research studies concluded that "calculator use did not hinder the development of mathematical skills" and that "students using calculators had better attitudes toward mathematics."[30]

As we teach our students how to use calculators, we must be careful not to focus exclusively on answers. Rather, we must focus on the thinking processes of students and their application of concepts and mathematical principles. Reasoning through a two-step problem, for example, requires much more than entering numbers in a calculator.

We must help our students understand what a calculator can do and how to use it, then give them opportunities to use calculators *throughout* the mathematics program. As noted by Huinker, a calculator can even be used with kindergarten and first-grade students to explore numerals, counting, number magnitude, and number relationships.[31]

A calculator can be used to reinforce underlying concepts and procedures—especially numeration concepts. For example, students can practice naming what some call the "product value of a digit" (face value × place value). Consider these instructions for a game.

> Everyone enter "1111" in your calculator.
> I have a set of cards; each has one of the digits 2 through 9 on it.
> When I draw a card, use addition or subtraction to change a 1 on your calculator to the number shown on the card. *You* decide which one to change.
> Then I will draw another card and you can change another of your 1s.
> After four cards are drawn and you have changed all four 1s, we will see who shows the greatest number on their calculator.

Basic multiplication products can be generated by using the repeat function of calculators.

$$6 \times 7 = ? \text{ Think of } 6 \times 7 \text{ as 6 sevens.}$$

Key  $\boxed{7}$  $\boxed{+}$  $\boxed{7}$  $\boxed{=}$  $\boxed{=}$  $\boxed{=}$  $\boxed{=}$  $\boxed{=}$
counting 2,   3,   4,   5,   6,

We can even use calculators to provide immediate feedback when students practice recalling basic facts. Calculators can be used to practice estimating quotients. Have each student estimate the answer for an example like $17,880 \div 894$, then have one student determine the exact answer with a calculator. Each student gets one point if his or her estimate has the correct number of digits, and two points if his or her first digit is also correct.

So-called broken calculator problems are often used to provide practice with different operations and fact recall. For example, students pretend that on their calculator the 7 key is broken. How could they solve the problem $7 \times 77$?

Indeed, a calculator has many uses—but its limitations must also be demonstrated. For example, it takes more time to multiply by a power of 10 on a calculator than to perform the multiplication mentally.

When our students use calculators, from time to time we should have them explain what they are doing and why specific choices are made.

---

**NCTM's Position Regarding Calculators**

School mathematics programs should provide students with a range of knowledge, skills, and tools. Students need an understanding of number and operations, including the use of computational procedures, estimation, mental mathematics, and the appropriate use of the calculator. A balanced mathematics program develops students' confidence and understanding of when and how to use these skills and tools. Students need to develop their basic mathematical understandings to solve problems both in and out of school.[32]

*Adopted July 2005*

---

# ■ Teaching Paper-and-Pencil Procedures

Conventional paper-and-pencil algorithms involve more than procedural knowledge; they entail conceptual knowledge as well. Many of the instructional activities described in this book are included because of the need for conceptual understanding. Students are not merely mechanical processors, they must be involved conceptually when learning and using paper-and-pencil procedures.

Even so, it must be recognized that as a student uses a specific paper-and-pencil algorithm over time, the procedure becomes more automatic. Students gradually use less conceptual knowledge and more procedural knowledge while doing the procedure, a process researchers sometimes call "proceduralization."

We must be careful not to introduce a paper-and-pencil procedure too early; we need to be *especially* careful not to use direct instruction about steps in a procedure too soon. Frequently, we can introduce an algorithm with a verbal problem and challenge our students to use what they already know to work out a solution—even if their prior knowledge is quite informal. When we let students use their own informal techniques initially, we will find that some students know more than we thought! Others will creatively use what they already know and the manipulatives we make available. By beginning this way, we will help students relate the algorithm we are teaching to their prior knowledge. We may even want to have a group of students investigate different ways of finding a sum, a product, and so on. Students should stay with the investigation long enough for several alternatives to be developed and shared; they could even write about their experiences.

Students who are permitted to work out solutions using informal knowledge before they are taught a specific computational procedure sometimes develop "invented" paper-and-pencil procedures. Place a high value on all invented procedures and the creativity involved; say something like, "That's great! Why does it work? Will your procedure give you the correct number every time? How can you find out?" Invented algorithms are often evidence of conceptual understanding. Invented computational procedures are not always efficient, but they are correct procedures if they always produce the number needed.

## Instruction in Grades 1–2

Mathematics educators agree that in grades 1–2 they want students to understand numbers and how numbers are related to one another. They want students to be able to represent quantities and to understand addition and subtraction and how those operations are related to one another. Fluency with addition facts is also a goal. There is less agreement on the place of computational procedures in the mathematics curriculum for grades 1–2.

Should the emphasis be on students inventing procedures or on students learning conventional algorithms? In *Principles and Standards for School Mathematics,* NCTM includes the following statements in its discussion of standards for numbers and operations for pre-K–2 (emphasis added):

- Students learn basic number combinations and **develop strategies for computing that make sense to them** when they solve problems with interesting and challenging contexts.
- Through class discussions, they can compare the ease of use and ease of explanation of various strategies. In some cases, their strategies for computing will be close to conventional algorithms; in other cases, they will be quite different.
- When students compute with **strategies they invent or choose because they are meaningful**, their learning tends to be robust—they are able to remember and apply their knowledge.
- Students can learn to compute accurately and efficiently through regular **experience with meaningful procedures.** They benefit from instruction that **blends procedural fluency and conceptual understanding.** . . . This is true for all students, including those with special educational needs.[33]

Clearly, NCTM recommends that we focus on meaningful learning. In the earliest grades this can involve both invented procedures and conventional algorithms, but *the stress should be on thinking and on procedures that make sense to students.* NCTM has published materials to help teachers teach so that students represent numbers in meaningful ways, understand operations, and make sense of computational procedures. Their series of books entitled *Navigating through Number and Operations* is one example.[34]

Trafton and Thiessen argue that children need to learn a wide variety of strategies for problem solving and computation; they emphasize that such strategies are not learned at one specific time or in a single lesson. Children learn strategies for solving problems and computing on their own timetable and not ours.[35]

When our students invent procedures and record them, we can ask questions that point toward more efficient refinements in the procedures students are developing. Invented algorithms can often be further developed into conventional algorithms, but some question the need to do this if the invented algorithm is correct and a reasonably efficient procedure. It is probably true that in grades 1–2 we should encourage students to invent procedures but also be open to helping them learn about conventional algorithms as warranted.

Some would delay teaching conventional procedures. In their proposed sequence for teaching computation, Reys and Reys suggest that conventional algorithms for addition and subtraction of whole numbers be delayed until grade 3, and taught then only if students have not already developed ways of computing that are efficient.[36]

Developing number sense should be the primary focus of instruction in grades 1–2 because well-developed number sense provides a foundation for computational fluency.[37] Conventional algorithms, whenever they are taught, should be yet another context that makes sense for investigating mathematics.

Conventional procedures can be taught so students understand the algorithms. When this is done, instruction typically involves the use of manipulatives.

## Developmental Instruction

Developmental instruction in conventional computational procedures must be distinguished from corrective instruction, which is discussed briefly in the section that follows. The term *developmental instruction,* as used here, is the initial sequence of instructional activities over time that enables students to understand, execute, and gain skill in using particular algorithms. *Corrective instruction* follows developmental instruction whenever a student has not learned a correct procedure; for example, a student may have learned an error pattern during initial instruction. Careful developmental instruction seeks to help students learn algorithms *without* learning error patterns.

Before we teach our students to compute on paper, we must make sure they are able to represent quantities with appropriate notation. Also, they need to be able to make suitable exchanges with manipulatives; when working with whole numbers, chip-trading activities can help our students develop these abilities.

As we introduce a particular algorithm and continue to provide instruction, we must engage our students in *thinking*—not in mindless copying and repetition. While our students are first learning a computational procedure, they need to make mental connections and build the procedure in their own heads.

We can begin by having our students use manipulatives to find solutions to problems; base-ten blocks are frequently used for addition and subtraction of whole numbers, and fraction parts are often used for addition and subtraction with fractions. Our students need to use manipulatives initially to solve problems—whether invented procedures are stressed, game-like activities are incorporated, or the instruction has a conventional algorithm as its goal. It is important that students begin with manipulatives, *then reflect on what they have done* with the materials.

If our goal is to teach a conventional algorithm, we must keep that procedure in mind as we guide the recording; a step-by-step written record of manipulations can become the algorithm itself. When our students are comfortable with this process, they will be able to visualize the manipulatives (but not actually han-dle them) as they write. In some cases, if students are to develop a more efficient algorithm, possibly a conventional algorithm, they will need to shorten the writ-ten record. We may want to say, "Mathematicians like to write fewer symbols whenever they can."

Instruction will be meaningful if it is done within a problem-solving con-text and the algorithm is developed as a step-by-step record of observations. The computational procedure will make sense to our students because it is a record of what they have actually seen. Typical elementary school students move very gradually from making sense through manipulatives to making sense through mathematical reasoning. Any student experiencing difficulty while attempting to learn a computational procedure may need to work more directly with manipu-latives for a while.

Admittedly, there are algorithms that cannot be developed as a record of observations—especially in the middle grades. Sometimes these procedures can be introduced as a shortcut. For example, the conventional algorithm for dividing fractions can be developed by reasoning through a rather elaborate but meaningful procedure involving complex fractions, applying the multiplicative identity and the like, then observing a pattern. The obvious implication of the observed pattern is that most of the steps can be eliminated; merely invert the divisor and multiply.

Teachers and curriculum designers are faced with the question, "When should different stages for an algorithm be introduced?" Traditionally, a rather rigid logical sequence was followed in textbooks; for example, addition of whole numbers with no regrouping was taught well before addition with regrouping. But when we teach computation in the context of solving problems, the problems of interest do not always occur within that traditional sequence. This should not deter us and our students from exploring solutions for interesting problems that will lead to more generalized written procedures. Usnick found that initial teach-ing of the generalized procedure for adding whole numbers (regrouping included) led to comparable achievement and effective retention.[38]

---

## Carry? Borrow? Regroup? Rename?

Which term is appropriate when adding or subtracting whole numbers? Obviously, *carry* and *borrow* are misleading mathematically, though the terms are often used. **They may promote mechanical manipulation of symbols instead of a procedure that makes sense to students**.

The term *regroup* is appropriate when manipulatives for a quantity are grouped differently. The term *rename* is mathematically correct; the quantity is actually given a different name. For example, when computing $273 - 186$, 2 hundreds $+$ **7 tens $+$ 3 ones** is renamed as 2 hundreds $+$ **6 tens $+$ 13 ones**.

Other terms that may cause students to focus only on a procedure are *reduce, cancel,* and *invert.* Make sure students understand the concepts involved.

When using manipulatives to teach a conventional algorithm, the critical step is progressing from manipulatives to written symbols. The resulting record or algorithm must make sense to our students if they are going to do more than push symbols around on paper.

We must be sure our students' paper-and-pencil procedures are correct before we encourage them to make the procedures automatic. When algorithms *are* correct, a certain amount of practice is required for the procedures to be remembered and used effectively; but practice with paper-and-pencil procedures needs to be planned carefully—as does practice for all methods of computation. NCTM notes in *Principles and Standards for School Mathematics*:

> **Practice needs to be motivating and systematic if students are to develop computational fluency, whether mentally, with manipulatives materials, or with paper and pencil. Practice can be conducted in the context of other activities, including games that require computation as part of score keeping, questions that emerge from children's literature, situations in the classroom, or focused activities that are part of another mathematical investigation. Practice should be purposeful and should focus on developing thinking strategies and a knowledge of number relationships . . .[39]**

*Continuing* diagnosis is very important. When we say, "Tell me something about this," we help our students develop the ability to communicate mathematical ideas—even as they give us diagnostic information. We must keep our "diagnostic eyes" open throughout instruction. However, it is also important to not overtest students—especially at-risk students. Although diagnosis should continue throughout instruction, we should never limit instruction to assessment activities. Sometimes teachers fall into that trap.

Our written and oral responses to students' written work in mathematics affect students—either positively or negatively. It is best to give an immediate *personal* response to what the student is doing rather than a list of things to be done next time.

"I have no trouble reading your numerals."
"Very interesting! How did you get your answer?"
"Did you think about your answer? Does it make sense?"

Sometimes, when teaching a specific algorithm, it is helpful to have a group of students analyze a completed example. It is important to emphasize thinking as students observe, describe, and hypothesize what was done. Students should discuss why it resulted in the correct number and try the procedure with different numbers. We may also want to ask some students to analyze incorrect computations, suggesting that they find and explain the errors.

Many of our students will make mistakes while learning to compute. Even so, mistakes can be an important, positive part of the initial learning process.

Interestingly, teachers respond differently to errors in different cultures. Our students who make mistakes and experience failures need to feel that we accept their failures along the way as an expected part of learning. Our attitudes toward errors are important. We should view them as opportunities for learning!

We need to monitor our own expectations of students, making sure we do not assume particular individuals cannot learn. Even so, we do need to be alert to any perceptual difficulties a student may have. In order to respond to instruction, students must be able to observe and also envision the physical properties of digits: vertical versus horizontal elongation, straightness versus curvature, and degree of closure. And our students must be able to perceive attributes of multi-digit numerals—properties such as position of a digit to the left or right of another digit. Poor spatial ability may affect an individual's capacity to respond to instruction emphasizing numeration concepts.

Other students may find it difficult to respond to instruction because of language patterns. The syntax of English language expressions is often different from the structure of mathematical statements, and we complicate the situation by using different but equivalent language expressions for the same concept. For example, *twelve minus four* and *four from twelve* express the same mathematical concept.

Teaching conventional computational procedures requires thorough developmental instruction; each student moves through a carefully planned sequence of learning activities. The amount of time needed for each type of activity will vary from student to student; and for any individual, the pace will likely vary from day to day. If we are to lessen the likelihood that students learn patterns of error, we will have to resist the temptation to cover the text or the curriculum guide by completing two pages a day or a similar plan. Careful attention will have to be given to ideas and skills needed by each student in order to learn the concept or algorithm under study. We *can* teach in a way that makes the adoption of erroneous procedures unlikely.

## Corrective Instruction

Corrective instruction may be necessary whenever one of our students has not been able to learn a computational procedure that produces correct answers in an efficient way. Corrective instruction must be built on a careful diagnosis of what the student has and has not learned and on what the student can and cannot do.

The student may have acquired a simple misconception that can be corrected with focused instruction. Sometimes the student is not adequately grounded in the concepts and principles needed to understand the algorithm. Then corrective instruction must begin by teaching foundational concepts and principles rather than the computational procedure itself.

For students who adopt error patterns, it is often wise to redevelop computational procedures as careful step-by-step records of observations while using manipulatives. Hopefully, this will help the student who has been pushing symbols around in a rote manner to make sense of the procedure.

Students need feedback that not only tells them which examples are correct but also assists in obtaining correct answers. Corrective feedback can take many forms. It can be presented orally along with personal comments that express confidence in the student's ability to learn, or it can be written on his paper. All too frequently, teacher feedback does not include *corrective* feedback; papers are merely scored and students are asked to rework the examples. When appropriate, we need to write on students' papers notes that provide personal, corrective assistance.

## Students with Special Needs

As we reflect on ways we can adapt instruction to the individual needs of students in our classrooms, we need to consider how we will differentiate instruction for students with learning disabilities and other special needs. They have specific needs, and if we are to help them we must be ready to intervene with a variety of strategies.

What difficulties do students with learning disabilities have when learning mathematics? And specifically, how do those disabilities affect learning paper-and-pencil computation procedures?

Students with learning disabilities, as well as other students who experience limited success, often have attention problems: They have difficulty listening to directions, attending to all the steps, and completing their work. How can we encourage attending behavior? Bender's suggestions for fostering attention skills include the following:[40]

- Display three or four positively stated classroom rules.
- Post a daily class schedule, even for short departmentalized periods.
- Focus on class cues. A bell can be rung for attention. Cue cards or charts can remind students how to begin a lesson (get out your book, etc.).
- Keep desks clear. Students should have on their desks only texts and materials needed for the lesson.
- Use peer buddies to make sure both are ready to begin the next activity or lesson.

Other characteristics common among students with learning disabilities also make it difficult for these students to learn mathematics. Steele describes the following:[41]

- Memory deficiencies—difficulty learning facts or remembering the correct sequence of steps for a particular skill.
- Auditory processing problems—difficulty understanding oral explanations of content and vocabulary.
- Visual processing problems—losing his or her place, confusing numbers such as 17 and 71, copying inaccurately, working problems in the wrong direction, and lining up work incorrectly with respect to place values.

- Abstract reasoning deficits—struggling more than usual with word problems and new concepts, and shutting down mentally when they see tasks they associate with failure.
- Organizational deficiencies—difficulty in selecting and using appropriate strategies. Sometimes these students master one strategy, then apply it regularly, even when inappropriate.

Students with learning disabilities frequently have difficulty imagining how what they see will change in appearance when moved. Drawings we normally use during instruction may not be adequate, even with explicit explanations. The students tend to be concrete in their thinking, and concepts must often be taught more directly.

How should we structure our lessons when teaching students with learning disabilities? Bender lists these suggestions:[42]

- Provide clear directions, particularly during transitions.
- Develop alternative instructional activities—for example, two worksheets that present the same material at different levels, and alternative assignments that cover the same material.
- Plan frequent breaks. Take "stretch breaks" (about thirty seconds) every fifteen minutes or so.
- Use physical activities. For example, movement can be involved when students learn basic combinations.
- Use clear worksheets. Make sure they are not cluttered and do not contain distractions.
- Decrease task length. A longer task can be presented as a set of shorter, do-able tasks.
- Develop alternative assessment tasks. As an alternative to paper-and-pencil assessment tasks, for example, have the student orally tell you how to do the computation, or show you the procedure with base-ten blocks.

If we are to provide effective instruction for our students who have learning disabilities, our instruction will need to be modified in many ways. Other suggestions are noted by Steele:[43]

- Present advance organizers. (The game board activities described in Appendix D are examples for paper-and-pencil computation procedures.)
- Review prerequisite skills or concepts. This should be done no matter how long ago they were taught.
- Model procedures enough times. Demonstrate a procedure slowly and repeatedly until it is clear.
- Use mnemonic strategies. These may be acronyms.
- Use peer tutoring. This may be especially effective for improving calculation skills.

> Those who will teach mathematics to special needs students will want to read the October 2004 issue of *Teaching Children Mathematics* 11(3), a focus issue on teaching mathematics to special needs students.

## CONCLUSION

Instruction in computation should be based on what students already understand and are able to do. For this reason continuing assessment and diagnosis is essential.

Students need a robust number sense. If they are to develop fluency with computation, they need to understand specific ideas and principles related to numeration, equivalence, and compensation. Students need to understand each of the four operations in order to make appropriate computations when they solve problems, whatever method of computation they use.

Instruction in computation must enable students to make connections. The basic facts of arithmetic should be introduced in a way that helps students make connections among facts, procedures, and concepts.

In the early grades, instruction in paper-and-pencil procedures should involve problem solving and manipulatives. The algorithms can be introduced as step-by-step written records of observations made while working with manipulatives.

As students become increasingly fluent with computation, they learn different methods of computation to use when appropriate: estimation, mental computation, paper-and-pencil algorithms, and calculators.

Mathematical concepts and procedures are taught and learned most effectively when instruction is enriched by instructional practices such as those described in the next chapter.

## FURTHER REFLECTION

Consider the following questions:

1. Students need to learn to compute, but they also need to *understand the operations* of arithmetic. Why do they need to understand the operations of arithmetic?
2. Why do students eventually need to master the basic facts for addition and multiplication?
3. Students need to be encouraged to use estimation, mental computation, paper-and-pencil procedures, and calculators—whichever is most appropriate. *When* is each method of computation the most appropriate method to use?

4. Write equations that show how the four operations on whole numbers are related. Show as many different relationships as you can.

5. State several compensation principles with words, and demonstrate each with an equation.

## REFERENCES

1. National Council of Teachers of Mathematics. (2000). *Principles and standards for school mathematics* (p. 16). Reston, VA: Author.
2. Ibid, p. 20.
3. Ibid, p. 79.
4. Ibid, p. 78.
5. Carpenter, T. P., Franke, M. L., & Levi, L. (2003). *Thinking mathematically: Integrating arithmetic & algebra in elementary school* (p. xiii). Portsmouth, NH: Heinemann.
6. Ibid, p. 42.
7. Ashlock, R. B., Johnson, M. L., Wilson, J. W., & Jones, W. L. (1983). *Guiding each child's leaning of mathematics* (p. 482). Columbus, OH: Charles E. Merrill Publishing Company.
8. Carpenter, T. P., Franke, M. L., & Levi, L. (2003). *Thinking mathematically: Integrating arithmetic & algebra in elementary school* (p. 22). Portsmouth, NH: Heinemann.
9. Ibid, p. 19.
10. National Council of Teachers of Mathematics. (2000). *Principles and standards for school mathematics* (p. 34). Reston, VA: The Council.
11. Based on R. B. Ashlock, M. L. Johnson, J. W. Wilson, & W. L. Jones. (1983). *Guiding each child's learning of mathematics* (pp. 478–485). Columbus, OH: Charles E. Merrill Publishing Company.
12. National Council of Teachers of Mathematics. (2007). Effective teaching for the development of skill and conceptual understanding of number: What is most effective? *Effective Instruction Brief*. Retrieved August 23, 2007, from www.nctm.org/news/content.aspx?id=8448, p. 1. (emphasis added)
13. Ibid, pp. 1–2.
14. For example, see C. Thrailkill. (2005). Connecting mathematics and literature. *Teaching Children Mathematics 12*(4), 218–224.
15. Schwartz, D. M. (1985). *How much is a million?* New York: Scholastic, Inc.
16. For example, see D. Birch. (1993). *The king's chessboard.* New York: Puffin.
17. O'Connell, S. (2005). *Now I get it: Strategies for building confident and competent mathematicians, K–6* (p. 22). Portsmouth, NH: Heinemann.
18. Battisa, M. T. (1999). The mathematical miseducation of America's youth: Ignoring research and scientific study in education. *Phi Delta Kappan 80*(6), 438.
19. Isaacs, A. C., & Carroll, W. M. (1999). Strategies for basic-fact instruction. *Teaching Children Mathematics 5*(9), 508–515.
20. It is easier for students to count *forward* than backward for the unknown addend. This is actually a how-many-more meaning for subtraction and leads to the helpful practice of using related addition facts to answer subtraction questions.
21. Teaching distribution of multiplication over addition (multiplying "in parts") can help students proceed independently when solving untaught or forgotten basic multiplication facts; they can derive facts from multiplication facts they remember. Show the multiplication by partitioning an array.
22. Kamii, C., & Lewis, B. A. (2003). Single-digit subtraction with fluency. *Teaching Children Mathematics 10*(4), 233.

23. Kamii, C., & Anderson, C. (2003). Multiplication games: How we made and used them. *Teaching Children Mathematics 10*(3), 135–141.
24. O'Connell, S. (2005). *Now I get it: Strategies for building confident and competent mathematicians, K–6* (p. 22). Portsmouth, NH: Heinemann.
25. National Council of Teachers of Mathematics. (2000). *Principles and standards for school mathematics* (p. 35). Reston, VA: The Council.
26. Hiebert, J. (1999). Relationships between research and the NCTM standards. *Journal for Research in Mathematics Education 30*(1), 15.
27. Reys, R. E. (1999). Basic skills should include mental computation. *Mathematics Education Dialogues 3*(1), 11–12.
28. Mochón S., & Román, J. (1998). Strategies of mental computation used by elementary and secondary school children. *Focus on Learning Problems in Mathematics 20*(4), 35–49.
29. Dessart, D. J., DeRidder, C. M., & Ellington, A. J. (1999). The research backs calculators. *Mathematics Education Dialogues 2*(3), 6.
30. Ellington, A. J. (2003). A meta-analysis of the effects of calculators on students' achievement and attitude levels in precollege mathematics classes. *Journal for Research in Mathematics Education 34*(5), 433.
31. Huinker, D. (2002). Calculators as learning tools for young children's explorations of number. *Teaching Children Mathematics 8*(6), 316–321.
32. National Council of Teachers of Mathematics (September 2005). Computation, calculators, and common sense: A position of the National Council of Teachers of Mathematics. *NCTM News Bulletin* (p. 6). Reston, VA: The Council.
33. National Council of Teachers of Mathematics. (2000). *Principles and standards for school mathematics* (pp. 84–87). Reston, VA: The Council.
34. National Council of Teachers of Mathematics. *Navigating through number and operations.* Reston, VA: The Council. The series includes Pre-kindergarten–grade 2 (2004) and grades 3–5 (2007).
35. Trafton, P., & Thiessen, D. (1999). *Learning through problems: Number sense and computational strategies* (pp. 44–45). Portsmouth, NH: Heinemann.
36. Reys, B. J., & Reys, R. E. (1998). Computation in the elementary curriculum: Shifting the emphasis. *Teaching Children Mathematics 5*(4), 236–241.
37. See S. Griffin. (2003). Laying the foundation for computational fluency in early childhood. *Teaching Children Mathematics 9*(6), 306–309. See also T. Fosnot & M. Dolk. (2001). *Young mathematicians at work: Constructing number sense, addition, and subtraction.* Portsmouth, NH: Heinemann.
38. Usnick, V. E. (1992). Multidigit addition: A study of an alternate sequence. *Focus on Learning Problems in Mathematics 14*(3), 53–62.
39. National Council of Teachers of Mathematics. (2000). *Principles and standards for school mathematics* (p. 87). Reston, VA: The Council.
40. Bender, W. N. (2002). *Differentiating instruction for students with learning disabilities* (pp. 20–21). Thousand Oaks, CA: Corwin Press, Inc.
41. Steele, M. M. (2002). Strategies for helping students who have learning disabilities in mathematics. *Mathematics Teaching in the Middle School 8*(3), 140–141.
42. Bender, W. N. (2002). *Differentiating instruction for students with learning disabilities* (pp. 20–21). Thousand Oaks, CA: Corwin Press, Inc.
43. Steele, M. M. (2002). Strategies for helping students who have learning disabilities in mathematics. *Mathematics Teaching in the Middle School 8*(3), 141–143.

# CHAPTER 11

# Enriching Instruction in Computation and Other Mathematical Topics

*Children's understanding grows in classrooms with
rich experiences,
time for reflective thought,
and opportunities to act on what they know.*[1]

There is much we can do to enrich instruction in mathematics and fully engage our students. As you read this chapter, reflect on your own teaching. Think about your use of representations, especially graphic organizers. And consider the specific helps described in regard to using mathematical vocabulary, talking and writing mathematics, and using portfolios to encourage progress. When teachers read the guidelines at the close of the chapter, they find it helpful to ponder each of them.

## ■ Teaching So Students Can Use What They Learn

Chapters 10 and 11 are designed to help you teach so your students can remember what they learn, then use the concepts and procedures later as needed. Sprenger has summarized instruction that makes this possible.[2] She focuses on the following steps:

- *Reaching students.* This involves attention and motivation, but it also involves instruction that is meaningful to students.
- *Reflecting on what is experienced and learned.* This includes making connections at every stage of the learning process.
- *Recoding material that is learned.* Students need to express what is learned in their own language. They need to be able use varied representations, and to explain using vocabulary appropriately.
- *Reinforcing what is learned.* It is imperative that students be provided with feedback.
- *Rehearsing what is learned.* If information is to get into long-term memory, it must be rehearsed. Practice should be diverse, and incorporate different learning styles and multiple intelligences.

- *Reviewing what was learned.* If we do not provide students with opportunities to review, most of what they have learned will be lost from memory. Have students use what they have learned; have them apply it to unfamiliar situations.
- *Retrieving what was learned.* Students often depend on cues to retrieve information. Guide the retrieval process; provide varied cues—including assessment items similar to those they are likely to encounter.

Mathematics will be meaningful for our students if our instructional activities and the content our students study make sense to them—and they *use* what they learn in varied situations. We can help our students by making sure they are able to use a variety of representations for the mathematics they are learning.

# ■ Using Representations

Teachers use the term *representation* in various ways. The term often refers to some kind of object: concrete objects or manipulatives that are frequently structured for instructional purposes; or *representation* may refer to objects such as notations, pictures, and drawings. Sometimes the term refers to signs, symbols, or icons that represent something. At other times it refers to drawings made by a teacher or a student. *Systems* of representation exist: Numeration systems are one example.[3] Not all representations are visual; the term may even refer to oral language, to actions or movements, or to mental images of what is observed in the world about us.

## The Role of Representations in Learning

Representations can help students learn concepts and procedures; this is true for older students as well as younger students. Representations, used appropriately, encourage our students to *think* about concepts and procedures. Eisner suggests we need to recognize that "different forms of representation develop different forms of thinking, convey different kinds of meaning . . ."[4] Attempts to teach procedures merely by demonstrating how to do it are inadequate for most students, even when accompanied by an explanation; this is especially true for young children. Demonstrations do not necessarily result in conceptual learning; very often they do not even result in procedural learning.

As was noted in Chapter 1, students look for commonalities among their contacts with an idea or a procedure; they notice common characteristics among their experiences and form an abstraction. Therefore, our students need experiences in which all perceptual stimuli are varied except those that are essential to the mathematical concept or procedure. A cardboard place-value chart may be of great value, but it should not be the only concrete aid we use for numeration activities; other models can be used also, possibly devices made with juice cans or wooden boxes.

Most often students develop an understanding of a particular concept while also developing an understanding of representations for that concept. It is not usually the case that a student learns an abstract concept, and later learns how to represent that concept. Nor is it typically the case that a student encounters a particular representation for the first time, and later is enabled to understand the associated concept. For concept learning to occur when representations are used, students need to be familiar enough with the objects (or whatever representation is used) that the representation is not a distraction in the learning process. In truth, the connections between concepts and their representations (including symbols) are quite interactive.[5]

## Using Representations When Teaching

Our students do not learn just because we are using certain materials. As Roberts cautions, "There is indeed no intrinsic magical power in the materials or models, but rather the power lies in the careful orchestration of the task by the teacher and thoughtful reflection by the students."[6]

The experiences we plan for our students help form their dispositions toward mathematics. Our use of representations, including manipulatives, can contribute to a positive disposition—if those experiences include exploration, problem solving, accurate modeling of the mathematics involved, and reflection by each student.

As an instructional tool a representation is most effective when it is as specific as possible and accompanied by explicit instruction. It may take more time for you to carefully make a drawing, for example, but your students are more likely to learn the mathematics and to learn more accurate mathematics because you took the time to draw your representation carefully. If students are making drawings, have them describe the connections between what they are drawing and what they are representing.

If our students believe that getting correct answers is all that is really important, they will believe that it is all right to push digits around whether it makes any sense or not. They will also push manipulatives around without thinking or relating them to a meaningful recording procedure. Our classroom talk must focus on *thinking*, even while students use concrete materials; expect them to make sense of the procedures we use and whatever we write down.

Do not let your students simply rely on you to verify answers. Instead, when they solve problems and compute, urge them to use reasoning and evidence to verify results. Sometimes they will be able to use mathematical reasoning to provide the needed evidence, at other times they can make a drawing or use manipulatives—if they are encouraged to do so.

In general, well-chosen manipulatives can provide a natural working environment for our students as they learn concepts and procedures. This is clearly true for whole numbers, which are very much part of each student's environment, but with fractions students have less direct experience and they are more apt to rely on rote procedures; so we need to take special care when selecting materials. Materials we can use to create more natural environments include chip-trading activities for whole numbers, and fraction bars for fractions. Extensive modeling with materials like these during the early phases of instruction usually helps students develop understandings they can apply flexibly.

We should help our students learn general concepts and procedures rather than ideas or processes specific to a particular model or example. For instance, students need to learn that "ten ones is the same amount as one ten," rather than "take ten yellows to the bank then put one blue in the next place." Similarly, if we do not focus on the general procedure, in a specific subtraction number sentence like $42 - 17 = 25$ a student may conclude that the five units in the answer is simply the result of finding the difference between the 2 and the 7. Models and examples should be varied so irrelevant characteristics are not observed as common attributes.

As our students use manipulatives to model concepts, we should involve them in experiences which "go both ways" whenever possible. This is especially important for numeration concepts. Have students work with manipulatives and then record what they observe with symbols, but also let them begin with symbols and interpret the symbols by modeling the concept. For example, provide a collection of base-ten blocks, and point to a unit block and explain, "This block is one"; then give a student a numeral card such as 1,324 and have the student show that amount with the blocks. In contrast, assemble a collection of base-ten blocks: five hundreds blocks, two unit blocks, one thousands block, and three tens blocks. Ask the student to write a numeral for the amount shown with the blocks.

Manipulatives are available for teaching mathematics to *all* students; this is especially true for younger students. Manipulatives can be made by the teacher or an aide, or purchased commercially. Some manipulatives have been available for *many* decades; the Montessori math materials are an example. Read about the Montessori Math Curriculum on the Internet and you will likely be surprised at the variety of creative resources available. Other manipulatives have become available only recently. For example, the National Library of Virtual Manipulatives includes interactive manipulatives in eModules—interactive online units that target objectives identified as important in state and national standards.

We must make sure that whatever manipulatives we design or select are accurate mathematically. Fraction representations, for example, are sometimes inaccurate. Although it is often wise to let students construct the models used, we need to make sure fractional parts are equal in area. Base-ten blocks are sometimes mysterious to students, especially the thousands block because they see only six hundreds on the sides. Wooden base-ten blocks are accurate mathematically, but we need to make sure students understand the mathematics accurately.

As our students use manipulatives to find needed sums, differences, products, and quotients, we must make it clear that we value their solution attempts. At the same time we can challenge students to provide evidence that what they are doing always works. Then, if we choose to guide them toward a paper-and-pencil procedure, we simply encourage them to record what they are doing. Ideally, their manipulations can be recorded on paper step by step.

Game-like activities using a pattern board are sometimes used after students have informally worked out solutions with manipulatives, if more direct instruction in conventional algorithms is desired. Such activities for addition, subtraction, and division of whole numbers are described in Appendix D. The pattern board serves as an organizing center; and a step-by-step record of what is done on the board turns out to be a conventional algorithm that can be seen as a mathematical representation of what was observed. The paper-and-pencil computation procedure makes sense to students because they have observed relationships and patterns; they have a visual referent for the algorithm itself.

As our students reflect on their experiences with representations, we will frequently want them to talk and write about what they have done and observed.

# ■ Developing Mathematical Vocabulary

Concepts and principles are named with words and expressed with words and symbols. And it is possible that many of our students will stumble over the specialized vocabulary associated with mathematics. A term may not be associated with the appropriate concept, or a concept understood may not be given the appropriate name. From time to time, something akin to the overgeneralizing and overspecializing illustrated in Chapter 1 is likely to happen as our students learn concepts and procedures. The result is muddled communication and confused thinking.

For younger students, a general teaching strategy is to introduce words and symbols as a way of describing and recording what students have already observed and know informally.[7] They use words informally; their math ideas are not expressed in final form initially—but that is also true of professional mathematicians. If we begin with students' very informal language—often the way students describe situations—we may be able to introduce more precise terminology in apposition to the informal language, gradually dropping the informal language.

For example, the term *addend* can be developed while students are examining sets separated into two subsets. The number of items in each subset and the total number of items are recorded. At first, the number of items in each subset is informally called the "number for the part." Later, something like "the number for this part, *or addend*, is 5," is appropriate. Eventually this leads to expressions like, "What is the other addend?" Often older students can simply be told, "We call the number for a part (or subset) an addend."

Some people seem to think that mathematics is culture-free because it involves numbers. But *learning* mathematics involves language, and, obviously, that is *not* culture-free. For example, in Japanese, the fraction called "one fourth" in English is *yon bun no ichi;* the denominator is read first, and the expression means "one of the four partitions." Japanese more clearly points to a part-whole interpretation of a fraction.[8]

We should not be in a hurry for our students to use precise mathematical terms. Before we emphasize precise terminology our students need opportunities to investigate, describe what they find, and explain ideas.

When our students learn mathematical vocabulary, they need to make connections with concepts and terms they already know. It is often helpful for them to connect with root meanings and related words. For example, the "nom" in denominator means "to name." A denominator names a fraction; it indicates the kind of fraction, the size of the parts. And "numer" in numerator suggests "number." A numerator tells the number of parts.

A concept web or a simple diagram may help those who are visually oriented. Figure 11.1 shows that the relationship between factors and multiples can be illustrated.

We may want to have students focus on mathematical vocabulary by writing on cards the terms they encounter. We can have students place the cards in categories such as the following—a few of the categories of difficulty described and illustrated by Rubenstein and Thompson.[9]

- Words that are also used in everyday English, but with different meanings
  (e.g., foot, reflection)
- Words with more than one mathematical meaning
  (e.g., square, second)
- Words that are homonyms with everyday English words
  (e.g., sum, arc, pi)
- Words or patterns with irregularities
  (e.g., four, but forty)

Sometimes we can make mathematical vocabulary clearer if we employ one of the key concepts of school mathematics—the idea that a number has many names. For instance, the term *factorization* is sometimes confusing. Factorizations

**FIGURE 11.1**  Diagram for factors and multiples.

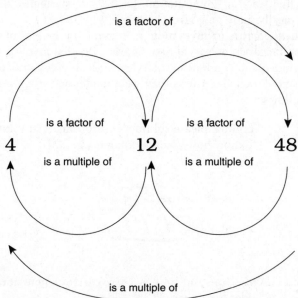

are particularly useful names for numbers, especially factorizations that consist solely of prime numbers; they are called "prime factorizations." Changing a fraction to an equivalent fraction involves another use of the idea that a number has many names. This process involves finding a different name for the same number, a name that is more useful for the purposes at hand.

As our students acquire and use mathematical vocabulary, we need to support classroom talk about mathematics that moves away from very specific contexts and moves toward applications of mathematical ideas in varied contexts.

---

For suggestions for teaching mathematical vocabulary, see the following.

- Murray, M. (2004). *Teaching mathematics vocabulary in context: Windows, doors, and secret passageways*. Portsmouth, NH: Heinemann.
- O'Connell, S. (2005). *Now I get it: Strategies for building confident and competent mathematicians, K–6* (Chapter 6). Portsmouth, NH: Heinemann.

---

## ■ Talking and Writing Mathematics

Talking mathematics and writing mathematics are teaching strategies that enhance learning. They give our students opportunities to relate the everyday language of their world to the language and symbols of mathematics. Both strategies can be used while teaching computation. Of the two strategies, the writings of students are typically more reflective.

Talking mathematics involves more risk taking on the part of students than does writing mathematics, at least at first. One activity that involves talking mathematics is for students to conduct an interview with an older adult to learn about specific paper-and-pencil algorithms they were taught and use now. Part of such an interview follows.

STUDENT:      Grandpa, please subtract this for me. And think out loud so I'll know how you are doing it.

$$\begin{array}{r} 253 \\ -179 \\ \hline \end{array}$$

GRANDPA:      OK. Nine and four is 13. Write four here and put the one under the seven.

$$-\frac{\begin{array}{r}253\\179\end{array}}{4}$$

Eight and seven is 15. Write seven here. . . .

STUDENT:      (later) That's different! Does it always work? . . . Why does it work? . . .

When students explain mathematical topics in a journal, it serves not only as a record of student learning, but also helps students clarify their thoughts. Journal writing can be done for different audiences. Often, journals are part of a written dialogue with the teacher in which students express how they feel about mathematics, what they know with confidence, when they believe that knowledge can be used, and questions they may have.

We may want our students to keep two journals: one to write what they know or have learned, and another to tell how they feel about specific experiences in mathematics. Journal writing can help students focus and ask appropriate questions; those who do not like to ask questions in class may be more likely to write their questions.

Journal writing is sometimes stimulated by prompts that we provide. Examples of appropriate prompts include: "I learned _____." "I was pleased that I _____." "I am most proud of _____." And "I wish _____." If our students have difficulty responding in writing to prompts, we may need to demonstrate on chart paper or the board for them to observe. Select a prompt and ask students to suggest what should be written. Involve them in thinking together about what is to be written, then show how to complete the prompt.[10]

We need to read the writings of our students diagnostically. For example, if a student demonstrates with manipulatives and explains what he did and why he did it in his journal, possibly by making a drawing but also writing words, we need to read his journal diagnostically and look for evidences of student learning and possible misconceptions. These personal stories can often be used to promote interaction—talking mathematics.[11]

Journals are not the only way to write mathematics. Activities such as the following can help students focus on what they are learning.

- Write out definitions in your own words.
- In your own words, write out the most important information about finding equivalent fractions.
- Write test questions about what you studied today.
- Describe any places you had difficulty and how you worked it out.
- Write questions about what you do not understand. (Merely writing them may help reduce anxiety.)
- Use a Solve and Comment Page for practice (see Figure 11.2).

**FIGURE 11.2** Solve and comment page.

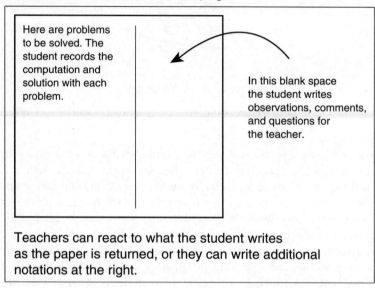

Here are problems to be solved. The student records the computation and solution with each problem.

In this blank space the student writes observations, comments, and questions for the teacher.

Teachers can react to what the student writes as the paper is returned, or they can write additional notations at the right.

Some of the following activities require students to produce written (or oral) explanations related to computation.

- Write how you would teach your cousin to add decimals.
- Write a letter to a student who was absent, and explain what is most important to understand about multiplying decimals.
- Use a hand puppet to explain to your younger sister how to subtract two-digit numbers.
- Make a poster or a bulletin board that explains how to divide whole numbers.

Students, individually or in groups, can respond to computations others have completed by talking and writing mathematics; both correctly and incorrectly worked-out examples can be included. Following is an example of a task that accompanies a paper with an error pattern similar to those illustrated in this book.

Score, analyze, and discuss each example.

For incorrect examples, describe in writing:
- what was done incorrectly,
- what should be done instead and why, and
- illustrate a correct procedure.

There are many occasions for talking and writing mathematics. Here is a list of additional things we can do to have our students write mathematics.

- Before a lesson, have students write in their journals to describe what they expect to happen. Later, students can write how they felt during the lesson.
- Have students do reflective writing to prepare for a discussion.
- Encourage students to write a math autobiography. You can stimulate similar writings with sentence starters.
- Have students write word problems of their own. You can supply the data, or they can supply their own.
- Have students write and solve word problems for which a particular computational procedure would be appropriate.
- Let students write a story that teaches a math concept. For example, a young child could write a story to teach "the number 7" or "place value."
- Encourage students to write a report or a book on a mathematical topic. Examples include numeration systems and algorithms used by different peoples.

As we teach we need to make frequent use of graphic organizers. They are another way our students can write and draw to show what they know.

## ■ Using Graphic Organizers for Instruction

Graphic organizers can enhance much of our instruction in mathematics, whether they are used for regular developmental instruction or for interventions with students experiencing difficulty. Because graphic organizers are another way our students can demonstrate their understanding, they are a means of assessment. Whenever we use graphic organizers to provide the support needed for a student to succeed with challenging work, we provide scaffolding for further learning. When students create or extend graphic organizers, they use writing and drawing to organize ideas and show what they understand.

Many types of graphic organizers can be incorporated into the teaching of mathematics, including computation. Here are some examples.

*Diagrams.* Many of the ways students represent and explain relationships are called diagrams; these are structural representations.[12] A number line is one example. Another example is a sequence chain, in which a sequence of boxes or a row of chain links shows successive steps in a process.

*Drawings.* Children can draw pictures of things their family buys at the grocery store, complete with price tags, and use them in constructing problems.

*Charts.* Fraction cards like $\frac{2}{6}$ and $\frac{5}{8}$ can be sorted in columns headed Less Than a Half, Names for One Half, and Greater Than a Half.

*Venn diagrams.* Phrase cards like $\boxed{100-99}$ and $\boxed{8 \div 8}$ and fraction cards can be placed in two overlapping circles, one labeled Fractions and the other labeled Names for One.

*Webs and concept maps.* Relationships among operations and among numbers are often shown with concept maps.[13] An example of a web to be completed with cards by young children appears in Figure 11.3.

**FIGURE 11.3** A web for students to complete by sorting cards.

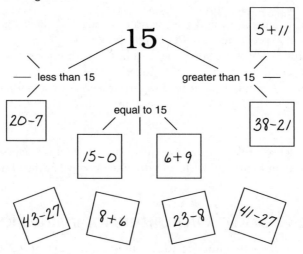

*Graphs.* Figure 11.4 illustrates a graph that students can make to record the results of their investigation regarding the number of basic addition facts for each sum.

**FIGURE 11.4** Graph for number of basic addition facts for each sum.

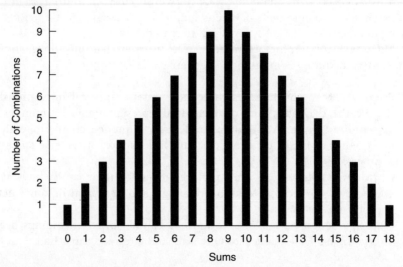

*Grids.* Grids typically display categories determined by two characteristics. Figure 11.5 illustrates a grid in which word problems on cards can be sorted by the operation required to determine the answer and by the most appropriate method for the computation.

**FIGURE 11.5** Grid for sorting word problem cards by most appropriate method of computation and by operation needed to find the answer.

|  | Estimate | Paper | Mental | Calculator |
|---|---|---|---|---|
| Add |  |  |  |  |
| Subtract |  |  |  |  |
| Multiply |  |  |  |  |
| Divide |  |  |  |  |

As you sort word problems, assume you have paper and pencil at hand, and it would take you about two minutes to locate a calculator.

*Procedural maps.* Figure 11.6 illustrates a procedural map for estimating the sum of two-digit numbers.

**FIGURE 11.6** Procedural map for estimating the sum of two-digit numbers.

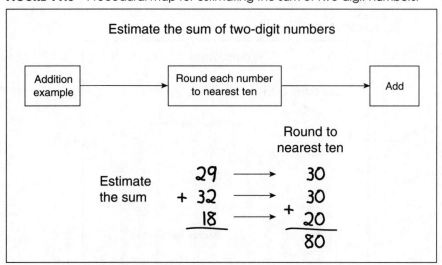

*Bar models.* Sometimes used to represent verbal problems, bar models are used extensively in early childhood texts associated with Singapore Math. Consider this problem.

> Bruce and Gary have 325 baseball cards.
> Bruce has 186 baseball cards.
> How many baseball cards does Gary have?

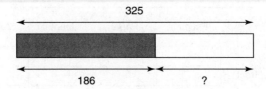

*Flowcharts.* Illustrations appear in Figures 11.7, 11.8, and 11.9. Flowcharts are of particular interest for teaching computational procedures. We can use concept maps and flowcharts to summarize what has already been taught. To use them to assess student understanding, have students write in empty blanks or boxes within the maps and charts.

To teach simple flowchart procedures, make a chart available for reference that shows the basic shapes and how they are used. Figure 11.7 is an example of such a chart. When teaching how to make a simple flowchart, focus on procedures for simple mathematical tasks. Figure 11.8 is an example of a flowchart developed to show how to choose the greatest of several whole numbers.

**FIGURE 11.7**  Basic shapes for flowcharts.

**FLOWCHARTS**

**Use these shapes.**

◯  **Start, or stop**

▭  **Do**

◇  **Decide (yes, or no)**

**FIGURE 11.8** An example of a flowchart.

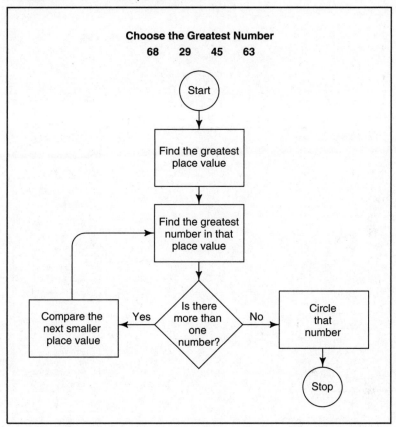

Sometimes teachers provide a flowchart in which all of the shapes are blank. They also give students each of the individual shapes that have instructions written in them. Students cut out the shapes and decide where to paste them on the blank flowchart.

After our students have learned how to make a flowchart, we can have pairs of students, and eventually individuals, create flowcharts for paper-and-pencil computation procedures. Figure 11.9 is a flowchart for adding fractions prepared by a fourth-grade boy. Make sure that student-generated flowcharts are tested; other students can follow the chart step by step to see if the chart is complete and accurate.

Near the end of the school year, some teachers have their students record computational procedures they have learned during the year by making flowcharts they can take with them to their new classrooms.

**FIGURE 11.9** A fourth grader's flowchart for adding fractions.

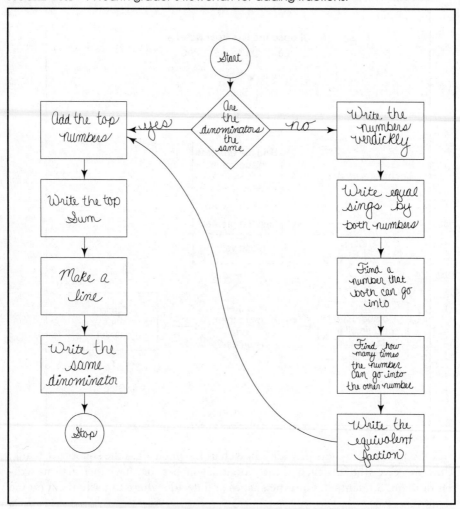

When our students use graphic organizers, we need to make sure they think carefully about what they are doing—especially if there is a potential for confusion. For example, sometimes math students use simple diagrams with legs to show basic facts and other addend pairs for a particular sum:

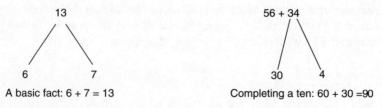

A basic fact: 6 + 7 = 13          Completing a ten: 60 + 30 =90

But when the same diagram is used to show place value, errors result if students are careless.

## ■ Using Classroom Discourse

We talk with our students as we teach mathematics. Indeed, classroom discourse can be viewed as an instructional strategy, whether we focus on concepts or procedures. It can also be viewed as a diagnostic tool when, during classroom discourse, teachers learn what individuals understand and can do and what is yet to be learned.

The National Council of Teachers of Mathematics (NCTM) likens a teacher's role in classroom discourse to orchestrating a piece of music: "[C]lassroom discourse has themes that pull together to create a whole that has meaning."[14]

As teachers we listen carefully and respond, then challenge thinking by asking questions that probe and guide thinking. We decide what to study in depth, and when to provide information or clarify. We create engaging tasks for students. We also monitor each student, and decide when and how to encourage.

Our students listen, respond, and ask questions of themselves and the teacher. But as they reason they make connections and representations. They present solutions and try to convince one another their solutions are valid.[15]

As teachers we will encourage classroom discourse in our mathematics classes if we involve students in thoughtful discussions about connections, representations, and graphic organizers; the writings of students can also be a focus of discourse. English language learners can benefit greatly from classroom discourse.

## ■ Using Portfolios to Monitor and Encourage Progress

Do your students have individual goals for learning mathematics? Can each student point to growth? Portfolios showcase student work and provide especially helpful insights into student growth and accomplishment.

Students may already have work folders for filing completed work or work in progress, but each of our students also needs to have a mathematics portfolio into which *selected* examples of mathematics work are placed. It is appropriate to require certain papers to be included in their portfolios, but students should be encouraged to select many or even most of the items—items *they* especially value or believe show growth or creativity.

During instruction we can have our students reflect on work that they completed early in the year, and compare it with more recent work, thereby enabling them to practice self-assessment. If we want our students to understand why a certain computational procedure works, for instance, we may want to have them select the item from their work folder that *best* demonstrates their understanding of *why* the procedure works and place it in their mathematics portfolio. Obviously, when we conference with parents, mathematics portfolios will be very useful.

Our purposes for having students develop mathematics portfolios will determine many of the types of items included. We may want to suggest that students include several of the following:

- Papers showing more than one way to solve a problem
- Papers showing why a traditional algorithm works
- Papers illustrating an alternative algorithm (or an algorithm invented by the student) and explaining why it works
- Papers that show how the student has corrected errors or misunderstandings
- Problems developed by the student; solutions may be included
- Papers displaying graphic organizers developed by the student, for example, a table of equivalent fractions
- Drawings of how manipulatives were used in solving a problem
- Individual or group reports of a project, such as a statistical survey with graphs
- Notes from an interview with someone about some aspect of mathematics
- Papers that show how mathematics is used in other subject areas
- Artwork involving geometric patterns or mathematical relationships
- Scale drawings
- Homework, especially solutions to nonroutine problems
- Performance assessment tasks given periodically
- Mathematical autobiographies
- Writings describing how the student feels about mathematics class or "doing mathematics"
- Papers that respond to "What I Learned in Math Class Today"
- Papers that respond to "What I Learned from My Mistake," written by students who have adopted error patterns in specific computation procedures
- Notes from the teacher describing evidence the student understood a particular mathematical principle
- Self-assessment sheets for groups and for individuals

Or we may want to have our students select from their work folders the five best items relative to a specific topic and place them in their mathematics portfolios, along with a letter that explains why each was selected.

## CONCLUSION

In conclusion, teachers have found the following guidelines to be helpful. They provide a summary to keep in mind when teaching students who are having difficulty learning to compute.

### Focus on the Student

1. *Personalize instruction.* Even when students meet in groups for instruction, individuals must be assessed and programs must be planned for *individuals.* Some individual tutoring may be required.
2. *Believe the student is capable of learning.* A student who has met repeated failure needs to believe that she is a valued person and is capable of eventually acquiring the needed knowledge and skill. If you are to help, you must believe this, too.
3. *Make sure the student has the goals of instruction clearly in mind.* He needs to know the direction in which instruction is heading. He needs to know where it will head eventually ("I'll be able to subtract and get the right answers") and where it is headed immediately ("I'll soon be able to rename a number many different ways").
4. *Encourage self-assessment.* From the beginning, involve students in the assessment process. Let them help set goals for instruction.
5. *Provide the student with a means to observe any progress.* Portfolios and journals, as well as charts and graphs, can serve this function.
6. *Ensure consistent expectations.* Make sure you and the student's parents have the same expectations in regard to what the student will accomplish. People in the United States tend to assume that difficulties with learning result from a lack of ability; in many other countries, they are more likely to assume that difficulties are a result of insufficient effort. Be sure you and the student's parents are together in regard to such expectations.

### Involve Parents

7. *Teach them strategies for engaging their children.* Many parents need to be helped if their children are going to be helped. (See Appendix C.)
8. *Raise expectations if needed.* Some parents think, "I was never any good at math." They need to believe their child can learn. Failure is not the norm.

### Teach Concepts and Skills

9. *Start with what the student knows and build on that knowledge.* She probably already knows more than you realize. Corrective instruction should build on a student's strengths; it should consider what she is ready to learn. Typically, students need to understand subordinate mathematical concepts before they can be expected to integrate them into more complex ideas.

10. *Emphasize ideas that help a student organize what he learns.* Students often assume the concept or procedure they are learning applies only to the specific task they are involved in at the time. Connect new learnings with what the student already knows. When organized, new learnings can be more easily retrieved from memory as the need arises; also, they can be applied more readily in new contexts. Stress ideas such as multiple names for a number, commutativity, identity elements, and inverse relations.

11. *Stress the ability to estimate.* A student who makes errors in computation will become more accurate with the ability to determine the reasonableness of answers.

## Provide Instruction

12. *Base instruction on your diagnosis.* Take into account the patterns you observed while collecting data. What strengths can you build on? Plan instruction that is data driven.

13. *Use a great variety of instructional procedures and activities.* Be sure to choose activities that differ from the way the student was previously taught because he may associate previous instruction with fear and failure. Students develop ideas from experiences embodying the idea, and they typically perceive the concept as that which is common to all of the experiences. Therefore, variety is often necessary for adequate concept formation.

14. *Involve students in higher-order thinking activities.* If paper-and-pencil computation is your instructional goal, you may want to focus on a large problem or task that is challenging and interesting to the student. If instruction is to be fruitful, your goal must be to thoroughly engage the student; prompt him to *think about* what is happening during instruction.

15. *Connect content to experiences outside school.* A student who can tie what she is learning to experiences outside school is likely to be motivated to learn and be able to apply what she does learn.

16. *Encourage the student to think out loud while working through a problem situation.* Have him show how and explain why certain materials and procedures are being used. Speaking out loud often enables a student to focus more completely on the task at hand.

17. *Ask leading questions that encourage reflection.* Allow sufficient time for the student to reflect.

18. *Let the student state his understanding of a concept or procedure in his own language.* Do not always require the terminology of textbooks. It may be appropriate to say, for example, "Mathematicians have a special name for that idea, but I rather like your name for it!"

19. *Sequence instruction in smaller amounts of content when needed.* Some students having difficulty need smaller "chunks." A large task may overwhelm such students. When instruction is based on a sequence that leads to the larger task, these students can focus on more immediately attainable goals.

Help them to see that immediate goals lead along a path going in the desired direction.

20. *Move toward symbols gradually.* Move from manipulatives to two-dimensional representations and visualizations to the use of symbols.

21. *Emphasize careful penmanship and proper alignment of digits.* A student must be able to read the work and tell the value assigned to each place where a digit is written. Columns can also be labeled if appropriate.

## Use Concrete Materials

22. *Let the student choose from materials available.* Whenever possible, a student should be permitted to select a game or activity from materials that are available and that lead toward the goals of instruction. Identify activities for which the student has needed prerequisite skills and that lead to the goals of instruction; then let her have some choice in deciding what she will do.

23. *Encourage a student to use aids as long as they are of value.* Peer group pressure often keeps students from using aids even when the teacher places aids on a table; the use of aids needs to be encouraged actively. Occasionally, a student needs to be prompted to try thinking a process through with just paper and pencil, but students often give up aids when they feel safe without them. After all, using aids is time consuming.

## Provide Practice

24. *Make sure a student understands the process before assigning practice.* We have known for some time that, in general, drill reinforces and makes more efficient that which a student *actually* practices. In other words, if a student counts on his fingers to find a sum, drill will only tend to help him count on his fingers more efficiently. He may find sums more quickly, but he is apt to continue any immature procedure he is using. Avoid extensive use of practice activities at a time when they merely reinforce processes that are developmental. By looking for patterns of error and by conducting data-gathering interviews in an atmosphere in which incorrect responses are accepted, you can usually learn enough to decide if the student is ready for practice.

25. *Include problems or puzzles to solve.* Some of our practice activities need to be problems or puzzles that require students to compute while solving them. In this way, students not only gain practice with computational procedures, but they also apply skills they are learning. Examples of such activities are included in Appendix E; although the activities are designed for cooperative groups, several can be easily adapted for individual practice.

26. *Select practice activities that provide immediate confirmation.* When looking for games and drill activities to strengthen skills, choose activities that let students know immediately whether the answer is correct. Many

games, manipulatives, and teacher-made devices provide such reinforcement. For example, magic squares are often used to provide practice with
computation for all four operations—with fractions and decimals as well
as with whole numbers.[16]

27. *Spread practice time over several short periods.* Typically, a short series of
examples (perhaps five to eight) is adequate to observe any error pattern. Longer series tend to reinforce erroneous procedures. If a correct
procedure is being used, frequent practice with a limited number of
examples is more fruitful than occasional practice with a large number
of examples.

## FURTHER REFLECTION

Consider the following questions:

1. How do graphic organizers help students make connections?
2. We are cautioned not to be too quick about requiring students to use precise mathematical terms. Why is this wise counsel?
3. Give several examples of students "going both ways" between mathematical ideas and their representations. Why is it important for students to
   be able to "go both ways"?
4. Explain what the following statement means, and provide a specific example: Students do not learn if they are merely using manipulatives; they
   learn when they *reflect* on what they are doing while using manipulatives.
5. Are problems and applications varied sufficiently in your classroom so
   that students can use the concepts and procedures they learn in entirely
   different contexts beyond the classroom? Explain your answer.

## REFERENCES

1. Zambo, R., & Zambo, D. (December 2007/January 2008). Mathematics and the learning
   cycle: How the brain works as it learns mathematics. *Teaching Children Mathematics*
   14(5), 268.
2. Sprenger, M. (2005). *How to teach so students remember.* Alexandria, VA: Association
   for Supervision and Curriculum Development.
3. For a discussion of how the term *representations* is defined, see S. P. Smith. (2003).
   Representation in school mathematics: Children's representations of problems. In
   J. Kilpatrick, W. G. Martin, & D. Schifter (Eds.). *A research companion to principles and
   standards for school mathematics* (pp. 263–274). Reston, VA: National Council of
   Teachers of Mathematics.
4. Eisner, E. W. (2002). The kinds of schools we need. *Phi Delta Kappan 83*(8), 581.
5. Brizuela, B. M. (2004). *Mathematical development in young children: Exploring notations*
   (pp. 100–101). New York: Teachers College Press.
6. Roberts, S. K. (2007). Not all manipulatives and models are created equal.
   *Mathematics Teaching in the Middle School 13*(1), 9.

7. For an explanation and for illustrations of this strategy, see K. Cramer and L. Karnowski. (1995). The importance of informal language in representing mathematical ideas. *Teaching Children Mathematics* 1(6), 332–335.
8. Watanabe, T. (2002). Representations in teaching and learning fractions. *Teaching Children Mathematics* 8(8), 457–463.
9. Rubenstein, R., & Thompson, D. (2002). Understanding and supporting children's mathematical vocabulary development. *Teaching Children Mathematics* 9(2), 108.
10. O'Connell, S. (2005). *Now I get it: Strategies for building confident and competent mathematicians, K–6* (p. 77). Portsmouth, NH: Heinemann.
11. See Whitin, D. J., & Whitin, P. E. (1998). The "write" way to mathematical understanding. In L. J. Morrow and M. J. Kenney (Eds.). *The teaching and learning of algorithms in school mathematics* (pp. 161–169). Reston, VA: National Council of Teachers of Mathematics.
12. For a discussion of diagrams, see C. M. Diezmann & L. D. English. (2001). Promoting the use of diagrams as tools for thinking. In A. A. Cuoco & F. R. Curcio (Eds.). *The roles of representation in school mathematics* (2001 yearbook) (pp. 77–89). Reston, VA: National Council of Teachers of Mathematics.
13. See A. J. Baroody & B. H. Bartels. (2000). Using concept maps to link mathematical ideas. *Mathematics Teaching in the Middle School* 5(9), 604–609.
14. National Council of Teachers of Mathematics. (1991). *Professional standards for teaching mathematics* (p. 35). Reston, VA: The Council.
15. See National Council of Teachers of Mathematics. (1991). Professional standards for teaching mathematics (pp. 35–54). Reston, VA: The Council. Also see M. Ben-Yehuda, I. Lavy, L. Linchevski, & A. Sfard. (2005). Doing wrong with words: What bars students' access to arithmetical discourses. *Journal for Research in Mathematics Education* 36(3), 176–247.
16. See G. A. Watson. (2003). The versatile magic square. *Mathematics Teaching in the Middle School* 8(5), 252–255.

# Glossary

**algebra** A generalized arithmetic in which letters (often squares or triangles in elementary schools) represent numbers. Information can be represented and problems solved.

**algorithms** Step-by-step procedures for accomplishing a task, such as solving a problem. In this text the term usually refers to paper-and-pencil procedures for finding a sum, difference, product, or quotient.

**alternative assessments** Nontraditional means of collecting information about student learning. They are often contrasted with more traditional paper-and-pencil tests.

**arithmetic** A branch of mathematics concerned with nonnegative real numbers and applications of the operations addition, subtraction, multiplication, and division.

**assessment** The gathering of information about student learning. When methods or strategies for assessment are varied, more satisfactory judgments can be made about past learning and about instruction that is appropriate.

**basic number facts (or basic combinations)** Simple equations or number sentences involving two one-digit whole numbers and their sum or product. Examples include $6 + 7 = 13$, $13 - 7 = 6$, $6 \times 8 = 48$, and $48 \div 8 = 6$. Altogether there are 390 basic facts of arithmetic, and they can be written either horizontally or vertically.

**buggy algorithms** Step-by-step procedures with at least one erroneous step; as a result the procedure does not always accomplish the intended task. When used to refer to paper-and-pencil computational procedures, buggy algorithms are often computational procedures with an error pattern.

**computation** The process of making a calculation. An estimate is sufficient for some situations; at other times an exact number is required. Computation can be done mentally, with a calculator (or computer), or by means of a paper-and-pencil algorithm—whichever is most appropriate.

**conceptual learning** In mathematics learning that focuses on ideas and on generalizations that make connections among ideas, in contrast to learning that focuses only on skills and step-by-step procedures without explicit reference to mathematical ideas.

**conceptual maps** Graphic organizers that show the interrelationships of ideas and processes for a particular area of content.

**concrete materials** Instructional materials that can be handled and moved about as mathematical ideas and processes are modeled. They are often three-dimensional but may be two-dimensional. Concrete materials are often called manipulatives.

**cooperative groups** Small groups of students who work together on mathematical tasks. Students communicate mathematical ideas and help each other learn.

**corrective instruction** May be similar to developmental instruction; however, it is not initial teaching of the concept or procedure. A student has somehow failed to learn or has learned misconceptions, and corrective instruction is needed.

**developmental instruction** Usually refers to the initial teaching of a concept or procedure such as an algorithm. It is planned instruction that gives careful attention to learning concepts as well as procedures. Developmental instruction for paper-and-pencil procedures usually involves the use of manipulatives.

**diagnosis** The process of investigating a student's condition in regard to learning mathematics. Data are collected to determine what the student knows and can do, and what concepts and processes are yet to be learned. Typically, a judgment is made about appropriate next steps for instruction.

**diagnostic interviews** Interviews conducted one-on-one with individuals in which the interviewer presents opportunities to demonstrate mathematical understanding and skill, and attempts to determine how the student is thinking. Modeling of mathematical concepts or procedures is often involved.

**diagnostic teaching** Moves back and forth between collecting data about students and providing instruction. It responds frequently, even within a single lesson, to evidences that individual students are or are not learning particular concepts and skills.

**digits** The symbols we use to create numerals. In our Hindu-Arabic numeration system we use 0, 1, 2, 3, 4, 5, 6, 7, 8, and 9. *Multi*-digit numerals are composed of two or more digits. The term digit comes from the Latin *digitus*, for "finger."

**equals** The same or identical in mathematical value, and is expressed with an equals sign (=). We say that 5 and 2 + 3 represent (or name) the same number; they express the same amount; they are equal; $5 = 2 + 3$, and $2 + 3 = 5$.

**equivalent expressions** Names for the same idea. For example, equivalent numerical expressions are names for the same number: $6 + 7$ and $13$ name the same number, as do $\frac{1}{2}$ and $\frac{2}{4}$.

**error patterns** Patterns observed within student work whenever an action is taken regularly that does not lead in every case to a correct result; some error patterns produce correct results part of the time. Error patterns are most commonly observed within the written work of students.

**evaluation** The process of making judgments about student achievement or about instruction needed. Evaluations should be based on data collected.

**formative evaluation** Assessment data are gathered before completion of a particular lesson or unit of instruction, and decisions are made about how instruction should continue.

**graphic organizers** Graphic representations that help learners organize information in their thinking. Examples include charts, diagrams, webs, conceptual maps, and number lines. They help students connect mathematical concepts and procedures.

**informal assessment** Assessment without the planning that typically precedes tests and performance tasks. Unplanned observations and incidental notations are examples of informal assessment.

**invented algorithms** Usually refers to paper-and-pencil computational procedures invented by students, often with encouragement and guidance from a teacher while students are solving problems with the aid of concrete materials.

**low-stress algorithms** Paper-and-pencil computational procedures that involve only minimal information held in short-term memory while executing the procedure. Typically, recall of number combinations is straightforward, and renaming is facilitated through nonstandard notation.

**manipulatives** Concrete materials used during instruction.

**mental computation** The process of making an exact calculation mentally, without the aid of a calculator, a computer, or a paper-and-pencil procedure. Mental computation relies heavily on important mathematical understandings; examples include the distributive property and principles related to numeration and compensation.

**minuend** The sum or total amount in a subtraction situation. In $35 - 17 = 18$, the 35 is the minuend.

**models** Representations of concepts and principles to be understood, processes to be learned, and problems to be solved. Concrete materials can be used to model mathematical ideas such as numerical concepts, spatial concepts, principles of numeration, and operations; and mathematical statements can model complex relationships and problem situations.[1]

**number combinations.** *See* basic number facts.

**number sense** Can be thought of as the informal "feel" that students develop for quantities, their relationships, and the effects of operating on numbers.

**numeracy** The disposition and ability to use mathematical knowledge and skills appropriately and effectively in everyday situations.

**numeration** Systems of counting or numbering, especially symbol systems used to represent numbers. Patterns among place values are a major focus of the study of our own Hindu-Arabic numeration system for recording whole numbers. Decimals are an extension of the system.

**operations** Mathematical processes whereby one number is derived from others. Arithmetic is concerned with four operations: addition, subtraction, multiplication, and division.

**overgeneralizing** The process of deriving conclusions that can be applied more broadly than justified. Students overgeneralize when they jump to a conclusion before they have adequate data on hand.

**overspecializing** The process of deriving conclusions that are restricted inappropriately. This may happen because students focus on irrelevant attributes of a limited number of instances.

**peer assessment** When students thoughtfully consider examples of work by other students, keeping specific criteria in mind.

**peer tutoring** When students instruct one another: questioning, explaining, and demonstrating concepts and procedures.

**portfolios** Collections of student work over time that can be used to aid student self-assessment. Typically, they provide varied sources of information for evaluating student learning.

**proceduralization** The process whereby a practiced procedure becomes more automatic over time; increasingly, less conceptual knowledge and more procedural knowledge is used as the procedure is executed.

**procedural learning** In mathematics learning that focuses on learning skills and step-by-step procedures; in practice it does not always include understanding of mathematical concepts and principles involved. However, procedural learning should be tied to conceptual learning and to real-life applications.

---

1. For a discussion of modeling, see National Council of Teachers of Mathematics. (2000). *Principles and standards for school mathematics* (pp. 70–71). Reston, VA: The Council.

**rational numbers** Numbers that can be expressed in the form $\frac{a}{b}$, in which $a$ and $b$ are integers and $b \neq 0$. In this text rational numbers are expressed with fractions, decimals, and percents.

**rubrics** Criteria for scoring a product or performance, usually organized so that levels are designated and indicators are described.

**self-assessment** When individuals reflect on their learning, examine what they have done, and thoughtfully evaluate their own learning. Self-assessment should note accomplishments as well as make comparisons with standards and criteria.

**standards** What students should know and be able to do. They are statements about what is valued in mathematics teaching and learning.

**subtrahend** The known addend in a subtraction situation. In $35 - 17 = ?$, the 17 is the subtrahend.

**summative evaluation** When assessment data are gathered after completion of a particular unit of instruction, and judgments are made about student learning. It usually involves a test, completion of projects, or a culminating performance task. Summative evaluations can point to the effectiveness of the instructional unit itself.

**whole numbers** Non-negative integers: $\{0, 1, 2, 3, \ldots \}$.

# Key for Additional Practice

1. The sum of all digits is determined, regardless of place value.
2. The minuend is subtracted from both the ones and the tens.
3. This student appears to use key words like *left* to indicate he should subtract; but the unknown is the total amount, and addition should be used to find the total amount.
4. When multiplying by the tens digit, both reminder numbers are added.
5. The numerators are added and recorded as the new numerator. The greater denominator is used as the new denominator because the lesser denominator "will go into" the greater denominator.
6. After the least common denominator is determined, the student computes the numerator by multiplying the original denominator times the whole number and then adding the original numerator.
7. The rule for placing the decimal point in a product is applied to a sum.
8. This student renames unlike fractions so they have a common denominator before multiplying the numerators. The common denominator is used for the denominator in the product. The student's procedure is very similar to the correct procedure for *adding* unlike fractions.
9. The whole numbers and common fractions are multiplied independently.
10. This student copies the example, and then she divides as if both numbers were whole numbers. After dividing, decimal points are placed within the dividend and the divisor as they were originally. Finally, a point is placed within the quotient above the decimal point in the dividend.
11. In these examples, the student *always* found the difference using absolute values; if the first addend was negative, the student affixed a negative sign.
12. All minus signs and signs of negation are counted. If there is an even number of signs, the absolute values are added. If there is an odd number of signs, absolute values are subtracted.
13. Rather than adding square roots, the student adds numbers under square root signs.

# Selected Resources

The annotated listing of resources that follows is divided into two categories: **Assessment and Diagnosis** and **Instruction**. Many of the resources listed in one category contain information for the other.

## Assessment and Diagnosis

ALLSOPP, D., LOVIN, L., GREEN, G., & SAVAGE-DAVIS, E. (2003). Why students with special needs have difficulty learning mathematics and what teachers can do to help. *Mathematics Teaching in the Middle School 8*(6), 308–314. The authors describe different kinds of problems that students with special needs have when learning mathematics, and suggest practical ways teachers can help. They stress the need to begin instruction at a student's current level of understanding.

BARLOW, A. T., & DRAKE, J. M. (February 2008). Assessing understanding through problem writing: Division by a fraction. *Mathematics Teaching in the Middle School 13*(6), 326–332. The authors show how verbal problems written by students can indicate levels of understanding of division by fractions.

BEHREND, J. L. (2001). Are rules interfering with children's mathematical understanding? *Teaching Children Mathematics 8*(1), 36–40. Behrend shows how students sometimes misinterpret our statements or "rules," and apply them inappropriately. The author also illustrates how instruction can be structured to confront misconceptions and provide opportunities to consider mathematical relationships and principles.

BEN-YEHUDI, M., LAVY, I., LINCHEVSKI, L., & SFARD, A. (2005). Doing wrong with words: What bars students' access to arithmetical discourses. *Journal for Research in Mathematics Education 36*(3), 176–247. Using interviews, the authors searched for factors that impede students' participation in arithmetic communication. With the help of arithmetical discourse profiles, they were able to make interesting and useful observations.

BRIGHT, G. W., JOYNER, J. M., & WALLIS, C. (2003). Assessing proportional thinking. *Mathematics Teaching in the Middle School 9*(3), 166–172. The authors illustrate and discuss items to assess proportional thinking. A helpful list of references is included.

COHEN, L. G., & SPENCINER, L. J. (2003). *Assessment of children and youth with special needs*, 2nd ed. Boston, MA: Allyn and Bacon. The authors address a full range of issues regarding assessment of students with special needs. Chapter 11 is concerned specifically with mathematics.

CORWIN, R. (2002). Assessing children's understanding: Doing mathematics to assess mathematics. *Teaching Children Mathematics 9*(4), 229–233. Corwin illustrates how a collection of coins can be used as a diagnostic tool.

Cox, L. S. (1975). Systematic errors in the four vertical algorithms in normal and handi-capped populations. *Journal for Research in Mathematics Education, 6,* 202–220. Cox documents the fact that many children use specific erroneous procedures. Data on the frequency of selected error patterns are included.

Dooren, W. V., DeBock, D., Verschaffel, L., & Janssens, D. (2003). Improper applications of proportional reasoning. *Mathematics Teaching in the Middle School 9*(4), 204–209. The authors illustrate improper applications of proportional reasoning as they report the results of interviews with 12-year-old and 16-year-old students working with the area of an enlarged irregular figure.

Drake, J. M., & Barlow, A. T. (2007 December/2008 January). Assessing students' levels of understanding multiplication through problem writing. *Teaching Children Mathematics 14*(5), 272–277. The authors illustrate how students' levels of understanding multipli-cation can be assessed as students write word problems in response to prompts.

Ellemor-Collins, D. L., & Wright, R. J. (2008 September). Assessing student thinking about arithmetic: Videotaped interviews. *Teaching Children Mathematics 14*(2), 106–111. The authors describe videotaped interview-based assessment, and tell when and how it can be used to inform instruction.

Graeber, A. O., & Baker, K. M. (1992 April). Little into big is the way it always is. *The Arithmetic Teacher, 39,* 18–21. The authors conclude that many children believe you "always take the little into the big" and "all operations are commutative." They also observe that children do not connect what they know about fractions with division of whole numbers. Suggestions for instruction in grades 4 and above are included.

Keiser, J. M., Klee, A., & Fitch, K. (2003). An assessment of students' understanding of angle. *Mathematics Teaching in the Middle School 9*(2), 116–119. The authors report assessment tasks and misconceptions in regard to the definition of an angle, and discuss implications for teaching and learning.

Leatham, K. R., Lawrence, K., & Mewborn, D. S. (2005). Getting started with open-ended assessment. *Teaching Children Mathematics 11*(8), 413–419. The authors describe and illustrate open-ended assessment items. Characteristics of these items (or problems) are listed and challenges teachers face when introducing them are explained. Benefits for students and teachers are also discussed.

Mack, N. K. (2007 November). Gaining insights into children's geometric knowledge. *Teaching Children Mathematics 14*(4), 238–245. Mack describes a variety of interesting student activities that can help teachers assess students' ability to identify, analyze, and relate properties of different shapes.

Martinie, S. L., & Bay-Williams, J. M. (2003). Investigating students' conceptual under-standing of decimal fractions using multiple representations. *Mathematics Teaching in the Middle School 8*(5), 244–247. The authors illustrate how student understanding of decimal fractions can be diagnosed by having students make several different represen-tations for the same concept.

Maxwell, V. L., & Lassak, M. B. (2008 March). An experiment in using portfolios in the middle school classroom. *Mathematics Teaching in the Middle School 13*(7), 404–409. The authors describe how they used portfolios for assessment in order to improve teaching and learning.

McMillan, J. H. (2004). *Classroom assessment: Principles and practice for effective instruc-tion,* 3rd ed. Boston, MA: Pearson Education, Inc. This rather comprehensive text includes sections on assessing students with special needs and assessing dispositions.

Molina, M., & Ambrose, R. (2008). From an operational to a relational conception of the equals sign: Third graders' developing algebraic thinking. *Focus on Learning Problems in Mathematics 30* (Winter Edition), 61–80. The authors found that different types of number sentences reveal different student conceptions of equals. They observed three stages in the development of how equals is perceived.

Parke, C. S., Lane, S., Silver, E. A., & Magone, M. E. (2003). *Using assessment to improve middle-graders teaching & learning.* Reston, VA: National Council of Teachers of

Mathematics. Sample performance tasks, task packets, and rubrics are presented, as are activities that address issues relevant to using assessment to improve teaching and learning. The material is also contained on an accompanying CD.

RESNICK, L. B., NESHER, P., LEONARD, F., MAGONE, M., OMANSON, S., & PELED, I. (1989). Conceptual bases of arithmetic errors: The case of decimal fractions. *Journal for Research in Mathematics Education 20*(1), 8–27. The authors document major categories of errors as children learn decimal fractions, and establish conceptual sources for the errors. They suggest that error patterns cannot be avoided during instruction, and encourage educators to use them as diagnostic tools to determine children's understanding.

ROMBERG, T. A. (Ed.). (2004). *Standards-based mathematics assessment in middle school. Rethinking classroom practice.* New York: Teachers College Press. Researchers and teachers describe challenges they faced as they attempted to implement formative assessment procedures that document students' growth in understanding rather than merely testing what students know.

RON, P. (1998). My family taught me this way. In L. J. Morrow & M. J. Kenney (Eds.), *The Teaching and Learning of Algorithms in School Mathematics* (pp. 115–119). Reston, VA: National Council of Teachers of Mathematics. Ron illustrates difficulties, and errors, common among European and Latin American students when learning algorithms taught in the United States.

SALVIA, J., YSSELDYKE, J. E., & BOLT, S. (2007). *Assessment in special and inclusive education,* 10th ed. (pp. 455–469). Boston, MA: Houghton Mifflin Company. This text covers various aspects of assessment, including diagnostic mathematics tests.

SHERMAN, H. J., RICHARDSON, L. I., & YARD, G. J. (2005). *Teaching children who struggle with mathematics: A systematic approach to analysis and correction.* Columbus, OH: Merrill/Prentice Hall. The authors focus on cognitive needs of children in grades 1–6 as they present three steps to assess students' math strengths and weaknesses and plan instruction accordingly.

STEELE, D. F. (2007). Understanding students' problem-solving knowledge through their writing. *Mathematics Teaching in the Middle School 13*(2), 102–109. The author focuses on four types of knowledge as she illustrates different student writings and what she learned from them.

STEFANICH, G. P., & ROKUSEK, T. (1992). An analysis of computational errors in the use of division algorithms by fourth-grade students. *School Science and Mathematics 92*(4), 201–205. The authors classify incorrect responses of fourth graders (division algorithm for whole numbers) and study the effects of instruction for the systematic errors identified.

STENMARK, J. K. (Ed.). (1991). *Mathematics assessment: Myths, models, good questions, and practical suggestions.* Reston, VA: National Council of Teachers of Mathematics: This very useful publication provides mathematics educators with a handbook for alternative forms of assessment.

TAYLOR, A. R., BRECK, S. E., & ALJETS, C. M. (2004). What Nathan teaches us about transitional thinking. *Teaching Children Mathematics 11*(3), 138–142. The authors describe and discuss an interview of a first-grader that illustrates what they call "transitional thinking."

VANDERHYE, C. M., & DEMERS, C. M. Z. (2007 December/2008 January). Assessing students' understanding through conversations. *Teaching Children Mathematics 14*(5), 260–264. The authors illustrate how listening to student conversations while they are solving problems can be a means of formative assessment that leads to needed changes in instruction.

WARD, R. A. (2000). Observing high school students' strategies and misconceptions as they use graphing calculators. *Focus on Learning Problems in Mathematics 22*(3&4), 28–40. Ward stresses the need to take time to help students learn the features and shortcomings of graphing calculators, *prior* to using it to learn mathematics.

WARREN, E. (2003). Language, arithmetic and young children's interpretations. *Focus on Learning Problems in Mathematics 25*(4), 22–35. Warren reports her research on how young children comprehend the language of mathematics, and discusses their understanding of words commonly used in addition and subtraction.

WICKETT, M. S. (2003). Discussion as a vehicle for demonstrating computational fluency in multiplication. *Teaching Children Mathematics* 9(6), 318–321. Wickett describes her class discussion that focused on a carefully constructed series of multiplication problems. Students were given many opportunities to demonstrate computational fluency.

WOODWARD, J., & HOWARD, L. (1994). The misconceptions of youth: Errors and their mathematical meaning. *Exceptional Children* 61(2), 126–136. The authors discuss a technology-based diagnostic system and related research. In view of the frequency of misconceptions among students with learning disabilities and the widespread use of technology, they suggest much more emphasis on conceptual understanding.

---

**Two series of books on assessment published by the National Council of Teachers of Mathematics:**

*Mathematics Assessment Samplers* for PreK–2, Grades 3–5, Grades 6–8, and Grades 9–12.

*Classroom Assessment for School Mathematics, K–12 Series*
Practical Handbooks for Grades K–2, Grades 3–5, Grades 6–8, and Grades 9–12.
Cases and Discussion Questions for Grades K–5 and Grades 6–12.

---

## Instruction

AMOS, S. F. (2007). Talking mathematics. *Teaching Children Mathematics* 14(2), 68–73. The author illustrates the value of talking mathematics, even in a highly diverse urban classroom, and notes how students can be grouped to promote discussion.

AZIM, D. (2002). Understanding multiplication as one operation. *Mathematics Teaching in the Middle School* 7(8), 466–471. Azim discusses the belief of many students that multiplication "works as two different operations," and describes activities that may help students think of multiplication as *one* operation that can be used with both integers and rational numbers.

BARLOW, A. T. (2004). How can a box help my students with multiplying polynomials? *Mathematics Teaching in the Middle School* 9(9), 512–513. Barlow describes how a two-dimensional grid can help students organize their approach to multiplying polynomials.

BAROODY, A. J. (2006). Why children have difficulties mastering the basic number combinations and how to help them. *Teaching Children Mathematics* 13(1), 22–31. The author contrasts conventional wisdom about learning and mastering the basic facts of arithmetic with instruction supported by research. Specific activities are suggested.

BAROODY, A. J., & BARTELS, B. H. (2000). Using concept maps to link mathematical ideas. *Mathematics Teaching in the Middle School* 5(9), 604–609. The authors describe concept maps and their roles in instruction. Illustrations are included, as are teaching tips on getting started.

BAY-WILLIAMS, J. M., & MARTINIE, S. L. (2003). Thinking rationally about number and operations in the middle school. *Mathematics Teaching in the Middle School* 8(6), 282–287. The authors emphasize that a *deep* understanding of fractions, decimals, and percents that are used frequently supports student understanding of those rational numbers that are used less often; this requires a lot of varied experiences. The authors also focus on the meaning of operations and proportionality.

BEATTY, R., & MOSS, J. (2007). Teaching the meaning of the equal sign to children with learning disabilities: Moving from concrete to abstractions. In W. G. Martin, M. E. Strutchens, & P. C. Elliott (Eds.), *The Learning of Mathematics: 69th Yearbook* (pp. 27–41). Reston, VA: National Council of Teachers of Mathematics. The authors describe lessons that shift from procedural learning to relational learning, and various assessments.

BECK, I. L., McKEOWN, M. G., & KUCAN, L. (2002). *Bringing words to life: Robust vocabulary instruction.* New York: The Guilford Press. The resources provided in this book for helping students understand what words mean can easily be applied to instruction in mathematics.

BENDOR, W. N. (2002). *Differentiating instruction for students with learning disabilities.* Thousand Oaks, CA: Corwin Press, Inc. The author provides practical help for special educators and inclusive classroom teachers who seek to help students with learning disabilities and other low achievers. Concepts, examples, and strategies described include webbing, cubing, brain-compatible tactics, scaffolding, self-management, performance assessment, and peer tutoring systems.

BLEY, N. S., & THORNTON, C. A. (2001). *Teaching mathematics to students with learning disabilities,* 4th ed. Austin, TX: Pro-Ed. This methods text has many practical suggestions for helping students with learning disabilities learn number combinations and algorithms.

BORASI, R. (1994). Capitalizing on errors as "springboards for inquiry": A teaching experiment. *Journal for Research in Mathematics Education 25*(2), 166–208. This report examines how errors among secondary students can be used instructionally.

BRESSER, R. (2003). Helping English language learners develop computational fluency. *Teaching Children Mathematics 9*(6), 294–299. Bresser describes 10 strategies for helping English language learners communicate and develop computational fluency.

BRIZUELA, B. M. (2004). *Mathematical development in young children: Exploring notations.* New York: Teachers College Press. The author argues that children not only learn how to make the symbols but also develop concepts about the representations themselves. Data are presented from children ages 5–9.

BUCHHOLZ, L. (2004). Learning strategies for addition and subtraction facts: The road to fluency and the license to think. *Teaching Children Mathematics 10*(7), 362–367. Buchholz emphasizes learning doubles, and describes strategies for both addition and subtraction facts, many of which build on knowledge of doubles.

BURNS, M. (2004). Writing in math. *Educational Leadership 62*(2), 30–33. The author provides reasons for using writing in math classes, and she illustrates a variety of strategies for incorporating writing.

BURNS, M. (2007). Nine ways to catch kids up. *Educational Leadership 65*(3), 16–21. The author emphasizes that extra help for struggling learners of mathematics has to be more than extra practice, and she describes nine strategies for successful interventions. There is much wisdom here for teachers.

CLARK, F. B., & KAMII, C. (1996). Identification of multiplicative thinking in children in grades 1–5. *Journal for Research in Mathematics Education 27*(1), 41–51. The authors found that multiplicative thinking appears early and develops slowly, and conclude that the introduction of multiplication in second grade is appropriate for some students, but not for all of them.

CLARKE, D. M., ROCHE, A., & MITCHELL, A. (2008 March). Ten practical tips for making fractions come alive and make sense. *Mathematics Teaching in the Middle School 13*(7), 372–380. The authors provide specific suggestions and activities for making fractions more readily understandable for students.

CRESPO, S. M., & KYRIAKIDES, A. O. (2007). To draw or not to draw: Exploring children's drawings for solving mathematics problems. *Teaching Children Mathematics 14*(2), 118–125. The authors reflect on research regarding student use of drawings to solve problems, and emphasize the importance of helping students make connections between the problems they are solving and what they are drawing.

CRESPO, S., KYRIAKIDES, A. O., & McGEE, S. (2005). Nothing "basic" about basic facts: Exploring addition facts with fourth graders. *Teaching Children Mathematics 23*(2), 60–67. After describing different strategies for finding the missing number in basic fact questions, the authors describe two teaching experiments and report their conclusions.

CUOCO, A. A., & CUOCO, F. R. (Eds.). (2001). *The roles of representation in school mathematics (2001 Yearbook)*. Reston, VA: National Council of Teachers of Mathematics. This yearbook explains how students form abstractions and develop misunderstandings about mathematics. It explains how students build mathematical representations, and the interplay between modeling and representation.

FALKNER, K. P., LEVI, L., & CARPENTER, T. P. (1999). Children's understanding of equality: A foundation for algebra. *Teaching Children Mathematics 6*(4), 232–236. Noting that elementary school students generally think that an equals sign means to carry out the operation that precedes it, the authors describe instruction in which early grade students came to understand the equals sign as expressing the relationship "is the same as."

FERRER, B. B., HUNTER, B., IRWIN, K. C., SHELDON, M. J., THOMPSON, C. S., & VISTRO-YU, C. P. (2001). By the unit or square unit? *Mathematics Teaching in the Middle School 7*(3), 132–137. The authors discuss why area and perimeter concepts are difficult for many students, and describe lessons that can help them understand these concepts.

FOSNOT, C. T., & DOLK, M. (three books). In *Young mathematicians at work: Constructing multiplication and division* (2001), the authors stress the development of "big ideas" and multiple strategies. In *Young mathematicians at work: Constructing number sense, addition and subtraction* (2001), they argue for deep number sense and development of a repertoire of strategies that emphasize "landmark numbers." In *Young mathematicians at work: Constructing fractions, decimals, and percents* (2002), they address equivalence, developing "big ideas," strategies, mathematical models, and "efficient computation." All three books draw from the work of Hans Freudenthal. The publisher is Portsmouth, NH: Heinemann.

FUSON, K. C. (1990). Issues in place-value and multidigit addition and subtraction learning and teaching. *Journal for Research in Mathematics Education 21*(4), 273–280. Fuson argues for a sequence for teaching and learning about place-value and multidigit addition and subtraction in which problems with and without trades are presented at the same time.

FUSON, K. C. (2003). Developing mathematical power in whole number operations. In J. Kilpatrick, W. G. Martin, & D. Schifter (Eds), *A research companion to principles and standards for school mathematics* (pp. 68–94). Reston, VA: National Council of Teachers of Mathematics. Fuson presents thoughtful research-based discussions with conclusions in regard to a number of issues related to building computational fluency with the four whole-number operations.

FUSON, K. C. (2003). Toward computational fluency in multi-digit multiplication and division. *Teaching Children Mathematics 9*(6), 300–305. Fuson discusses and illustrates the teaching of various algorithms for the four operations on whole numbers, and notes that some algorithms are more effectively taught for understanding than others.

GORAL, M. B., & WIEST, L. R. (2007). An arts-based approach to teaching fractions. *Teaching Children Mathematics 14*(2), 74–80. The authors describe and reflect upon lessons on fractions that incorporate poetry, movement, and music.

GRAVEMEIJER, K., & VAN GALEN, F. (2003). Facts and algorithms as products of students' own mathematical activity. In J. Kilpatrick, W. G. Martin, & D. Schifter (Eds), *A research companion to principles and standards for school mathematics* (pp. 114–122). Reston, VA: National Council of Teachers of Mathematics. The authors describe the learning of facts and algorithms as a process building on number sense. They focus on guided reinvention by students and semi-informal algorithms.

GREGG, J., & GREGG, D. U. (2007). A context for integer computation. *Mathematics Teaching in the Middle School 13*(1), 46–50. The authors use an allowance context with the debit-credit model for integers, and illustrate how it can be used with operations on integers.

HANSELMAN, C. A. (1997). Stop using foul language in the mathematics classroom. *Mathematics Teaching in the Middle School 3*(2), 143–160. Hanselman argues against use of terms like *reduce, cancel, and invert* that cause students to focus only on the procedure, with little or no conceptual understanding.

HENRY, V. J., & BROWN, R. S. (2008). First-grade basic facts: An investigation into teaching and learning of an accelerated, high-demand memorization standard. *Journal for Research in Mathematics Education 39*(2), 153–183. This research report includes suggestions for improving basic-facts learning among early childhood students.

HEUSER, D. (2005). Teaching without telling: Computational fluency and understanding through invention. *Teaching Children Mathematics 11*(8), pp. 404–412. The author describes first- and second-graders exploring alternative computation procedures in a workshop environment.

HOVEN, J., & GARELICK, B. (2007 November). Singapore math: Simple or complex? *Educational Leadership 65*(3), 28–31. The authors illustrate how the bar model is used in Singapore textbooks to enable students to solve math problems and think symbolically.

HUTCHINGS, B. (1978). Low-stress algorithms. In D. Nelson & R. E. Reys (Eds.), *Measurement in school mathematics*. Reston, VA: National Council of Teachers of Mathematics. Hutchings describes and illustrates low-stress procedures for whole-number computation, algorithms that are especially useful with students experiencing difficulty with standard procedures.

HYDE, A. (2006). *Comprehending math: Adapting reading strategies to teach mathematics, K–6*. Portsmouth, NH: Heinemann. The author focuses on strategies like asking questions, making connections, visualization, inferring and predicting, determining importance, and synthesizing.

JENKINS, H. (2005). Getting into the game. *Educational Leadership 62*(7), 48–51. The author describes benefits from children playing games, and discusses the learning potential of games in classrooms.

JUDD, WALLACE (2007). Instructional games with calculators. *Mathematics Teaching in the Middle School 12*(6), 312–314. In this reprint, the author illustrates how calculators can be used to learn mathematical concepts. Games are described that can be adapted to many levels.

KAMII, C., & ANDERSON, C. (2003). Multiplication games: How we made and used them. *Teaching Children Mathematics 10*(3), 135–141. The authors describe how they made and used games involving basic multiplication combinations in a third-grade classroom. Some games are adaptations of other games, even commercial games.

KAMII, C., & LEWIS, B. A. (2003). Single-digit subtraction with fluency. *Teaching Children Mathematics 10*(4), 230–236. The authors note that a child who knows the sum of two single-digit numbers solidly can deduce quickly the part that is unknown when presented with the related subtraction combination. They argue that "we must de-emphasize fluency in subtraction in the first two grades and heavily emphasize addition."

KARP, K., & HOWELL, P. (2004). Building responsibility for learning in students with special needs. *Teaching Children Mathematics 11*(3), 118–126. The authors describe how instruction can be individualized by removing barriers, structuring the environment, incorporating more time and practice, and providing clarity.

KAZEMI, E. (1998). Discourse that promotes conceptual understanding. *Teaching Children Mathematics 4*(7), 410–414. Kazemi emphasizes the need to expect students to justify procedures—not just to state them—and discusses how this relates to the way teachers react to student errors.

KLINE, K. (2008 October). Learning to think and thinking to learn. *Teaching Children Mathematics 15*(3), 144–151. Kline describes ways classroom discourse can engage students and help them think more deeply.

KNUTH, E. J., ALIBALI, M. W., HATTIKUDUR, S., MCNEIL, N. M., & STEPHENS, A. C. (2008 May). The importance of equal sign understanding in the middle grades. *Mathematics Teaching in the Middle School 13*(9), 514–519. Students tend to view equals signs as indicating an operation rather than a relation. The authors tell why it is important for students to develop a relational view of the equals sign and, from their research, how to help students do that.

LAPPAN, G., & BOUCK, M. K. (1998). Developing algorithms for adding and subtracting fractions. In L. J. Morrow & M. J. Kenney (Eds.), *The teaching and learning of algorithms in school mathematics* (pp. 183–197). Reston, VA: National Council of Teachers of Mathematics. The authors describe experiences that enable students to learn about addition and subtraction with fractions in contexts that make sense to them.

LEUTZINGER, L. P. (1999). Developing thinking strategies for addition facts. *Teaching Children Mathematics* 6(1), 14–18. Leutzinger illustrates how students can use number combinations they know to determine ones they do not know.

LI, Y. (2008 May). What do students need to learn about division of fractions? *Mathematics Teaching in the Middle School* 13(9), 546–552. Students need to learn more than just the algorithm. The author shares a Chinese perspective which emphasizes connections with multiplication and applications.

LITWILLER, B. (Ed.). (2002). *Making sense of fractions, ratios, and proportions.* Reston, VA: National Council of Teachers of Mathematics. This yearbook provides insights into students' thinking and shows the importance of proportional reasoning as a foundation for many applications of mathematics. A supplementary booklet provides activities for teachers to use in their classrooms.

MACK, N. K. (2004). Connecting to develop computational fluency with fractions. *Teaching Children Mathematics* 11(4), 226–232. Mack shows how we can help students make connections with prior knowledge as they learn to add and subtract fractions.

MANOUCHEHRI, A., & ENDERSON, M. C. (1999). Promoting mathematical discourse: Learning from classroom examples. *Mathematics Teaching in the Middle School* 4(4), 216–222. The authors present and discuss a vignette of classroom discourse, and make suggestions for creating classroom discourse.

MILLER, J. L., & FEY, J. T. (2000). Proportional reasoning. *Mathematics Teaching in the Middle School* 5(5), 310–313. The authors illustrate how understanding and strategies for proportional reasoning can be built through guided collaborative work on authentic problems.

MORRIS, A. K. (2003). The development of children's understanding of equality and inequality relationships in numerical symbolic contexts. *Focus on Learning Problems in Mathematics* 25(2), 18–57. From her research, the author presents guidelines for introducing the equals sign in K–1, guidelines that stress comparing quantities, and developing the concept she calls "quantitative sameness."

MORROW, L. J., & KENNEY, M. J. (Eds.). (1998). *The teaching and learning of algorithms in school mathematics.* Reston, VA: National Council of Teachers of Mathematics. This yearbook focuses on issues and history, and also on curriculum and instruction at the elementary, middle, and high school levels.

MUNIER, V., DEVICHI, C., & MERLE, H. (2008 March). A physical situation as a way to teach angle. *Teaching Children Mathematics* 14(7), 402–407. The authors describe situations in the classroom, on the playground, and elsewhere that can help students develop the concept of angle.

MURRAY, M. (2004). *Teaching mathematics vocabulary in context: Windows, doors, and secret passageways.* Portsmouth, NH: Heinemann. Murray uses samples of student work to illustrate vocabulary as an integral part of teaching and learning mathematics. She provides very practical guidance for vocabulary development in the mathematics class.

MURREY, D. L. (2008 October). Differentiating instruction in mathematics for the English language learner. *Mathematics Teaching in the Middle School* 14(3), 146–153. Murrey provides language acquisition principles and strategies. Illustrations for teaching mathematics are included.

NATIONAL COUNCIL OF TEACHERS OF MATHEMATICS. (2000). *Principles and standards for school mathematics.* Reston, VA: The Council. Six foundational principles are established, then ten standards for grades PreK–12 are set forth and illustrated for each of four grade bands: PreK–2, 3–5, 6–8, and 9–12. There are five content standards and five process standards.

NURNBERGER-HAAG, J. (2007). Integers made easy: Just walk it off. *Mathematics Teaching in the Middle School 13*(2), 118–121. The author describes how students can literally walk off problems on number lines; students can walk off problems involving all four operations with integers. Response forms for student notes are provided.

OBERDORF, C. D., & TAYLOR-COX, J. (1999). Shape up! *Teaching Children Mathematics 5*(6), 340–345. The authors describe typical misconceptions in the elementary grades, and make suggestions for instruction that can avoid such misconceptions.

O'CONNELL, S. (2005). *Now I get it: Strategies for building confident and competent mathematicians, K–6*. Portsmouth, NH: Heinemann. The author provides a wealth of instructional strategies designed to help teachers teach concepts and skills while emphasizing problem solving and applications. An accompanying CD contains several classroom resources.

O'LOUGHLIN, T. A. (2007 October). Using research to develop computational fluency in young mathematicians. *Teaching Children Mathematics 14*(3), 132–138. O'Loughlin describes how she developed instructional interventions using "strings" to help students with specific conceptual and skill needs.

OLSON, J. C. (2007). Developing students' mathematical reasoning through games. *Teaching Children Mathematics 13*(9), 464–471. The author emphasizes playing the game yourself, planning how to introduce the game, and patience. The Product Game is illustrated for intermediate students.

PARKER, M. (2004). Reasoning and working proportionally with percent. *Mathematics Teaching in the Middle School 9*(6), 326–330. Parker describes a way to represent percent visually during instruction.

PERKINS, I., & FLORES, A. (2002). Mathematical notations and procedures of recent immigrant students. *Mathematics Teaching in the Middle School 7*(6), 346–351. The authors describe differences they observed in notation and algorithms used by students from Latin America and the United States.

PHILIPP, R. A. (1996). Multicultural mathematics and alternative algorithms. *Teaching Children Mathematics 3*(3), 128–133. Philipp describes alternative algorithms for operations with whole numbers. They are often associated with specific cultures.

POSTLEWAIT, K. B., ADAMS, M. R., & SHIH, J. C. (2003). Promoting meaningful mastery of addition and subtraction. *Teaching Children Mathematics 9*(6), 354–357. The authors emphasize understanding what the basic facts mean as they describe "Hiding Assessment," number talks, and math stations.

RAMBHIA, S. (2002). A new approach to an old order. *Mathematics Teaching in the Middle School 8*(4), 193–195. Rambhia demonstrates how students can use a table format to apply the rules of order for operations.

RANDOLPH, T. D., & SHERMAN, H. J. (2001). Alternative algorithms: Increasing options, reducing errors. *Teaching Children Mathematics 7*(8), 480–484. The authors illustrate alternative algorithms with whole numbers for each of the four operations.

RATHMELL, E. C. (1978). Using thinking strategies to teach the basic facts. In M. N. Suydam & R. E. Reys (Eds.), *Developing Computational Skills* (pp. 13–38). Reston, VA: National Council of Teachers of Mathematics. Thinking strategies are described for use when organizing instruction in number combinations for addition and multiplication.

RODDICK, C., & SILVAS-CENTENO, S. (2007 October). Developing understanding of fractions through pattern blocks and fair trade. *Teaching Children Mathematics 14*(3), 140–145. The authors describe a unit on fractions that uses fair trades with pattern blocks to illustrate equivalent fractions.

RUBENSTEIN, R. N. (2000). Word origins: Building communication connections. *Mathematics Teaching in the Middle School 5*(8), 493–497. Rubenstein illustrates how roots, meanings, and related words can make confusing mathematical terms easier to understand and remember.

SAXE, G. B., et al. (2007). Learning about fractions as points on a number line. In W. G. Martin, M. E. Strutchens, & P. C. Elliott (Eds.), *The Learning of Mathematics: 69th Yearbook* (pp. 221–237). Reston, VA: National Council of Teachers of Mathematics. The authors describe research on how students make sense out of points on a number line, and how teachers can help their students learn the big ideas of fractions on number lines.

SHERMAN, H. J., RICHARDSON, L. I., & YARD, G. J. (2009). *Teaching children who struggle with mathematics: Systematic intervention and remediation,* 2nd ed. Boston, MA: Pearson Education. The authors present steps to assess students' math strengths and weaknesses, and plan instruction designed to meet students' individual needs.

SLIVA, J. A. (2004). *Teaching inclusive mathematics to special learners, K–6.* Thousand Oaks, CA: Corwin Press, Inc. Sliva lists characteristics of students with learning disabilities and describes the impact on learning mathematics. Assessment is addressed and strategies for instruction are described.

SPRENGER, M. (2005). *How to teach so students remember.* Alexandria, VA: Association for Supervision and Curriculum Development. Sprenger discusses steps to help students receive information in working memory, store it in long-term memory, and use what they've learned when they need it. Forms for graphic organizers are provided in an appendix.

STEELE, M. M. (2002). Strategies for helping students who have learning disabilities in mathematics. *Mathematics Teaching in the Middle School 8*(3), 140–143. Steele describes characteristics of students with learning disabilities in mathematics and also instructional modifications that can help them learn.

STEIN, M. K., & BOVALINO, J. W. (2001). Manipulatives: One piece of the puzzle. *Mathematics Teaching in the Middle School 6*(6), 356–359. The authors describe factors associated with successful use of manipulatives, and caution that the use of manipulatives does not automatically result in learning.

STRONG, R., THOMAS, E., PERINI, M., & SILVER, H. (2004 February). Creating a differentiated mathematics classroom. *Educational Leadership 61*(5), 73–78. The authors describe different mathematical learning styles and how instruction and tests can be varied to accommodate them.

SUN, W., & ZHANG, J. Y. (2001 September). Teaching addition and subtraction facts: A Chinese perspective. *Teaching Children Mathematics 8*(1), 28–31. The authors describe how spoken language differences affect the learning of numeration and basic facts. The primary strategy taught by Chinese teachers for addition facts is "make 10." Teachers strongly emphasize using addition facts to do subtraction.

SWEENEY, E. S., & QUINN, R. J. (2000). Concentration: Connecting fractions, decimals, & percents. *Mathematics Teaching in the Middle School 5*(5), 324–328. The authors describe a series of lessons. A game is created, and there are assessments.

THORNTON, C. A., & BLEY, N. S. (2001). *Teaching mathematics to students with learning disabilities.* Austin, TX: Pro-Ed, Inc. Practical approaches are described for helping learning disabled students understand math concepts and develop everyday math skills. The authors believe these students *can* learn math concepts and skills, but they often learn differently.

TRUELOVE, J. E., HOLAWAY-JOHNSON, C. A., LESLIE, K. M., & SMITH, T. E. C. (2007). Tips for including elementary students with disabilities in mathematics classes. *Teaching Children Mathematics 13*(6), 336–340. The authors describe specific interventions for cognitive problems, emotional and behavioral disorders, and physical disabilities.

USISKIN, Z. (1998). Paper-and-pencil algorithms in a calculator-and-computer age. In L. J. Morrow & M. J. Kenney (Eds.), *The teaching and learning of algorithms in school mathematics* (pp. 7–20). Reston, VA: National Council of Teachers of Mathematics. Usiskin lists principles for teaching algorithms of all types. Algorithms are valuable, but they have inherent dangers.

USNICK, V. E. (1992). Multidigit addition: A study of an alternative sequence. *Focus on Learning Problems in Mathematics 14*(3), 53–62. Usnick studied the effects of two instructional sequences for the standard addition algorithm: a traditional sequence in which examples with no regrouping are introduced and practiced before examples with regrouping, and an alternative sequence with regrouping introduced initially. The alternative sequence was as effective as the traditional sequence.

WARD, R. A. (2009). *Literature-based activities for integrating mathematics with other content areas*. Boston, MA: Pearson. Each chapter focuses on mathematics instruction for a different content area. Within each chapter, activities are described for areas of mathematics that reflect NCTM standards.

WATANABE, T. (2002). Representations in teaching and learning fractions. *Teaching Children Mathematics 8*(8), 457–463. Watanabe illustrates varied ways of representing fraction concepts, and notes how fractions are read differently in different languages.

WATSON, G. A. (2003). The versatile magic square. *Mathematics Teaching in the Middle School 8*(5), 252–255. Watson describes how the magic square can be adapted easily to provide computation practice for all four operations, with both whole numbers and rational numbers.

WEISS, D. M. (2006). Keeping it real: The rationale for using manipulatives in the middle grades. *Mathematics Teaching in the Middle School 11*(5), 238–242. Drawing from research, the author argues for the occasional use of manipulatives along with in-depth coverage of content, even for the older student.

WIEST, L. R. (2002). Multicultural mathematics instruction: Approaches and resources. *Teaching Children Mathematics 9*(1), 49–55. Wiest illustrates how cultures have differed with reference to computation procedures, and lists resources for multicultural mathematics instruction.

WILLIS, J. K., & JOHNSON, A. N. (2001). Multiply with MI: Using multiple intelligences to master multiplication. *Teaching Children Mathematics 7*(5), 260–269. The authors describe mathematics teaching strategies and learning activities for each of the intelligences identified by Howard Gardner.

WITZEL, B. S., & RICCOMINI, P. J. (2009). *Computation of Fractions: Math Intervention for Elementary and Middle Grades Students*. Upper Saddle River, NJ: Pearson Education Inc. The authors present 30 detailed lesson plans for varied topics.

WU, Z. (2001). Multiplying fractions. *Teaching Children Mathematics 8*(3), 174–177. Wu focuses on the conceptual challenges of multiplying fractions. For many students the meaning of multiplication must be expanded as they work with fractions.

ZAMBO, R. (2008 March). Percents can make sense. *Mathematics Teaching in the Middle School 13*(7), 418–422. Zambo provides specific suggestions and activities for making percents more readily understandable for students.

---

### *Navigations Series* published by the National Council of Teachers of Mathematics

A book and CD is available for most standards within each grade band, for example:

*Navigating Through Number and Operations in PreK–Grade 2*
*Navigating Through Geometry in Grades 6–8*

# Appendix A

# Using Alternative Algorithms

If we are willing to accept the idea that there are many legitimate ways to subtract, divide, and so on, we could choose to introduce an algorithm that is fresh and new to those students who are experiencing difficulty. By doing so, we may circumvent any mind-set of failure. We will also help students realize that there are many different ways of getting correct answers when computing. Algorithms have differed historically, and they often differ among cultures today. Accordingly, numerous examples of alternative algorithms can be found in the literature of mathematics education.

Three examples of alternative algorithms follow. With students who experience difficulty learning to compute, we may find that a low-stress procedure such as the first algorithm is learned with relative ease. Like traditional algorithms, low-stress procedures often can be taught as sensible records of manipulations with sticks, blocks, or number rods. The advantage of such algorithms is that they separate fact recall from renaming and thereby place fewer demands for remembering on the student who is computing.

---

**Check It Out**

Do You Understand Your Algorithms?

by J. Pickreign & R. Rogers in the August 2006 issue of *Mathematics Teaching in the Middle School.*

- Origins of the word *algorithm*
- Connections with the array model
- Multiplication and division alternatives

---

## ADDITION OF WHOLE NUMBERS: HUTCHINGS'S LOW-STRESS METHOD[1]

A.

$$4$$
$$3_7$$

B.

$$6$$
$$_1 7_3$$

C. ↓

$$5$$
$$_1 9_4$$
$$_1 8_2$$
$$4_6$$
$$_1 7_3$$
$$\overline{33}$$

D. ↓

$$^{2}\;^{2}$$
$$4_6\,7_9\,6$$
$$_1 8_{41}\,5_4\,9_5$$
$$_1 9_3\,6_{10}\,4_9$$
$$\underline{_1 7_0\,9_9\,8_7}$$
$$3\;0\;9\;7$$

As illustrated in examples A and B, sums for basic facts are written with small digits to the left and to the right instead of in the usual manner.

When a column is added, the one ten is ignored and the ones digit is added to the next number. In Example C, $5 + 9 = 14$, $4 + 8 = 12$, $2 + 4 = 6$, and $6 + 7 = 13$. The remaining three ones are recorded in the answer. The tens are counted and also recorded. Multicolumn addition proceeds similarly, except the number of tens counted is recorded at the top of the tens column.

Many students for whom regrouping in addition is difficult find this alternative rather easy to learn. It often brings success quickly, even with large examples. Other students, including those with perceptual problems, may be confused by the abundance of "crutches." This is especially true when the examples are not written with large digits, which is the case with many published achievement tests.

## SUBTRACTION OF WHOLE NUMBERS: THE EQUAL ADDITIONS (OR EUROPEAN-LATINO) METHOD

A. ↓

$$4\;5\,'3$$
$$-\;1_8\,\cancel{7}\;8$$
$$\overline{\phantom{00}5}$$

B. ↓ ↓

$$4\;\cancel{5}\;3$$
$$\underline{_2\cancel{1}\;_6\cancel{7}\;8}$$
$$2\;7\;5$$

A principle of compensation is applied: when equal quantities are added to both the minuend and the subtrahend, the difference remains the same. In this computation, ten is added to the sum, i.e., to the 3 in the ones place. To compensate for this addition, 10 is also added to the known addend; the 7 in the tens place is replaced with 8. Similarly, one hundred is added to the sum; that is, the 5 in the tens place becomes a 15. To compensate, one hundred is added to the known addend; the 1 in the hundreds place is replaced with a 2.

## SUBTRACTION OF RATIONAL NUMBERS: THE EQUAL ADDITIONS METHOD

Problem:

$$-\,7\tfrac{1}{4} \quad \text{add 1} \quad \left(\tfrac{4}{4}\right) \longrightarrow 7\tfrac{5}{4}$$

$$\underline{3\tfrac{3}{4}} \quad \text{add 1} \quad \left(1\right) \longrightarrow \underline{4\tfrac{3}{4}}$$

Difference: $\quad 3\tfrac{1}{2} \qquad\qquad\qquad\qquad 3\tfrac{2}{4}$

The principle of compensation is applied; 1 is added to both the minuend and the subtrahend in order to subtract easily.

# REFERENCE

1. Hutchings, B. (1976). Low-stress algorithms. In D. Nelson & R. E. Reys (Eds.). *Measurement in school mathematics*, pp. 218–239. Reston, VA: National Council of Teachers of Mathematics.

# Appendix B

# Involving Peers

Teaching and learning mathematics in our classrooms can be enhanced as we provide opportunities for our students to interact with one another. Peers can be involved in both assessment and instruction.

## ASSESSMENT

Chappuis and Stiggins rightly assert, "Classroom assessment that involves students in the process and focuses on increasing learning can motivate rather than merely measure students."[1] Whenever students are involved in peer assessment, they need to keep relevant criteria in mind—criteria that make sense to them. As they assess, students need to *thoughtfully* consider examples of work by their peers (in reality or simulation).

There is great value in students using what they know about mathematics to help others. At the same time, we as teachers learn much about both the student assessors and the peers whom they assess.

Here is an example of a task that a student assessor could present to a peer to learn what the other student knows and can do, and what kind of help the student needs; such tasks are likely to stimulate a productive discussion.

> Here is the way Gary multiplied. What could you tell Gary or show him to help him understand?
> $$\frac{5}{8} \times 3 = \frac{15}{24}$$

Sometimes a checklist can be used to guide peer assessment. In the following example the assessor circles the Y (yes), the ? (I'm not sure), or the N (no).

Name of student _____
Date on paper _____

1. Are digits written in place-value columns?                                Y     ?     N
2. Can the student explain the procedure used?                              Y     ?     N
3. Will the procedure used always produce the correct answer?               Y     ?     N
4. Did the student check the answer?                                         Y     ?     N
5. Can the student describe a situation in which this computation            Y     ?     N
   could be used?

Comments




Signature of student evaluator _____

Peer involvement in instruction can take the form of peer tutoring, or it can involve groups of students working together cooperatively. Peer tutoring, a strategy we may find helpful when we teach computation, occurs when students instruct one another by challenging, explaining, and demonstrating concepts and procedures. Often the tutor learns even more than the student being tutored.

If we plan carefully, peer tutoring can foster many of the emphases of *Principles and Standards for School Mathematics*: Problems will be solved, mathematical ideas will be discussed, reasoning will justify procedures, manipulatives and drawings will be used for representations, and connections will be made with prior learning. But these things will not happen unless we prepare carefully.

Barone and Taylor recommend at least a two-year age difference between tutors and their tutees.[2] They suggest ways to implement peer tutoring with young children, but many of their ideas apply to peer tutoring by older students as well. We need to select engaging instructional activities to be taught, then prepare tutors by teaching them the activity before they teach it to their peers. We can even have tutors teach the activity to other tutors while we observe, and have tutors switch roles. After tutoring sessions it is helpful to have both tutors and tutees write in their journals.

If more than one limited-English-proficient student in your mathematics class is using the same native language, the use of this language can often be facilitated if those students learn cooperatively in small groups.[3]

Students working in cooperative groups need to be responsible for the learning of each person within the group (perhaps there is to be a team score). But we need to hold each individual accountable for his or her own learning. Individuals also need to be held accountable for contributing to the group.

Typically, groups should be heterogeneous groups—often groups of four students. Cooperative groups can be structured by the tasks we give them. Tasks related to computational knowledge and skills include the following.

- Assign a set of computations to each student in a group of students. After individuals compute, they total their answers for the group, and compare that number with the specific number you provide.
- Discuss specific questions; for example, "What is the most important step in the procedure we studied? Why?"
- Solve a problem that involves deciding the appropriate method of computation, including procedures recently learned.
- Go over homework completed by individuals. Check answers with one another. Where answers differ, determine why, and determine which answer is correct. Students often assume they are correct and have to be convinced by others that they are not.
- Review for a test. Assign a sample test for the group to complete together.

When our students are in groups explaining a procedure to one another, we can tell them to make sure *each* member of their group understands and can do the procedure.

Remember that our students do *not* learn just by using manipulatives; they learn by *thinking* about what they are doing when they use them. They need to reflect on what they are doing with manipulatives and explain their reasoning to one another.

It has been said:

**Never tell a child what that child might be able to tell us. Similarly, try not to tell a child what some other child might be able to tell the child for us.**

We need to carefully observe our students as they work, and focus on their thinking as we observe them—not on their answers alone.

Sample activities for cooperative groups of students are described in Appendix E. The activities focus on computational procedures.

# REFERENCES

1. Chappuis, S., & Stiggins, R. J. (2002 September). Classroom assessment for learning. *Educational Leadership* 60(1), 40–43.
2. Barone, M. M., & Taylor, L. (1996). Peer tutoring with mathematics manipulatives: A practical guide. *Teaching Children Mathematics* 3(1), 8–15.
3. Lee, H., and Sikjung, W. (2004). Limited-English-Proficient (LEP) students and mathematical understanding. *Mathematics Teaching in the Middle School* 9(5), 269–272.

# Appendix C

# Working with Parents

We must work with parents; it is an important part of our program of assessment and instruction for our students. Many parents need help to respond appropriately to their children as they are learning mathematics, and students need opportunities to show parents what they are learning.

With appropriate guidance, parents can stimulate their children's interest in mathematics. Parents can show children that the mathematics they are learning is very much part of adult daily life. They can describe how their jobs use mathematics, share their own strategies for estimating and solving problems, and show how they think through a specific problem. Several publishers of textbooks have tips for parents.

## FAMILY MATH NIGHTS

School-sponsored family math nights can be collaborative celebrations of mathematical learning. They can be math-awareness workshops, or math labs that focus on various topics students are studying, or even carnival-like occasions filled with mathematical activities. Whatever the form, whenever you plan a family math night, prepare to provide parents with the help they need. Remember that many parents need help.

- They need to realize their child is capable of learning mathematics, especially when they think, "I was never any good at math."
- They need to understand the goals of mathematics instruction in your classroom.
- They need to know strategies that will engage their children. Examples include games that provide practice they are ready for, children estimating amounts while cooking, and estimating distances between places.

- They need to know how to link new knowledge and skills to what their child already knows and can do.
- They need suggestions for getting their child organized and for establishing a pattern of regular home study.

Also, many parents need help asking appropriate questions while working with their children:

- Did you estimate an answer?
- How does this relate to . . . ?
- Is there a drawing you can make that would help?
- How did you get your answer?
- How can you convince me your answer makes sense?

## MONTHLY MATH CHALLENGES

To encourage engagement in mathematics, send home a math challenge each month. Encourage students and parents to work on the challenge together. A certificate of participation can be awarded to all who participate (if you desire, a prize can be given to one chosen at random). If this is a schoolwide activity, have a different challenge for grades K–3, grades 4–6, and grades 7–8; when it is a schoolwide activity the principal needs to issue the certificates.[1]

## TAKE-HOME PAGES

Teachers can provide take-home pages that pose a question families often ask, then respond in a way that helps parents understand *why* instruction takes the form it does. For example, in the November 2005 issue of *Mathematics Teaching in the Middle School,* a sample take-home page addresses the question: Isn't it more efficient for children just to learn rules and have understanding come later when they are more mature?[2]

## STUDENT-LED CONFERENCES

Student-led conferences are not a substitute for teacher-parent conferences, but they *are* one way that parents can find out about their child's experiences with mathematics at school. These conferences also help students understand what is important, and help students take responsibility for their own learning.

When student-led conferences are planned, students usually decide what part of their work the conference will focus on; they select work samples for their parents or guardians to see. During conferences, have students explain the criteria used for deciding that a particular work sample is well done. Encourage students to talk about their struggles as they learn mathematics—not just their successes. Student-led conferences need to be well planned, and students need to be prepared for their role in the conference.

> To help parents highlight mathematical concepts (number, measurement, and geometry) with young children, read Hansen, L. E. (2005). ABCs of early mathematical experiences. *Teaching Children Mathematics 12*(4), 208–212.

# REFERENCES

1. Jennings, L., & Likis, L. (2005). Meeting a math achievement crisis. *Educational Leadership 62*(6), 65–68.
2. Martinie, S. (2005). Rules or understanding. *Mathematics Teaching in the Middle School 11*(4), 188–189.

# Appendix D

# Game-Like Activities with Base Blocks or the Equivalent

Game-like activities using base blocks or the equivalent and a pattern board can be incorporated into developmental instruction as a bridge between having students informally work out solutions with manipulatives and providing more direct instruction in conventional algorithms. Because each game-like activity models the steps in a specific algorithm, these activities can also be used for corrective instruction whenever a student has not successfully learned a particular algorithm taught by other means; it may provide the scaffolding needed by the student.

The pattern board serves as an organizing center for materials. It is the place where the "game is played" because each activity has a goal analogous to winning a game. Each activity also has rules much as a game has rules: rules about how to interpret the problem by placing base-ten blocks on the pattern board. There are also rules about how to proceed with the activity toward the goal.

Initially, the activity should be completed without any paper record being made; but when students have learned to do the activity, that which is done on the pattern board can be recorded *step by step*. That record, a mathematical representation of what the student observes, can be the conventional algorithm.

After initial experiences with the activity, one student can manipulate the blocks on the pattern board while another student intervenes and records what is done step by step. Then the two students can exchange roles. Eventually, have students use only the paper-and-pencil computation procedure to find the needed number, visualizing the pattern board and activity as they do so. The computation procedure makes sense to students because they have observed relationships and patterns, giving them a visual referent for the algorithm itself.

As students are involved with such game-like activities, encourage them not only to talk about things that are observed repeatedly but also to look beyond simple repetitions for more complex structures. Observe and discuss structures such as our numeration system ("Each place to the left has a value that is ten times as great.") and *repeated* sequences of steps that are observed within an algorithm. If the game-like activity for addition is played with other number-base blocks before base-ten blocks are used, students can observe that the games for different bases are structured alike, except for the trading rule.

The sample game-like activities that follow use base-ten blocks. Activities are described for addition, subtraction, and division of whole numbers.

## ADDITION OF WHOLE NUMBERS

The purpose of this game-like activity is to obtain the sum of two numbers in a manner that will picture the conventional computation procedure.

### The Pattern Board

This is a grid with four columns for materials. It also has four rows: three rows above a heavy line and one row below the line. (You may want to lightly shade the top row because it has a special use.) Label columns right to left: Units (or Ones), Tens, Hundreds, and Thousands.

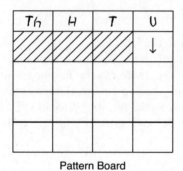

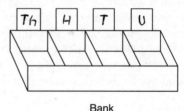

|  Pattern Board  | Bank |
|---|---|

### Materials for Quantities

Base-ten blocks are used, although there is value in using blocks for other bases initially—before written records are made. Other bases help students focus on the trading pattern.

### Bank

This is wherever materials for quantities are stored and sorted. It is where trades for *equal* quantities are executed (e.g., 10 tens for one 100).

### Goal of the Activity

The goal is to show the total amount of wood (or plastic) with as few pieces as possible. This will indicate the standard numeral for the sum.

## Rules

1. Show the two quantities in the problem (the two addends) on the two rows above the heavy line. The top row of the pattern board should be empty as you start. For 618 + 782, the pattern board would look similar to this:

2. Start with the units column and proceed to the left.
3. Within a column, move the total quantity of materials *below* the heavy line.
4. As you move materials below the heavy line, *trade 10 ones for one ten* if you can. If you do trade, place the one ten in the top row in the tens column. (When using another number base, trade *that* number "if you can." For example, in base three, trade three ones for one three if you can. Different headings for columns are required.)

## Example

Beginning with the units (at the arrow), the child collects 10 units if she can (because this is a base-ten game) and moves all remaining units below the heavy line. If she has been able to collect 10 units, they are traded at the bank for one ten. The ten is then placed above the other tens in the shaded place. (At first, many students want to verify the equivalence of what goes into the bank and what comes out by placing the 10 units in a row and matching them with one ten.)

As the student continues, she collects 10 tens if she can, and then moves all remaining tens below the heavy line. If she has been able to collect 10 tens, they are traded at the bank for one hundred, and the hundred is placed above the other hundreds in the shaded place. Finally, the child collects 10 hundreds if she can and moves all remaining hundreds below the heavy line. If she has been able to collect 10 hundreds they are traded at the bank for one thousand, and the thousand is placed in the shaded area at the top of the column for thousands. It is not possible to collect 10 thousands, so the one remaining thousand is brought below the heavy line.

As a student records the procedure, she records the number of blocks in each region every time trading is completed. (Making the record can be likened to writing a story.) When the record is finished, the algorithm is completed.

## SUBTRACTION OF WHOLE NUMBERS

The purpose of this game-like activity is to obtain the difference between two numbers in a manner that will picture the conventional decomposition computation procedure for subtraction.

### The Pattern Board

This grid is identical to the pattern board described for the addition activity.

### Materials for Quantities

Base-ten blocks are recommended.

### Bank

Materials for quantities are stored and sorted at the bank. It is where trades for *equal* quantities are executed (e.g., one ten for 10 ones).

### Goal of the Activity

Think of subtraction as finding the unknown amount in one of two (disjoint) parts of a quantity, whenever the total amount and the amount in one of the two parts are known. The goal of this activity is to determine that unknown amount.

> Note: It is important for developing the decomposition algorithm that the verbal problem setting be a "take-away" problem rather than a comparison problem. The two addend quantities should be parts of the given quantity for the sum. An example:
>
> **Gary hopes to sell a total of 243 baseball cards at the fair. He has already sold 185 cards. How many remain to be sold?**

### Rules

1. Show the total quantity (the sum or minuend) in the second row above the heavy line. As you start, the mostly shaded first row of the pattern board should be empty.
2. Use numeral cards to show the known addend on the row above the heavy line. *Do not use base blocks* because this amount is really part of the amount

already shown for the sum. Place numeral cards to show the number of ones, tens, and so on. For 243 − 185, the pattern board would look similar to this:

$$\begin{array}{r} 243 \\ -185 \\ \hline \end{array}$$

Pattern Board Used for Subtraction

3. Start with the ones column and proceed to the left.
4. Within a column, move the total quantity of base blocks to the parts below—one above the heavy line (known addend) and one below it (unknown addend). Place the amount indicated *on* the numeral card, and the remaining amount below the heavy line.
5. If there are not enough blocks in the column to place on the numeral card, *trade one ten for 10 ones* or *one hundred for 10 tens,* and so on, so you will have enough. Then place blocks on the numeral card and any remaining blocks below the heavy line.

**Note:** When the student is ready to record the computation, proceed with the activity step by step. Let the student trade and remove blocks while you make a step-by-step record of the student's moves in an evolving algorithm. Then reverse the process: While you trade and remove blocks (thinking aloud), let the student make the record. Two students can take turns being manipulator and recorder.

## DIVISION OF WHOLE NUMBERS

The purpose of this game-like activity is to obtain the quotient of a three- or four-digit number divided by a one-digit number in a manner that will picture the conventional computation procedure.

## The Pattern Board or Play Area

The play area may or may not be a board as such. A space is needed to display base-ten blocks for the dividend of the problem, and a number of collecting spaces are needed as determined by the divisor. For example, if the divisor is 4, then four collecting spaces are needed. These can be blank sheets of paper, box lids, and so on. For $1412 \div 4$, the play area might look similar to the following:

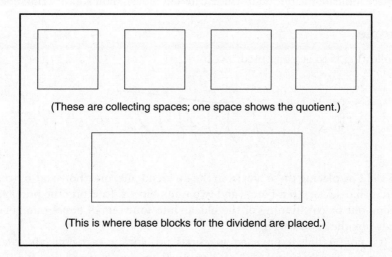

(These are collecting spaces; one space shows the quotient.)

(This is where base blocks for the dividend are placed.)

## Materials for Quantities

Base-ten blocks are recommended.

## Bank

This is wherever materials for quantities are stored and sorted. It is where trades for *equal* quantities are executed (e.g., two hundreds for 20 tens).

## Goal of the Activity

The goal is to show the amount for the unknown factor, that is, the amount in each equivalent set.

## Rules

1. Show the total amount (dividend, product) with base-ten blocks.
2. Provide collecting spaces as determined by the divisor.
3. Begin with the largest available block of wood, then work progressively with smaller blocks.

4. For a given block size, parcel out an equal number of blocks in each collecting space. **Parcel out only once.**[1] Think: *What is the greatest number of blocks
I can put in each collecting space and still have enough for all the spaces?*

5. If there are not enough blocks of a given size to put even one block in each
collecting space, then trade those blocks for an equal amount of wood of the
next smaller size. For example, trade two hundreds for 20 tens.

6. When you have proceeded as far as you can, the blocks in one collecting
space indicate the quotient. Undistributed blocks indicate the remainder.

## Example

The following is to be computed:

Show 1412 by placing these blocks in the dividend pile: one thousand-block, four
hundreds-blocks, one ten-block, and two units-blocks. Interpret the problem as a
parceling out or partitioning of the blocks into four sets of equal number—sets
indicated by the collecting spaces.[2]

It is not possible to put even one thousand-block in each collecting place, so
exchange the one thousand-block for an equal amount of wood, i.e., for 10 hundreds-blocks. Then, before you parcel out the 14 hundreds-blocks, think something like, "What is the greatest number of hundreds-blocks I can put in each of
the four collecting places? Two in each of the four places is okay, but more can be
parceled out. Three in each of the four places is okay. Four in each of the four
places is 16, more than I have. I will put three in each place." Parcel out the
blocks; two hundreds-blocks remain.

Exchange the two hundreds-blocks for 20 tens-blocks; there are now 21
tens-blocks altogether. Proceed similarly, placing five tens-blocks in each of the
four places, with one tens-block remaining. Exchange the tens-block for 10 units,
for a total of 12 units. This time place three units in each of the four collecting
places. The quotient is 353.

The algorithm can be recorded as this activity is observed—step by step.

1. If the student deals out blocks one at a time, much as he or she would deal out playing
cards, then only a mechanical procedure for getting an answer is learned; it will not
picture the algorithm. Emphasize the need to think about the greatest number because
you get to parcel out only once.

2. Any accompanying verbal problem should be a partitive problem, that is, a problem in
which the known factor indicates the number of equivalent subsets. The verbal problem should *not* be a measurement problem, a problem in which the known factor indicates the number in each subset.

# Appendix **E**

# Activities for Cooperative Groups

Cooperative groups of students typically work with text-based tasks or with tasks designed by the teacher. While students are exploring new relationships and processes, they create their own mental scaffolding for the concepts and processes involved. Students are then ready for guided lessons from the teacher.

Make sure students in each group understand their task and how to proceed. Ask someone in the group to tell you, in their own words, what they will be doing and procedures for working together in the group.

The following are examples of activities for two or more students to complete cooperatively. Most activities focus on some aspect of a specific computational procedure, though they can often be adapted to other algorithms. Interact with your students as they work, and prompt them on what they are doing.

## A. WHOLE NUMBER NUMERATION

Show 352 with a set of wooden base-ten blocks. Also show the same amount of wood using one less ten rod. Explain how you know the two sets of blocks contain the same amount of wood. (Similar tasks can be designed with decimals.)

## B. WHOLE NUMBER COMPUTATION

1. How many digits are in each answer? Write why there are that many digits. Use estimation or mental computation, *not* paper and pencil or a calculator.

   A. 347 + 642
   B. 479 − 183
   C. 67 × 98
   D. 3688 ÷ 7

2. Find the missing digits in each of these.

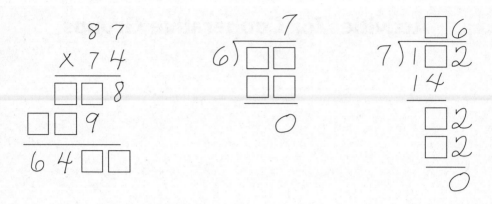

3. Are A, B, and C done correctly?
　　　Decide how Brenda subtracted.

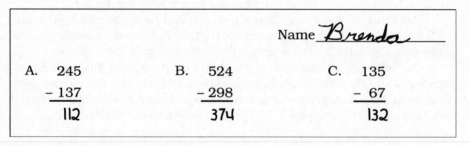

Use your subtraction procedure to subtract D and E correctly.

　　　D.　458　　　E.　241
　　　　　−372　　　　　　−96

Write what you observed in Brenda's paper.

Write how your subtraction procedure is different.

4. A palindrome is a number, word, or phrase that reads the same forward or
backward. Two-digit numbers can be turned into palindromes in one step by

adding the same digits in reverse order once, or in more than one step, as may be required. The following are examples of palindromes formed with one, two, and three steps:

| | | |
|---|---|---|
| 38 | 19 | 59 |
| + 83 | + 91 | + 95 |
| 121 | 110 | 154 |
| | + 011 | + 451 |
| | 121 | 605 |
| | | + 506 |
| | | 1111 |

How many steps are required to convert each of the following two-digit numbers into palindromes? Complete the chart.[1]

| Number | Resulting Palindrome | Number of Steps |
|--------|---------------------|-----------------|
| 38 | | |
| 57 | | |
| 69 | | |
| 68 | | |

5. Sometimes it is easier to multiply two whole numbers in your head instead of using paper and pencil. Many students find it easier to multiply $40 \times 600$ in their heads rather than using paper and pencil, but they would use paper or a calculator for $47 \times 618$. Some students would also multiply $4 \times 198$ in their heads.

Write how you can know it will be easier to multiply in your head when you are to multiply two whole numbers.

6. Solve this puzzle by finding the missing digits. Solve the puzzle in at least two different ways.

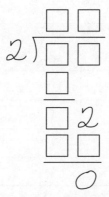

## C. COMPUTATION WITH FRACTIONS

1. Which number is greater? Write why you believe it is greater.

   a. $\frac{1}{2}$ or $\frac{5}{8}$
   b. $\frac{1}{3}$ or $\frac{3}{8}$
   c. $\frac{3}{4}$ or $\frac{7}{8}$

2. Find the missing number.

$$\frac{3}{8} + \frac{\square}{8} = \frac{1}{2}$$

3. In two different ways, show that

$$4\frac{1}{4} \times 4 \quad \text{does } \textbf{not} \text{ equal} \quad 16\frac{1}{4}.$$

## D. PROBLEM SOLVING

1. Give each group a collection of at least 10 clippings; each clipping is an advertisement for an item selling for less than $10. Have each group select exactly six items that have a total cost of more than $15 and less than $20. They must prove to you that they have completed the task correctly.
2. Each group needs a chart with a four-by-three grid, labeled as shown below. Make sure each cell on the chart measures at least four-by-six inches. Also provide each group of students with about 15 blank four-by-six-inch cards.

|          | Estimate | Paper | Mental Computation |
|----------|----------|-------|--------------------|
| Add      |          |       |                    |
| Subtract |          |       |                    |
| Multiply |          |       |                    |
| Divide   |          |       |                    |

Students assume a calculator is not available, and they create word problems for each cell in the grid. They write each problem on a four-by-six-inch card and fasten it within the appropriate cell.

Before you assign this task, you may want to review how we know when estimation is the appropriate way to compute a needed number and (when an exact answer is needed) how we know that mental computation would be more appropriate than using a paper-and-pencil procedure.

3. Give each group of students a different word problem to solve. After they have solved the problem, they are to make a poster to explain
   • how they decided what operation to use, and
   • how they computed the answer.

## E. ASSESSMENT OF GROUP ACTIVITIES

1.

| Name_____ |
| --- |

**About Our Group**

|  | 😊 | 😐 | 🙁 |
| --- | --- | --- | --- |
| 1. We listened to each other. |  |  |  |
| 2. We worked together. |  |  |  |
| 3. There were good ideas. |  |  |  |
| 4. We finished our task. |  |  |  |

What was well done?

What should have been different?

2. Have students write about their participation.
    - In my group, I am happy with the way I . . .
    - In my group, I can improve by . . .
    - My group should . . .

---

1. Based on D. Schiller & M. Charles. (2004). Moving forward and backward with palin-dromes. *Mathematics Teaching in the Middle School 10*(2), 76–80.

# Appendix F

## Introducing Total-and-Parts Meanings for Operations

Adding, subtracting, multiplying, and dividing are not operations on sets; they are operations on numbers. These operations have nothing to do with moving objects about—putting them together or moving one object away from other objects. If teachers use words that imply that these operations involve moving objects, students are apt to be confused later when solving equations and other problems. Adding, for example, is finding the total amount or "number altogether"; it is not "putting things together." Why is addition used to find the missing number in the situation described by the equation $\Box - 14 = 38$? Addition is used because what is needed is the total amount, *not* because objects are put together. Objects may actually have been removed from a set of objects.

In view of this, with younger students it is often helpful to think of the operations as follows:

- Addition finds the total amount (the number altogether) when the numbers in both parts are known.
- Subtraction finds the number in one part when the total amount and the number in the other part are known.
- Multiplication finds the total amount (product) when both of the numbers *about* parts are known: the number of equivalent parts, and the number in each part.
- Division finds one of the numbers about parts (either the number in each part, or the number of equivalent parts) when the total amount (product) and the other number about parts is known.

These concepts or meanings for the operations assume that sets of objects are used to picture situations—objects such as blocks or discs. With addition and subtraction, the *parts* are two disjoint subsets; with multiplication and division, the *numbers about parts* are the number of equivalent subsets and the number in each of the equivalent subsets. These meanings for the operations are sometimes called total-and-parts meanings for the four operations.

Eventually, of course, these expressions need to be replaced by more precise terminology:

- Addition finds the missing sum when both addends are known.

    addend + addend = sum

- Subtraction finds the missing addend when the sum and one addend are known.

    sum − addend = addend

- Multiplication finds the missing product when both factors are known.

    factor × factor = product

- Division finds the missing factor when the product and one factor are known.

    product ÷ factor = factor

If students use the first sets of meanings comfortably, the second set can begin to be used alongside (or in apposition to) the first set. For example, say, "Yes, you know the numbers for both parts, so you use addition. Addition finds the sum when you know both addends." Eventually, the second set of meanings will be used comfortably and with understanding.

# Appendix G

# A Diagnostic Interview

Begin by preparing an interview protocol—a plan for what you expect to do and say as you conduct an in-depth, one-on-one diagnostic interview with a student regarding selected areas of mathematics. It is a script for what *you* will say and do, but it does *not* state the child's responses.

Then try it out with a student—actually conduct a diagnostic interview with a student within your certification range. The amount of time required to conduct the interview will vary with the age of the child.

After you conduct the interview, write a report of the *actual* interview—what really was said and done, not what you planned to say. Your report should also include your analysis of the results and a prescription, as described in the sections that follow.

## PLANNING THE INTERVIEW

First, read Chapter 9; it provides helpful background information.

On your plan, *note the grade level* of the student you plan to interview. Your plan or protocol should be a list of specific questions or tasks, including *both* what you expect to say *and* what you expect to present to the student (numerals, manipulatives, etc.). In other words, for each question or task, describe as *completely* as possible your anticipated "stimulus" to which the student will respond in some way.

Write out your plan so specifically that someone else could use your protocol as a script and would do the same things. You can prepare your plan on a set of cards or on paper—the cards are probably more flexible because they permit you to insert and delete tasks easily.

You may choose to focus on particular state standards or objectives; if you do, identify them in your report. Try to ask questions that will evoke a response that can help you understand how well the student understands. In general, *questions answered with yes or no are not as helpful as probing questions that require a more complete response.*

Try to include a *variety of assessment tasks* for any one skill or understanding (such as "identifying place values" or "understanding what fractions mean"). You will probably involve the student with manipulatives as well as paper and pencil.

Sometimes probing questions can follow a question that has one correct answer. Note questions 2 and 3 in the following sequence.

1. [Give the student a card showing 7 + 6 = _____; point to the blank.] **What number is the sum, the total amount?**
2. [Wave your hand over the base-ten blocks and counters.] **How could you use these materials to show me that the sum is 13?**
3. **Could you show me that the sum is 13** *in a different way?*

Order your assessment tasks from simple to complex. That way you can skip over some of the simplest tasks unless they are needed, and you can stop when it is no longer appropriate to administer more complex tasks.

For the topics you have chosen, try to prepare as thoroughly as possible; assume that the student may know and be able to do *less* than you expect, but remember that the student may know and do *more* than you expect. When planning, it is often wise to anticipate assessing knowledge and skills at one or more grade levels below and also at one grade level above the grade level of the child you plan to interview.

## CONDUCTING THE INTERVIEW

As you conduct the interview, you will probably want to record it so you have a complete record of what the student said during the interview.

Before you begin the interview, make sure you have at hand all materials you will need. Seat the student across a table from you, and *make sure the student is facing away from any potential distractions,* such as other students.

So you can write the report at a later time, make sure your records are adequate during the interview. Before you conduct the interview, study the directions that follow.

## REPORTING THE INTERVIEW

Write your report in three parts as follows:

### 1. The Interview as Conducted

This is a complete account of what *actually* happened: what you said and did, what the student said and did—everything—and in the sequence it *really* happened.

### 2. Analysis of the Results

In this section, focus on the following questions for the topics in mathematics you examined:

a. What does *the student actually understand*? How well developed, how mature, is that understanding? What skills does the student possess?

b. What does *the student not yet understand*? What skills does the student not now possess?

c. What have you learned about *the student's dispositions toward mathematics*?

d. If you conducted such an interview again, *how would you modify your interview protocol*?

### 3. Prescription

In this important section tell what you believe the student is actually *ready to learn* as determined by your interview, and state *why* you decided he or she is ready to learn it.

# Criteria for Assessing the Report

## The Interview as Conducted

- The report is a complete account of the interview as *actually* conducted.
- Accurate mathematical content is evident throughout.
- Questions and tasks for the student are clearly stated.
- What the interviewer did with manipulatives and symbols is clearly presented.
- Student responses are clearly stated.
- Varied representations and applications were used.
- The interviewer probed to provide an in-depth diagnosis.
- The interview was thorough for the mathematical area or topic chosen.

## Analysis of the Results

- The report specifically states what the student already understands and the skills possessed.
- The report also lists specific concepts and skills the child does *not* yet possess.
- The report describes evidences of particular dispositions toward mathematics.
- The report states how the interview would be modified if conducted again.

## Prescription

- The report describes mathematical content and skills the child is now ready to learn.
- The report provides evidence the child is ready to learn the content and skills listed.

# Appendix H

# A Thematic Unit
# Can Make Connections Clear

In some schools thematic units of instruction are stressed. It is possible to design and teach a unit that focuses primarily on a topic in mathematics yet makes explicit connections with other topics—topics in mathematics and beyond. A thematic unit so designed can involve many creative instructional activities that make connections clear to students.

As an example, consider a unit that focuses on multiplication; it begins with multiplication of whole numbers. We know that multiplication is related to addition; furthermore, subtraction and division can be viewed as special cases of addition and multiplication. These relationships suggest a unit of instruction that focuses on multiplication—with connections to other operations and to other topics.

A unit that focuses on multiplication will need to review the meaning of the operation of multiplication. The unit could also include instruction involving:

- *Divisibility.* Divisibility rules build on factors, which are connected with multiplication.
- *Prime and composite numbers.* Prime and composite numbers are related to the number of factors, factorization, and eventually to prime factorization. Patterns can be observed that relate to definitions for prime and for composite numbers.
- *Exponents.* Exponents are merely shorthand for a special case of multiplication.
- *Multiplication of fractions.* The connection between the meaning of multiplication with whole numbers and that same meaning applied to rational numbers expressed with fractions should be noted. The algorithm can be connected to two-dimensional diagrams (for example, place a square half shaded on top of the same square $\frac{2}{3}$ shaded and turned 90 degrees) to show that the results of the algorithm are not hocus pocus but connect with reality, but be sure to express the result in terms of the basic unit (the square).

- *Multiplication by canceling factors.* When you analyze this, it involves multiplying by a name for one.
- *Dividing fractions.* Again, both the meaning and the algorithm deserve attention. Connect the meaning for division (probably measurement division) illustrated with whole numbers to rational numbers expressed as fractions. This is important because it shows that the algorithm for dividing fractions connects with the real world, but it can be tricky. For example, $\frac{1}{2}$ divided by $\frac{1}{3}$ (How many one-thirds in one-half?) results in the answer $1\frac{1}{2}$ because in $\frac{1}{2}$ there is all of a third, and also half of another third. The algorithm itself is actually shorthand for a rather involved process that involves multiplying a reciprocal with rather fancy names for fractions.

Connections with mathematics can lead to other topics—including applications beyond the school.